HINDU SYMBOLOGY
AND OTHER ESSAYS

Swami Swahananda

SRI RAMAKRISHNA MATH
16, Sri Ramakrishna Math Road
MADRAS-600 004   ::   INDIA

Published by :
© The President,
Sri Ramakrishna Math,
Mylapore, Madras 600 004.

Printed in India at
Sri Ramakrishna Math Printing Press,
Mylapore, Madras 600 004.

CONTENTS

SYMBOLISM IN RELIGION

A SYMBOL is a sign or an identifying mark. The original Greek word *symbolon* means a sign by which one knows or infers a thing. It typifies, represents or recalls 'something by possession of analogous qualities or by association in fact or thought'. Symbols are signs for expressing the invisible by means of visible or sensuous representations. All our contact with the world outside is based on symbols. Our language is nothing but symbols. The scripts are still more so. Our art, our poetry, in fact, every aspect of life is based on symbols. 'We think in symbols, we act in symbols, we live in symbols, we learn in symbols'. As Carlyle's professor in *Sartor Resartus* puts it, 'The universe is but one vast symbol of God; nay, if thou wilt have it, what is man himself but a symbol of God'.

Though man and his life also ultimately are symbolic, there are more evident symbols in man's creation. These symbols are mainly of two types, based on the ear and the eye, though other senses also take part in them. The sound symbol and the form symbol are the substitute or suggestion of an abstract thing. They are more concrete in nature. Thus superimposing an idea on a thing or invoking a deity in an image is nothing but a symbol.

This symbol-making tendency is innate in man. Symbols are used for the easy transmission of culture. But when the symbols lose their freshness, or their intrinsic meaning is forgotten, they become ordinary expressions. A symbol retains its value through antiquity, fresh interpretation and sincere belief. 'In a symbol', as Carlyle pointed out, 'there is concealment and yet revelation'. It conceals partly the essential content from an ordinary person but partly reveals it by suggesting it. When the abstract is quite clear to a discerning mind, a symbol loses its concealing quality, but even then it is used by advanced men for suggesting the abstract. Of course, then it does not have any binding force on them. Conveying of truth through fiction, poetry, allegory or metaphor is as old as human language. Symbology is, as it were, the kindergarten of abstract thoughts. Because of its allegoric nature, a symbol gives rise to esoterism. This is true of every branch of learning. An uninitiated cannot decipher a chemical formula. But this tendency is more in evidence in religion. Religious truth, being intangible by nature, has given rise to much of symbology. Every religion has its own body of symbols which suggests the ultimate reality, the deity and other spiritual truths.

Some modern psychologists have made a thorough study of symbology. We do not have any idea of presenting their views here. But we may note in passing that in his *Psychology of the Unconscious* Jung has dealt with the symbolism of ancient religions and of the mythology of many races, in connection with the life of ordinary people of the present day. Dr. Mees, who has made a searching study of symbols, says:

> It is now recognized that dreams form the mythology of the individual as much as mythology represents the dream-life of a race....Symbols, and in particular religious symbols, are not mere objective pictures, but are highly subjective, in that they form the most sacred and intimate part of our being.

Some authors have made special studies of similarity of symbols in different countries. In *Symbolism of the East and West* by H. Murray-Aynsley, similarities in sun, fire and other worships, use of sacred stones, sacred trees to typify a new birth of the soul, etc., have been noted. Regarding the symbol of the Svastika familiar to us, the writer points out that it is an emblem of the Sun and Fire and is used in Hindu temples at the present day to kindle the sacred fire. It was used by the Greeks and Romans down to a late period and has been found on ancient Egyptian articles and in the ruins of Troy. Even now it is used in Spain. Nazi Germany again made people familiar with it. It is an all-absorbing study. But we shall restrict ourselves only to symbols pertaining to religion.

In Christianity

Though symbols are often seen in every religion, a more detailed study has been made about symbols in Christianity and Hinduism, where they are used profusely. Later Christianity denounces idols, etc., officially, but it is full of such idols and images. 'An idol is a representation of a deity in symbolic or human form, adored or worshipped as a tangible manifestation of the divine presence. Idols are images but many images are not worshipped.' Amulets and fetishes, though symbols, are not adored in Christianity. In olden days the sun, the moon, etc., have been recognized as nature deities, for they are the tangible symbols of spirits. Symbols have some relation with characteristics or attributes. The old religions of Babylonia and Egypt treated the idols as real embodiments of gods. Israel afterwards rejected them. Christianity created a host of images. Islam was iconoclastic but it also was forced to recognize a few symbols. Symbolism was used for mystification in the Old Testament, and for sacred mysteries in Gnostic theologies. Augustine and other early Christian Fathers interpreted scriptural narratives as symbolic. Christ and other teachers of men used parables for conveying spiritual truths.

In Christianity the symbols are the outward and visible signs of divinity, doctrines, spiritual ideas, sacred seasons, historical characters, etc. Their development began in the days of persecution. Symbols were used as a code language carrying meaning only to those who knew the secret. Afterwards, when Christianity became popular among the masses, it was necessary to have symbols to convey information to the ignorant folk. Figures in woodcarving and stained glass were then used with symbols for easy identification. The Lord was signified by a nimbus, or circle about His head, and from this circle emanated four rays, forming a cross. St. John was depicted with an eagle, Peter with two keys, Andrew as leaning on a cross and Paul with a sword and a book. These were done recalling some well-known facts in their lives. The Old Testament worthies were also represented in a like manner. Thus Isaiah was given a saw, the supposed instrument of his martyrdom, Moses his two tablets of stone, Noah an ark, St. Stephen the stones.

The geometrical figures were used as suggesting marks. The assurance of eternal life was signified by the circle, the Trinity by an equilateral triangle, and regeneration by an octagon. Numbers also were used for signification based on the Biblical saying, 'God has arranged all things in number'. Thus 1 represents the unity of God and Spirit, 2 the diversity of earth and matter and 3 the Trinity and the extension of Godhead.

In course of time each character gathered round itself different symbols. Thus Christ was symbolized by a fish, a candle, a crown, a lamb, etc. Each representation reveals a wealth of meaning. Thus the fish stands for 'Jesus Christ, Son of God, the Saviour', based on the corresponding Greek word.

The Holy Spirit is represented by the dove and by various forms of the candle stick. The cross stands for Christ's suffering and redemptive love. Of other innumerable symbols, the star represents the Epiphany, the ox stands for patience and sacrifice, the anchor for hope, the peacock for resurrection and the butterfly for immortality.

The greatest symbol of Christianity is the cross. Though it had its basis on the system of crucifixion then prevalent at Rome, it now not only signifies the death of Christ but also the redemption of man. Here the idea is that the 'blood of Christ' cleanses man of the original sin. The cross has also signified that Christ's followers should, like their Master on the cross, bear pain, suffer with patience and also suffer all ignominy for Him. 'Perhaps it was the chief triumph of Christianity that it transformed the cross into the symbol of all that is grandest and most sacred.'

In other Semitic Religions

Among all the religions, Islam had strong objection to all symbolism. It has been pointed out that in Arabic there is no exact equivalent for 'symbol'. The Muslim rulers, however, used different colours of flags to indicate sovereignty and power. With the passage of time the Byzantine crescent and star became the Islamic symbol. Though because of Islamic objection to limner's art, symbolism is very scanty in its architecture, in India the Muslim rulers became staunch supporters of art. Symbolism is so all-pervading that though in the field of faith there was objection, yet unconsciously many symbolic acts have crept in. Scholars have given various symbolic meanings for postures in Namaz, etc., as for example, raising the hand during prayer means that the votary wants to be free from all possessions so that he might approach the Almighty. The Sufis, however, have specialized in symbolic language. They even explain much of the *Koran* as elaborate symbolism. In Sufi terminology, 'breeze' signifies the means whereby union with the Desired One is attained, while 'bell' signifies the angel of Death and 'dark night' the world.

In the Jewish tradition symbolic actions as well as symbolic ideas occur frequently. The Biblical Sabbath is an example in point. In the process of symbolization the present values do not entirely depend on past origins. 'Religious ceremonial often becomes ennobled by the newer ideas read into it by progressive ages. And conversely, when an institution is lost (as with the Biblical sacrifices), the whole system may be retrospectively idealized by symbolic adaptation'. Thus when fasting replaced sacrifices, it itself was considered as sacrifice. The parallel may be seen in the Hindu idea of considering the human life itself as a Yajna. The rites in religious traditions have also been pointed out as symbolic survivals of literal acts. Many particulars of the Jewish sacrificial system, the ritual of the temple, synagogue and home, are thus treated in the symbolical manner.

In Hinduism

Of all the religions, it is Hinduism that has consciously and boldly accepted symbolism. Other religions of Indian origin also have done that. According to Hindu philosophy, the Divine has both personal and impersonal aspects. Symbols of the personal aspects 'satisfy the philosophic sense of the devotee, yet make easy the grasping of the absolute'. The Higher Reality is Brahman which is indefinable. A votary can draw nearer and nearer to it through approximation. In fact, all descriptions of it are its aspects only. So symbols or likenesses are used as intermediaries between the inadequate and limited capacity of man and the created language and the incommunicable nature and fullness of Brahman. But symbols of Brahman are not false. They are a portion or aspect of the truth.

Hinduism has profusely made use of symbolism in religious worship with a definite purpose. Its main aim is to set forth in visible or audible likeness what cannot be really or fully expressed or conceived. All language in the last resort is symbolic and religious language in an especial degree, for it endeavours to present a reality too deep for words. The image or symbol of God serves the purpose of providing in material and suitable form a convenient object of reverence. But Hinduism never considered them as ultimate. They were the stepping stones to a higher conception, something like the signposts or guides to better and higher thoughts. That is why Hinduism does not look askance at the so-called idols, totems or fetishes. It considers them as symbols, for they remind us of the reality and that is their function, for the Highest Reality cannot be approached through the senses. As Swami Vivekananda explained it when he was appealed to on one occasion to condemn the fetishism of the Hottentot:

Don't you see that there is no fetishism? Oh, your hearts are steeled, that you cannot see that the child is right! The child sees person everywhere. Knowledge robs us of the child's vision. But at last, through higher knowledge, we win back to it. He connects a living power with rocks, sticks, trees and the rest. And is there not a living power behind them? It is *Symbolism,* not fetishism! Can you not see?

Hinduism recognizes that all finite things are symbols of the infinite. But to be spiritually beneficial, true symbols should be selected as against the comparatively false ones. 'A mirage is a delusive symbol whereas a wave is a true one, for it is made of the same substance.' For worship higher

symbols are used, symbols which have acquired a sort of life,
having been visualized and used by innumerable saints and
holy men.

For worship various substitutes of Brahman have been
accepted. Of the most important types a few may be mentioned. Brahman has been described as Satchidananda,
Existence-Knowledge-Bliss   absolute or as Hiranyagarbha
the golden germ, or as Svayambhu, the self-created and self-
existent One. But even these conceptions are difficult and
in essence elude our comprehension. So the Upanishads
prescribe for meditation the more tangible symbols of Prana,
the vital energy, Vayu, the wind, Akasa, the all-pervading
ether, Aditya, the sun dispelling darkness, or the golden
Purusha in the eye. Mind, the repository of all thoughts,
itself has been presented as a symbol.   Pranava, the
syllable Aum, has been described as the best sound   symbol
of Brahman. Some of the symbols are quite comprehensive
and suggestive, but Brahman transcends them all. Though
the Vedic Rishis worshipped many deities, such as Indra,
Varuna, Mitra, Savita and others, they, even in those days,
had the knowledge of the Supreme Reality at the back of them
all. This is clear from sayings like 'Truth is one, sages call
it variously.' That shows that Hinduism used the symbols
knowing them as partial manifestations of the Highest Reality.

All gods in the Hindu Pantheon have some identifying
marks. Many have quite a good number of them, some representing their characteristics, some their 'vehicles'. Thus
the goose of Brahma, the eagle of Vishnu, the bull of Siva,
the peacock of Kartikeya, the elephant of Indra, the owl of
Lakshmi, the swan of Saraswati, are all vehicles, by which we
can identify them. Of the three main Gods, the Trimurti,
Brahma has four faces to give out the four Vedas; Siva is
represented by a linga, a stone emblem which along with the

salagrama of Vishnu is the least anthropomorphic symbol of Divinity. Siva's trident bespeaks of His government and authority. The crescent moon depicted on His forehead indicates His greatness. It recalls the sovereignty that was assigned to Him when the moon was discovered during the churning of the ocean. The *Bhagavata* (XII. 11) gives the symbolic meanings of Vishnu's weapons, apparel, etc. He has a discus, a club, a conch-shell, indicating His authority and power. The auspicious mark, Srivatsa, usually represented on His breast in the form of a curl of hair represents His brilliance and capability; the garland symbolizes the variegated Maya, the sacred thread, the three-lettered Aum. The Tulasi in a house represents Vishnu's presence and protection. In this way, it may be shown that every article on the person of a deity represents its particular quality or power. The Vibhuti Yoga of the *Gita* gives a number of animate and inanimate objects which can be identified with the Deity. The image of Kali dancing on the breast of Siva is also symbolic of Time manifesting itself in the background of the Timeless. The Tantras have given rise to innumerable symbols. Of these the Yantras, the geometrical diagrams of various forms, are very popular.

With all these symbolic representations, Hinduism tries to bring the Divine within the grasp of the devotee. The vision of the Deity changes with the inner growth of the devotee. Thus the Deity is seen sometimes outside, sometimes as the indwelling spirit, then as immanent in all creation and ultimately as the transcendental Brahman. And that is the ultimate goal to which all spiritual disciplines can lead an aspirant.

HINDU SYMBOLOGY

Symbology is All-pervading

SYMBOLIZATION is the basic principle of all manifestations. An abstract idea or feeling requires some symbols or symbolic actions for self-expression. While symbolism can be traced everywhere, it is more manifest in religious practices. Hinduism specialized in the use of this art of symbology. Even its highest philosophy is surcharged with this idea. Hence we find that the philosophy of Advaita defines God as the highest reading of the Absolute. The other gods and goddesses are still more concretized. Even if we give up this extreme position we find more evident symbols in Hinduism. The ancient scriptures are variously explained by scholars. There is nature symbolism as well as spiritual symbolism. Take the Puranic fight of Indra and Vritra, kings of the gods and demons respectively. It has been explained that Indra, the god of rain, pierces Vritra, the clouds, and brings about rain. The fight in the famous celestial song of the Lord, the *Gita* of Sri Krishna, or the fight between the gods and demons mentioned in the Upanishads, has been explained as the spiritual fight between good and evil forces in the individual's mind or in the world at large.

There are other scholars who have given a purely mystical explanation of the Vedic lore. Some of the words have been pointed out as 'the perceptible outer image or symbol of a truth, an idea of an object of the inner world'. Thus the esoteric meaning of *go*, cow, is the inner illumination, *asva*, horse, is the symbol of strength, life force, *apah*, waters, symbolize the sap of life, and so on.[1] So when we speak of symbolism in Hinduism we must include all these also.

Hinduism has a peculiar method of raising every worship to the highest level through reinterpretation. It is not clear whether we had, or when we outgrew, the primitive stages of animism, fetishism, etc. However, at present we find all the different rites and ceremonies are given a philosophical inter-pretation and thus linked with the direct religious pursuit. Vedanta systematizes the heterogeneous deities by viewing them as symbols of Brahman, and different rituals and faiths as ways leading to the Divine. Thus when the entire super-structure of Hindu worship is built on this idea of symbolism, it is rather difficult to give a fair account of all of them but we may have a glimpse of the more evident and popular symbols.

Sound Symbols

Every sect, every faith has some symbols and these representations overlap one another. According to the Hindus there is one ultimate reality—Brahman. That ultimate reality in relation to the world is Isvara. He has the three functions of creation, maintenance and destruction of the universe and then He is represented by Brahma, Vishnu and Siva. The other deities are subservient to these deities.

Two types of symbology may be noticed in Hinduism. First, the sound symbols found in the mantras and secondly, the form symbols of different types of figures, revealed by conceptions of deities, the anthropomorphic forms of which are often worshipped. The images are built according to the dhyana-slokas (meditation verses) of the particular deities. The images of the deities as well as the mantras

---

1 *Rig-bhashya Bhumika* (pp. 79-80) by T. V. Kapali Sastry.

referring to them are embodiments of consciousness, through which God may be communed with. They are based upon the idea of the Mantra Sastra, which points out that every form has a corresponding sound at the back of it and every sound must have a form.

Om

The most important mantra is the Pranava or Om. It represents the undifferentiated Brahman. 'Brahman is one-syllabled Om', says the *Gita* (8.13). As God, its three letters A, U, M (Aum is the correct spelling) represent His three aspects viz., Brahma, Vishnu, Rudra and their Powers. The vibration of Om is of the sound-Brahman or the first manifestation of the primordial Person. Om is the ground sound and ground movement of nature. Out of Om everything else has evolved. So Om is a symbol of universality. Swami Vivekananda had an idea of a universal temple where no image would be installed but only 'Om'.

The Natha-yogins had specialized in the worship of Om along with that of Siva. To them 'Om is the First Sound, the most elementary Sound, the one unproduced, undifferentiated natural Sound, the most spontaneous self-expression of Energy or Power in audible form.'[2] Om is the Name of the Supreme. Every uttered sound is particular, produced from the strokes of the vocal organs, and broken into parts. But Om is an Anahata-nada, a universal continuous sound behind all broken sounds. It is in the heart, and the search for it is the search for Brahman. As an effective help repetition of Om with steady and lengthened utterance is prescribed. According to the Nathayogins the heart, the seat of Anahata sound, is not located in the particular part of the body but it gradually

---

2 *Nathayoga* (p. 62) by Akshaya Kumar Banerjee.

shifts from lower yogic centres to the higher ones and ultimately to the sahasrara where union of Sakti with Siva is attained. Om, again, has been identified with the three Gunas —Sattva, Rajas, Tamas—constituting the world. It is also regarded as the original Bija-akshara syllable source.

Bija-Mantra

The Tantric Mantra Sastra regards several Aksharas as Bijas or seeds. Akshara is imperishable. It is not really a letter but a combination of a few letters represented in Sanskrit practically as one letter. *Aim, klim, hrim*, etc., are such Bija-aksharas. These sound vibrations have great myst.cal significance. By vocal pronunciation or mental thinking they give illumination. They represent the deities and generally they are added to the Ishta-mantra, name of the chosen Ideal, given for repetition by the Guru. Bija-aksharas are sometimes said to be three or seven in number. They are Bhuh, Bhuvah and Suvah or these three plus Mahat, Janah, Tapah and Satya. They represent also the seven worlds of the same names.

Gayatri

Another important mantra is the Gayatri mentioned in the Rigveda. Every twice-born repeats it thrice a day. In imitation of this mantra Gayatris for other deities also have been prescribed. The Gayatri mantra consists of twenty-four letters. Various interpretations have been given to it. Generally speaking, it means: 'We meditate on the glory of that Being who has produced this universe; may He enlighten our minds.'[3] The Being who is the Sun in the heavenly firmament is the Indweller in the heart of the Sadhaka.

---

3 *Complete Works of Swami Vivekananda* Vol. I (p. 191).

Contemplating on Him and supplicating Him to direct our minds signify surrender to the Lord through whom only the correct understanding and highest realization are possible.

Impersonal and Personal Symbols

There are various conceptions of the Godhead. Broadly classified they come under two heads—personal and impersonal. Impersonal Brahman admits of thought symbols only. To realize the impersonal Absolute, meditation is enjoined considering the soul as a spark, or a river flowing into the sea, or a fish or pot in the ocean of the Absolute, or a bird in infinite space or a ray of light reflected in the body. Meditation on the God of the microcosm leads to the realization of God in the macrocosm.[4]

The personal God, however, admits of innumerable forms. God as the Indwelling Spirit is also a thought symbol. The idea of visualizing the chosen deity in the heart has developed from this conception. The worship of the incarnations of God again is also very common and they are regarded as the veritable representations of God on earth.

Some Form Symbols

The personal God is viewed as the Indweller sitting on the lotus of the heart of man. This is based upon the yogic idea of lotuses with different numbers of petals in the yogic plexuses within the Sushumna, the path for the Kundalini.

Lotus

Fundamentally a symbol is necessary to conceive and meditate on the Lord who in essence is beyond the ken of

---

4 cf. *Cultural Heritage of India*, Vol. IV. (p. 444).

thought and mind. So each system develops through centuries of spiritual practice certain symbols, representations
and diagrams in accordance with the genius of the people.
For this reason, the physical heart which is the most important
organ of the human body is symbolized as a lotus, for it
resembles the lotus flower which is the most beautiful flower.
The devotees are asked to meditate on the chosen deity who
is seated, as it were, on the lotus of the heart, which is the
centre of our very life itself. So externally also the deities
are conceived as sitting on the lotus. The lotus has so much
impressed the collective unconscious of the Indian poets and
seers that they see the beauty of lotus everywhere—in palms,
soles of the feet, eyes, etc. Every symbol has two aspects—
Adhyatma and Adhibhautika. Lotuses are also conceived
outside as well as within the human body where the yogic
centres of realization, inner and outer, are located.

Yantra

As an image is a human, demi-human or divine representation of reality and mantra a sound equivalent, the Yantra
is a diagramatic representation of reality in lines. According
to the votaries of Yantra, the Yantra with its lines, circles and
triangles is a better symbol of reality. As for example, the
well-known Srichakra, which is a Yantra, represents elements,
elementals, the various presiding deities, the complete phonetic
system, Chakras, as well as union of Siva-Sakti in the centre.
Such a comprehensive unity can be conceived only in a
Yantra which with its endless lines and circles can encompass
the whole universe. There is an intimate relationship between
Yantra and mantra and the deity dwells in the Yantra when
real potency is given through invocation.

The Sakti of the Absolute, the Mother of the Universe,
is represented in Her formless aspect by Sriyantra or Sri-

chakra. It represents the Purusha-cum-Prakriti aspect.
But its worship harmonizes the personal and impersonal
aspects of Brahman.

Woodroffe describes in *Shakti and Shakta* (p. 424) the
Evolution of Power, illustrating it by Yantric symbolism.
Brahman or Siva has two aspects. In the Saguna aspect He
is related to Sakti. From Sakti, Nada or sound emanates,
and out of Nada, Bindu. The two triangles represent the
union of Siva and Sakti. The crescent moon is the symbol
of Nada which is not manifested sound or movement, but an
inchoate state of both. The bindu or point is full-moon-like,
for it is Power ready to evolve into manifested sound and
movement. Bindu also means seed, for it is the seed of the
universe as the result of the union of its ultimate principles as
Siva and Sakti. The Bindu is shown as a circle, so as to
display its content and a line divides the Point, one half
representing the 'I', and the other, the 'This' aspect of experience. The Bindu is compared to a Chanaka gram which
contains two seeds so close to one another within their common sheath as to seem to be one seed.

The supreme divinity is represented in the Srichakra
by this central point or Bindu. The triangle around the
Bindu represents all things threefold, Sattva, Rajas, Tamas;
past, present, future; waking, dream and sleep.

Then follow several Avaranas or Chakras, in each point
of which definite powers or Saktis are invoked and worshipped.
By worship the Yantra or Chakra is transformed from a
material object of lines and curves into a mental state of
union with the universe, its divinities and supreme deity.
Sun, Moon and Fire are the three Bindus and Brahma, Vishnu,
Rudra are the three lines. Sun, Moon and Fire do not refer
to the luminaries but the technical terms of the Mantra Sastra
denoting the creative trinity.

Mantra

In the Yogic tradition the mantras are regarded as the special self-manifestations of the Supreme Power, and every letter of every mantra is presided over by a Sakti or Matrika, says the Tantra. The repetition of the Divine Name with every breath is the essence of Yogic mantra-yoga. This is called Ajapa-japa. By nature a Jiva repeats the Hamsa mantra (*ham* while infilling and *sa* during expiration). It means 'I am He'. In the Tantra, Om is regarded as the subtle form of the sacred formula, Hamsa. As all living creatures depend on breathing, their creator Brahma has Hamsa as the carrier, another meaning of it being a water fowl, which explains why Brahma is put on a swan or water fowl.

For spiritual progress an Ishta-mantra is also prescribed other than the Gayatri or the Hamsa mantra. This sacred formula of the chosen deity is selected by the Guru in accordance with the nature of the devotee and his emotional disposition. That is, he considers whether he has Sattva, Rajas or Tamas as his preponderant quality and whether he likes to worship God as Lord, parent, friend, servant, child or lover. The mantra is inspirited by the Guru's own spiritual power plus the power of the first propounder who visualized it. It is the verbal representation of the Supreme. While performing Japa, not only the significance is to be known but its spiritual meaning also must be deeply contemplated.

Sivalinga and Salagrama

Half-way between the sound symbols and the anthropomorphic symbols there is another type called the aniconic symbols. These symbols of Siva and Vishnu are known as the Sivalinga and Narayana-sila or Salagrama. Linga means symbol, sign. It also means the place of mergence, in which all manifestations are dissolved and unified. Some have tried to trace its origin to phallus worship but no such association is traceable in the ideas of devotees. Some have endeavoured to identify the conceptions of Linga and Yoni in Tantra as fatherhood and motherhood. We do not know whether the human parallels were taken from life or due to some confusion from any cult, but it is clear to philosophical minds that they refer only to the fatherhood and motherhood of the universe in a figurative sense. The tapering Siva-linga situated on the base represents Purusha and Prakriti of Sankhya. Linga here clearly means the unchanging axis round which the whole creation moves. It has also been pointed out that the temples of Siva are generally built in the imitation of the Himalayan peaks with their bases on the earth and summits soaring towards the transcendent sky. Similarly a devotee, though he is in the world, must keep his mind on Siva. That is the idea behind the Linga, as some point out.

The Salagrama of Narayana represents the Absolute with attributes. It is black and egg-shaped and represents Hiranyagarbha or the primordial Golden Egg, the undifferentiated Totality. It is out of Hiranyagarbha that the whole universe becomes differentiated in course of time.

Ceremonial Worship

There is much of symbolism in ceremonial worship. Worship of deities in different methods is done by different sects. But some of the processes are common among them. During worship, the worshipper sits on a seat in a particular Yogic posture conducive to high thinking. After bowing down to the guru, the spiritual teacher and Ganesa, the Lord of success, he purifies his hands, etc., as well as the area and the ingredients with appropriate sacred formulas. After purifying the earth, sky, etc., he thinks of a fence of fire,

putting water in a circle all around, meant to protect him
from all physical and psychical obstacles. Then the purification of the elements constituting the body, called Bhuta-
suddhi, is performed with Pranayama consisting of inhaling,
retaining and exhaling the breath.

The practice of Bhuta-suddhi done during ceremonial
worship makes the worshipper pure. The Tantric idea is,
'Worship God by becoming God'. Bhuta-suddhi is done
thus: first, inhaling through sushumna, one's own Jiva is
transferred to the feet of the Lord in the thousand-petalled
lotus in the head. Then with the seed-mantra of air the
dross in the spiritual body is dried up. Next, with the seed-
mantra of fire the dross is burnt up; then the drossless body
is bathed in ambrosia and then a purified body is generated;
now the worshipper is free from all dross and equal to the
spirit of Lord Himself.

These practices are not meaningless formality but have
spiritual usefulness as will be clear when we observe the
life of Sri Ramakrishna who noticed the wall of fire around
himself and also saw the Papa-purusha, the evil and dross
personified.

After Bhuta-suddhi the Sadhaka performs Nyasas touching
the different parts of the body with mantras. Then he thinks
of the deity occupying his body, mind, Pranas and sense
organs. Then investing the Absolute with the form of his
chosen deity, he meditates on Him as sitting in the heart.
Then the deity is brought out to the Linga or flower, etc.,
representing the deity and taken back after worship. Different
Mudras or gestures pleasing to the gods are then shown.
They help in concentration also. Now, different articles are
offered to the deity. Next, offering handfuls of flowers
and performing Japa, the fruits of worship are offered to the
deity Himself. With bowing down, the worship comes to an

end. For special worship, however, more elaborate rituals
are prescribed.

One thing to be noted in the ceremonial worship is that
among the Vaishnavas the stress is more on the seva or
Kainkarya, the service of the deity exactly as we do to a very
respectable beloved human being. The Smartas have a great
belief in the potency of the mantra and they believe that as
soon as a thing is offered with a suitable mantra properly
uttered, the deity accepts it.

Articles of Offering

The Upacharas or the articles offered are really the
manifestations of Prakriti. So 'the esotericism of the
Upacharas is to conceive the return of the manifested universe
to the unmanifested homogeneous unitary state, which is the
Absolute, as a result of the effect of time, which itself is eternal
and absolute. In its exoteric form, this truth assumes the
shape of offering of the five fundamental forms of existence
and becomes the Panchopachara.'[5] When material food
is offered, the pranahuti mantra is uttered. It denotes that
the offering is really of the life-principle or the Para-Prakriti.
The Amrita mantra denotes the immortal factor or 'spirit'
as the material offered. In panchopachara, materials are
used only in elaborate worship but the entire worship can be
performed mentally also according to Manasa-puja.

Every deity is worshipped with 5, 10, 16 or 64 Upacharas
or articles. They also have esoteric meanings. The five
Upacharas of sandal paste, flower, incense, light and food
signify trust, adoration, love, knowledge and identity.
Another item alternative to food is water. It represents
adherence. These, however, are offered taking the deity as

---

5 *Ibid* (p. 461).

a very honoured guest. The worship in temples is conducted considering the deity as the king of the universe. The Arati is done waving before the deity the five articles of light, water, cloth, flower, and chamara (yak's hairy tail). These represent the five basic elements constituting the world or the five basic forms in which all the material things are manifested.

Installation Ceremony

The system of Yoga has profoundly influenced all rituals. As for example, its influence is very evident in the ceremony of installation of an image of a deity. When an idol is placed in a temple, first an excavation is made and some articles are placed successively with appropriate mantras. A support stone, a pot of deposit, a lotus bud, a form of a tortoise—all made of stone normally, are placed. Then follow an open lotus flower and a tortoise in silver, then the same in gold, and a hollow copper tube like the spinal cord. The enumerated articles are identified with the different Yogic centres in the body. 'This arrangement depicts the temple itself as the body of the Yogin. The actual idol is placed where the Sahasrara lotus would be. Thus a perfect and complete Yogic representation is given to the installed image.'[6]

Human Body as Temple

This practice of considering the human body as a symbol, as a temple of God is very common among the Hindu sects. 'The body of ours is a temple of the Divine', says the *Maitreyi Upanishad* (II. 1). God resides in the heart of man and the sanctum sanctorum of the temple represents his heart. The heart is a cave and the king of the dark chamber is God; hence the sanctum sanctorum is purposely kept dark without

6 *Ibid* (p. 452-3).

any windows or ventilators; except for a small lamp in front burning day and night. The latter represents the lamp of wisdom that would be lit in the heart and kept burning constantly.

Lights in the temple represent the light of the soul, the ever resplendent atma-jyoti. The clarified butter often supplied to the lamp stands for regular spiritual practice. The system of burning camphor before the deity means that our ego, etc., are to be set on fire with the flame of divinity. When all desires, etc., are consumed in the flame, the Jiva becomes one with the Lord. The Suprabhata song sung early in the morning for the purpose of waking up the Lord is really the waking up of the sleeping divinity in man.

Many temples in South India arrange the floating festival, in which the deity is placed on a lighted boat in the temple tank and taken around. The idea is, the world is an unchartered ocean in which men are about to sail. If the Lord be the helmsman there is no fear, for He is the real saviour.

Generally every temple has three prakaras or rounds representing the three bodies—gross, subtle and causal. Some temples have five rounds representing five sheaths of Atman—Anna, Prana, Mana, Vijnana, and Anandamaya. The seven rounds in the seven-walled city of Srirangam, the abode of Lord Ranganatha represent the seven Dhatus of which the body is made.

Every temple has a Bali-pitha in front. It suggests to the devotee to sacrifice all his ego and desires before he enters the temple. The circumambulation done in some of the temples of Siva is not in the clockwise direction but one goes up to one half and then turns back and completes the circuit. Thus the figure of Om is traced.

The car festivals are arranged in temples once a year. The car festival of Lord Jagannath of Puri is very famous.

The idea behind this festival in which the deity is put on a chariot and drawn by devotees, is that the human body is a chariot and God resides in it as the indweller. The *Kathopanishad* (I.3.3.) says that Atman should be considered the master of the chariot and body, the chariot.

Conclusion

We have described a few of the Hindu symbols. The forms of deities will require a separate treatment which we propose to do later. The various symbols of religion have deep inner meaning. It is often so grand and poetic that to understand it is to find out the sublime but subtle truths of philosophy. A symbol is not a mere shadowy vision; it is the living revelation to saints and seers in their deep ecstatic contemplation. Thereby it has acquired its spiritual validity and usefulness.

The goal of sadhana is the transformation of the worshipper into the likeness of the worshipped. It is based on forms which experience has shown to be fruitful. So there is no question of inventing a ritual or a symbol. That can be done only by an incarnation of God. The generally recognized effective forms of God are the traditional ones, for they have been used for ages.

Spiritual growth comes through intense thought of God in different forms. 'As are one's thought and faith, such one becomes', says the *Chandogya Upanishad* (3.14.1). The symbols help us to have this thought. If we know the spiritual meanings of symbols, they help us in keeping the mind in the thought of God. As a result, we shall climb gradually on the spiritual ladder and ultimately have the vision of the Supreme.

DIVINE FORMS
(A SYMBOLIC INTERPRETATION)

THE Hindu tradition accepts many gods and goddesses as manifestations of the Absolute. Though each of the deities represents one dominant aspect of God, generally the evolutionary process of creation is also symbolized in the images. Images are the forms of God visualized by saints and seers in their hours of communion. Art has also contributed to their beauty and richness. Different images have been portrayed by later artists, and they are part of the priceless treasures of our heritage. Images, being the focal point of all devotional expressions, have satisfied devotees of varied temperaments. But images are not mere naturalistic representations of the artists. They are the symbols of the Divine. meant primarily to orient our thoughts and feelings, and not for gratifying the aesthetic sense. As the image is a production of the saintly artist, every single detail of the form is expressive of some deeper universal truth. And this truth presented in artistic forms is more lovable. The images give tangible forms to the abstract concepts of philosophy and mystic realization. They are the link between the Infinite and the finite, the Eternal and the transient, the Formless and the formful. If we know the significance of the images, we can easily reach the deeper truth, for meditation becomes easier. As Wilson pertinently observes in his translation of the *Vishnu Purana*, in a conception of an image we have

a representation of one mode of Dhyana or contemplation in which the thoughts are more readily concentrated, by being addressed to a sensible emblem, instead of an abstract truth.

From a perceptible substance to the imperceptible idea—that is the method followed here. The human representations of God, with divine peculiarities, of course, become so palpable to the devotee that the latter sees Him as his near and dear one. Hundreds of instances are there in mystical literature where devotees have seen God in tangible form as Mother, Child and the like.

For understanding the conceptions of Hindu deities not only philosophy but much of Puranic knowledge is also necessary. Every deity has been represented in different forms according to different traditions but we shall have to give the interpretations of some more prevalent forms, just as samples. It should also be remembered that interpretations slightly vary according to the conceptions of the particular sect. Let us now describe only a few of the main deities who are worshipped throughout India.

Siva

Siva is one of the most popular deities in India. The divine human representation of Siva is based on a grand conception. Siva is depicted with a Trisula. With His holy three-pronged Trident He killed the Tripurasura, the demon of ego inhabiting the three bodies—gross, subtle and causal. The three prongs are Vairagya (non-attachment), Jnana (knowledge) and Samadhi (absorption). His third eye is the eye of Knowledge. With His three eyes He sees the past, present and future. Siva as the Lord of the universe rides on the bull of dharma having the four feet of truth, purity, kindness and charity. Siva's symbol of destruction is the battle-axe. The moon, when it means Time, also stands for dissolution. It may mean the dawn of wisdom also.

Siva is the Ishta-devata of the Yogis. Hence Yogic symbolization is very pronounced in this form. The three eyes here represent the sun, the moon and the fire or Ida, Pingala and Sushumna. The Ganges represents nectar in the Sahasrara. The moon is the Chandramandala, the white region of the Yogis, the Damaru, drum, the Nada-Brahman. According to the Yogis the Sahasrara is in Kailasa, the abode of Siva, and the entire India is the body having six important Yogic centres, important for Saivites.

In South India there are five separate Siva temples representing the five elements. They are in Kanchi (earth), Tiruvanaikavu near Trichi (water), Kalahasti (air), Tiruvanna-malai (fire) and Chidambaram (ether).

To the devotees of Siva fire or the constantly burning Dhuni implies the fire of Vairagya, burning all attachments and desires. They besmear the ashes of the Dhuni on their body as does the Lord Himself, for ashes are left over after the diverse names and forms disappear and the real unity under-lying all the differences is attained. Maha-yogi Siva is in this sense the all-destroyer, for He dissolves all diversities in the absolute unity.

Nataraja

The Nataraja form represents the five functions of God. The drum stands for creation, the hand for Abhaya, the promise of freeing from fear, fire for destruction, the foot on the ground for veiling and the uplifted foot stands for unveiling and enlightenment. The place of dance is this universe where He dances the cosmic dance. There are five steps leading to the temple representing Saivite Ishtamantra which has five syllables. While Nataraja represents the form aspect, the secret is, at the background of form is the formless and this is shown by not having any image at all.

B. Rajam Iyer gives a fine, poetic description of Nataraja in his *Rambles in Vedanta*. Nataraja means the Lord of the stage of this transitory world. He is the real Guru concretely represented, for He teaches by being what He teaches. It is this idea that is the key-note to the Nataraja symbol. The drum in His right hand means that God or the Guru holds in His hand the cause of all the world, i.e., sound. The deer on one side is the mind with all its fickleness. The tiger skin He wears represents egoism, for the latter must be killed for spiritual progress. The Ganges on His head represents wisdom which is cooling and refreshing and the moon represents the ethereal light and blissfulness of the Atman. One foot crushes the giant Muyalaka, the endless illusion which is the cause of birth and death, while the other foot is raised upward representing the Turiya state which is beyond and above the three states of waking, dream and dreamless sleep and leaves behind the mind, Maya and the world. The second right hand representing the idea of peace indicates the blessed calmness of wisdom. The fire in one of the left hands shows the light of the Atman that is brought by the Guru, which is to be experienced. The place of the dance, the theatre is Thillai-vanam, a forest on account of the many components of the body. The cremation ground is the platform, where all passions and all names and forms are burnt away. When we see this inner meaning of the image of Nataraja, it will be clear that this image is a grand symbol of the highest teaching, an object that can inspire and elevate.

Vishnu

The form of Vishnu is Yogic and the symbolism is based on the Vedantic fundamentals. There is a grandeur in the poetic conception of Ananta or the Sesha-sayana form of Vishnu lying on a serpent. Many temples are dedicated to Him in this

form. The Srirangam and Trivandrum temples are very
famous. Ranganatha, like Nataraja, means the Lord of the
stage of the world, of the cosmos or better still, of the body and
the senses. He sleeps on the milky sea representing the
sweet, undisturbed, nectar-like calmness of the effulgent Turiya
state. He sleeps on Sesha, the huge serpent with upraised
hood, symbolizing the intelligent human consciousness.
Another name of the serpent is Ananta, represented as infinite
time. But it goes beyond that. Sesha also means what
remains at the end, the undying eternal. Ananta means
endless. The serpent in Yogic tradition stands for the Coiled
Power, Kundalini. The basis of the all-pervading Vishnu
must be infinite but the three coils of Ananta show the finite
too. The image in the temple is made of five metals as the
entire universe is made of five basic elements.

Ananta is on the milky sea, for 'until the heavenly calm
of the inner soul is realized, the beauty of the inner consciousness cannot be seen.'[1] Vishnu means all-pervading and
His sleep represents the Nirvikalpa state or the non-kinetic
state of the Absolute. Vishnu is sleeping on no particular
side, for He fills every side. He is in water and no clouds of
sin, grief or imperfection can touch Him. He has dark
colour to signify that He cannot be known by the senses.
Vishnu in the milky sea is the personal God with the background of the abstract Brahman.

The *Vishnu Purāna* (1.22) gives an interpretation of the
ornaments of Vishnu. The Kaustubha gem on His broad
chest represents the pure and everlasting soul of the world.
The pradhana, the chief principle of things, is the Srivatsa
mark on the forehead of the Lord. The Gada (mace) represents the intellect that saves against the arrows in the war of

---

1 *Cultural Heritage of India* IV (p. 455).

life. The conch-shell represents the great function of creation, for creation is due to vibration—*sabdanishtham jagat*. The bow represents the sense-organs with the faculty of grasping.

Creation and enjoyment are the Lila or sport of the Lord. Ahankara or egoism is the basis of that. The Chakra (discus) symbolizes the mind for its speed and swiftness. The multi-coloured garland or necklace Vaijayanti represents the variegated universe. The Achyuta, the sword, fells the Aswattha tree of Samsara mentioned often in old books. Lakshmi represents the luxuriance of the world, the Lord's glory. She sits near the feet, the Avidya-pada, the sphere of ignorance, which is the mother of creation of the world.[2] The whole conception is very grand and is not mere idolatry, as direct philosophical descriptions of the Lord will clearly show.

In the standing posture of Vishnu, one of His hands is towards the feet and the other towards the devotee, as if the Lord is asking the devotee to surrender himself completely and take refuge at His feet so that He might give him the boon of freedom from fear. The hands of other deities also are often represented likewise.

His two Saktis, Bhumi and Lakshmi represent Sattva and Rajas, while His Yogic sleep represents Tamas and stands for His third Sakti called Nila by the Pancharatras. So Anantasayana represents the Absolute with differentiated Gunas about it. These Saktis are also regarded as the three aspects of the Grace of the Lord.

Subrahmanya

Subrahmanya or Skanda is a very popular deity, especially in the Tamil area. He has different names. Muruga has been regarded as a deity of the hilly regions. He has six

---

2 cf. *Rambles in Vedanta*

3

principal shrines, all on hillocks. They are in Tiruchendur, Palani, Swamimalai, Alagarkoil, Tirupparankunram and Tiruttani. In mystic tradition, He is known as Guha, for He resides in the cave (Guha) of the heart. Lord Subrahmanya, the Commander-in-Chief of the gods and son of Siva and Devi, is seated on a peacock. Sometimes He is depicted with two divine consorts, Valli and Devasena or Devayani. The peacock represents the Rajasic ego, so fond of pomp and grandeur, represented by variegated colours. The spear in the hand represents wisdom. Valli is the power of will and Devasena, the power of action. Iccha, Kriya and Jnana—all the three saktis should be exercised to kill the demon of ego in us represented by Surapadma with hundred heads. If one of his heads is cut off, another head appears. The hydra-headed monster of egoism likewise cannot be completely vanquished but can be subdued. Then it becomes one's vehicle or vahana.

His victory over the demons and liberation of the gods from captivity were the prime purpose of His manifestation. The three demons, Surapadma, Simhamukha and Taraka represent the three basic factors of nescience, viz., self-centred ego, wrath and illusion. Skanda, with His spear representing illumination, destroyed the forces of nescience.

Skanda is called Shanmukha, for He has six faces. Nakkirar, an old Tamil writer, gives the significance of each one of the six faces of Shanmukha. 'One removes the darkness and ignorance of the world and bathes it in light; the second grants boons to the devotees; the third protects the Yajna; the fourth discourses upon the Knowledge of the Self; the fifth destroys evil demons; and the sixth glances lovingly at the face of Valli, His bride from the hills.'[3]

_____

3 *C.H.I.* IV (p. 310).

The offering taken ceremoniously to His temple has a Yogic meaning. Kavadi (or ornamented bamboo poles, to which are hung small pots containing milk, sugar, honey, flower and fruits) stands for the spinal column on two ends of which are two lotuses.

Ganesha

Ganesha is the god of plenty and wisdom, of fortune, peace and spiritual success. He destroys all obstacles of man and opens the gate of realization. Calm and tranquil by nature, He represnts the conquest of manifested animality which is transformed into spirituality. Sometimes Ganesha is worshipped with two wives, Success and Prosperity or Intelligence, though both Kartika and Ganesha are said to be unmarried in most of the traditions. A rat is His vehicle, which is emblematical of sagacity. In Tamil tradition, He stands for Om for His figure with an elephant's trunk resembles the form of Om.

Kali

Of all the forms of the Goddess it is Her form of Kali that has given rise to much of symbolic interpretation, for many forms are more Puranic than philosophical. The Mother-worshippers generally represent Siva and Sakti together. Siva represents the transcendent aspect of the Absolute Spirit and Mother Kali the world-producing Supreme Power, the dynamic aspect. Kali's dance on the breast of Siva indicates that the whole universe of ever-changing diversities is an appearance of the one changeless

Supreme Spirit. Amidst all changes Siva remains unchanged. Mother Kali is worshipped for the realization of the Absolute within oneself in all the vicissitudes of life.

Normally Mother Kali is represented with four arms stretched out over all the four directions. She holds the bleeding head of a demon in the lower left hand, a sharp dazzling sword in the upper left hand, a banner of universal fearlessness in the upper right hand and an offer of blissful boons in the lower right hand. Thus one hand destroys the lower forms of manifestation, the relatively unreal ones and the other preserves the world order. So She is both the just Ruler and the affectionate Mother. With the other two arms She brandishes the swords and offers boons and freedom from fear. There are terrible evil forces ready to cut asunder and there is Her grace too. Both are Her aspects. The former ones are necessary to lead the creatures to the latter so that ultimately they may be released from the transmigratory existence.

The gifts of fearlessness, hope, strength, etc., are being promised by the Abhaya-mudra of Her right hand. The Jiva who is able to see through the world-process knows that She is ever awaiting Her devotees to confer on them eternal bliss. This hand is pointed towards the face of Siva, who is of the nature of highest bliss. Sivahood, realization of the Absolute, is the *summum bonum* of life. Thus with one hand She creates limitations; with another She cuts them asunder and frees the soul.

The legs of Kali are in a dancing pose. And She is dancing on the calm Siva. Kali is the embodiment of Time standing and dancing the cosmic dance on the breast of the Timeless Eternity, Mahakala. Kali is all black, Siva is all white. Her black colour is the mother of all colours while the white colour of Siva is the fulfilment and unity of all the

coloured existences. Through Sadhana for Siva, Kali becomes
Gauri, having a fair complexion. As She is infinite and eter-
nal, She is without any limitation. This is represented by
Her nakedness.

Kali wears a garland of human skulls. Destruction does
not mean annihilation; only the lower planes of existence are
replaced by the higher ones. The garland of the human
souls and their contributions to the world system is on the
breast of Time. The past, present and future pertain to Her
transitory, finite self-manifestation. Though dancing eternally,
She is never outside the breast of Siva. She is represented with
a protruding tongue which is bitten by the teeth. This is
due to Her wonder and admiration at Her own appearance
and performance. The Divine Power is as if ashamed because
of Her restlessness in creating the universe in spite of Her
transcendent nature and hence Kali bites Her tongue, as is the
common human practice. Her eyes are gleaming in joy
because of Her performance and union. Her third eye is
ever-waking, for it is the eye of Her perfect knowledge of
identity with the Absolute.

Devi

Of the other forms of the Divine Mother, mention may be
made of Rajarajesvari and Durga. Rajarajesvari is conceived as having the perfect Rajoguna form. She also represents knowledge in its abstract sense and is often known as
Srividya or auspicious knowledge. 'Her weapons are the
sugarcane bow, arrows of flowers, the noose and the goad.
Kamikagama explains the sense underlying these. The
sugarcane bow stands for the mind or the faculty of per-
ception; the five arrows of flowers represent the five Tanmatras
or the Bhuta forms that can affect the five senses. Knowledge
of any type can arise only as a result of action of the pheno-

menal universe on the mind through the senses. The knowledge that arises thus may be beneficial or dangerous; it
may be used for the good of the world or for its ill. The
noose stands for binding or attaching, and means that one
should attach oneself to the beneficent form of knowledge.
The Ankusa or the goad shows that dangerous knowledge
should be kept under control as an unruly elephant.'[5]

Another form of the Mother is Durga, specially popular
in Bengal. The festival of Navaratri is observed throughout
India, from Kashmir to Kanyakumari and Kamakhya to
Hinglaz. Of course, Devi is known differently in different
places. The worship of Durga is a very elaborate affair
requiring various preparatory rituals of worship. The Bodhana
worship or awakening of the Goddess done earlier is the
awakening of the 'sleeping' Divinity within the worshipper
or the Coiled Power of the Yogis. The Vilva tree, where She is
prayed to dwell, is a symbol of the Sushumna canal, the
path of Kundalini.

Conclusion

In this way the spiritual and philosophical significance
of different deities in the Hindu tradition may be brought out.
But the already described ones, we hope, are enough to show
how the old teachers and philosophical votaries have interpreted the symbolical character of gods and goddesses
Their worship is the potent method of realizing the ultimate
Reality. Three kinds of worship are described in the scrip
tures: Svarupa, Sampad and Pratika. To realize the Absolute
in one's Self through discrimination and renunciation is the
first method. To meditate on perceptible objects like the sun
wind, vital breath, etc., resembling Brahman in respect o

---

5 *C.H.I.* IV (p. 460).

luminosity, motion, sustaining power, etc., is the second. To serve a symbol or substitute of Brahman is the third method. Image or Pratima comes under it. The Sastras declare Brahman to be the only existence. So images are really Brahman Himself and worship of images is really worship of Brahman. Moreover, forms of deities were intuited by saints and often visualized by later men of realization. With the deeper understanding of the symbolical nature of images, the awareness of God is more easy and immediate. Herein lies its significance.

THE TANTRIK CONCEPT OF MOTHER WORSHIP

'Brahman and Sakti are identical. Him who you call Brahman, I call Sakti,' said Sri Ramakrishna. But this conception of the Mother as the Supreme Reality took a long time to develop fully, though here and there some Sadhakas or Rishis might have found out the clues or inklings, as is evident from the Rigvedic Devi-sukta, 'I am the empress of the whole universe'.[1] In fact all the later thoughts in the Puranas and the Tantras have been traced back to the Vedas which are the sources of knowledge.

About the origin of Mother worship, Swami Vivek-ananda says:

Mother worship is a distinct philosophy in itself. Power is the first of our ideas. It infringes upon man at every step. Power felt within, is the Soul, without, nature. And the battle between the two makes human life. All that we know or feel is but the resultant of these two forces. Man saw that the sun shines on the good and the evil alike. Here was a new idea of God as the Universal Power behind all. The Mother-idea was born.

This conception of the Mother developed through the process of history. The Rigvedic Gnas or the fertility god-desses or the Devapatnis like Dhishana, Sarasvati, Hotra, Bharati, Indrani represent the earliest conceptions of Sakti. The goddesses of plenty are gradually identified with Lakshmi,

---

1 अहं राष्ट्री संगमनी वसूनाम् (10.10.125,3.)

the goddesses of the river with Sarasvati and the Gna goddesses merge in Vak. The creative functions of Sarasvati in the Brahmanas under a motherly conception is the precursor of the later Sakti-cult. The Vak-sakti is fully developed in the Svetasvatara Upanishad which is considered to be the main source of the personalistic conceptions.[2] This view of the relation of Sakti to Saktiman, Isvara, was adopted by the later schools of philosophy. The Kashmir School of Saivism developed the idea of Sakti. The great Adyanatha supplied the definition of Sakti as the power by which Siva externalises His consciousness as the object of His self-enjoyment. The Vira-saiva idea of Sakti was much influenced by the Kashmir School and it added the idea of Mahamaya. Among the orthodox schools, Mimamsa discusses Sakti only in connection with the idea of Adrishta, the idea of causality, and in connection with the capability of words to show class-idea. Samkhya admits Sakti in connection with Prakriti as at best the source of matter, gross and subtle. Sankara in Advaita Vedanta admits Sakti as a determinative category in the cause and also in connection with the description of Maya. These orthodox schools do not view Sakti as the 'Supreme Divine Power' belonging to God as developed by the Saiva-schools. But the idea of Sakti as the Mother who creates, sustains and destroys and bestows grace as well, was developed by the Tantrika worshippers called the Saktas.

The Saktas are so-called because they are the worshippers of Sakti. Their rule of conduct is called Saktadharma, their doctrine, Saktivada or Sakti Darshana, even though Sakti had important roles in the Tantras of the Saivas, the Vaishnavas and the Buddhists. According to the Saktas,

---

2 देवात्मशक्तिं स्वगुणैर्निगूढाम् (sv. u. I.3.)

Siva is the unchanging Consciousness and Sakti is Its changing Power appearing as mind and matter. Siva-Sakti is therefore Consciousness and Its power. The former is God as He is, and the latter is God as He appears to us. This then is the doctrine of the dual aspects of Brahman acting through its threefold powers of will, knowledge and action.[3] In the static, transcendent aspect (Siva) the one Brahman does not change and in the kinetic, immanent aspect (Sakti) It does. There is thus changelessness in change.

In creation a change is produced without change in the producer. The Sakti 'goes forth', in a series of emanations or transformations which are known in the Saiva and Sakta Tantras as the 36 Tattvas as against the 24 Tattvas of Samkhya.

All possible conceptions have been identified with the Devi, Who is the Mother Supreme. Thus She is the great Sakti and is the ordainer of the Universe. *Kubjika Tantra* says, 'Not Brahma, Vishnu and Rudra create, maintain and destroy, but Brahmi, Vaishnavi, Rudrani. Their husbands are but as dead bodies.' Sankara writes in *Saundarya Lahari* (sloka 1), 'If Siva is in union with Sakti, He becomes the Lord of the Universe; if not He cannot even move.' This is quite in keeping with the Rigvedic idea, 'I am the empress of the whole universe.'

She is all-pervading, says the *Chandi*.[4] Devi shows grace to Rama and Arjuna as recorded in the two great epics.

She is not simply a goddess with names, but is the very essence of all the gods, as shown in the creation of Chandika in the *Chandi*.

Mother has two sets of forms—a set of gentle forms

---

3 इच्छा, ज्ञान, क्रिया—*iccha jñana kriya*
4 नित्यैव सा जगन्मूर्तिस्तया सर्वमिदं ततम् ।

in which She is surpassingly beautiful and another set of terrible forms in which She is surpassingly fearful. A Sadhaka must be able to see Her in both. This is a very peculiar conception of the Tantra. Swami Vivekananda wanted to introduce this worship of the Terrible. Kali is the symbol of the Terrible who requires sacrifices. She is called the lover of sacrifices, of blood (Balipriya, Rudhirapriya). We must give our blood to satisfy Her. This is nothing but complete self-surrender at the feet of the Mother, which is variously known as the Death of the Old man or *manonasah* or *cittavritti-nirodhah*. This is true in our everyday life. That man is successful who can sacrifice the attraction of the moment for an ideal.

Mother is Trigunamayi as well as Gunatita. The different conceptions vary according to the preponderance of the Gunas. Thus Kali is Kaivalyadayini, Tara is Sattvagunatmika, Tattvadayini. Shodasi, Bhuvanesvari, Chhinnamasta are Rajopradhana Sattvagunatmika, the givers of Gaunamukti and Svarga. Dhumavati, Kamala are Tamopradhana whose action is sought in magical Shatkarma. Mother is the meeting ground of all the opposites. Nay, She Herself is all the contradictory things, both good and bad.

She is Maya, for of Her the Maya which produces the Samsara is. As lord of Maya She is Mahamaya. As Maya She binds, as Mahamaya She liberates when pleased.[5] As Avidya Sakti she puts snares; as Vidya Sakti She frees from snares. She is Prakriti, and as existing before creation She is the Adya (Primordial) Sakti. She is the Vachaka-sakti, the manifestation of Chit in Prakriti, and the Vachya-sakti or Chit itself.

---

5 सैषा प्रसन्ना वरदा नणां भवति मुक्तये (Chandi: I. 56.)

Mother is in all manifestations,[6] says the Svetasvatara Upanishad.

But She is more manifested in the female forms.[7] She is famous as Ten Mahavidyas and stays in fifty-one holy places in different forms.

Like Sri Krishna in the Gita, She also promises to incarnate when vice prevails. Thus in the *Chandi* she says: 'Whenever there is trouble of this kind caused by the demons, I shall incarnate myself and destroy the enemies.'[8] The whole conception of Nava-sakti (nine manifestations of the Goddess) is based on this idea of incarnation.

Mainly, Mother has three forms viz.: (1) 'Para' which none knows, says *Vishnu Yamala;* (2) Sukshma (subtle) form which consists of Mantra; (3) Sthula (gross) form which She takes up for the convenience of the devotee's meditation.

There are various conceptions of the Devi, but to the devotees She is popular as the Mother with infinite grace. Thus *Bhairavi Stotra* (S1.5.) says that some think of Her as Sthula, some as Sukshma, some as the guardian of speech, some as the cause of the Universe, but the devotee considers Her as the ocean of infinite grace. And the Mother with great grace is worshipped with various rituals which are given by the Tantra Sastras.

Though the Tantra Sastra is divided into three parts, viz., Sadhana, Siddhi and philosophy, it is mainly considered to be a Sadhana Sastra, not actually books on philosophy. Philosophy is necessary, but experience is the highest test.

---

6 त्वं स्त्री त्वं पुमानसि (IV.3.)

7 स्त्रियः समस्ताः सकला जगत्सु (Chandi: IV.6.)

8 इत्थं यदा यदा बाधा दानवोत्था भविष्यति ।
   तदा तदाऽवतीर्याहं करिष्याम्यरिसंक्षयम् ॥ (XI.55)

'Religion is Realisation' as Swamiji puts it. For that, Sadhana—exertion, practice—is necessary. Tantra therefore developed a most wonderful and elaborate system of rituals partly its own and partly of Vaidika origin. The watchword of Tantra is Kriya or action. It believes not only in Bhava-dvaita but in Kriyadvaita, not only in feeling but in behaviour also. 'Advaita Vedanta is the whole day and life of the Sakti-sadhaka.' Thus he begins his day saying that he is the Devi Herself and none else. *Kali Tantra* enjoins, 'Having thus meditated, the Sadhaka should worship Devi with the notion of Soham'[9] and *Kubjika Tantra* says, "A Sadhaka should meditate upon himself as one and the same with Her."[10] Similarly we find *Nila Tantra* directing the Sadhaka to think of himself as Tarini, *Gandharva Tantra* telling him to meditate on the Self as one with Tripura not different from Paramatman and *Kalikula-sarvasva* as one with Kalika and so on. *Kularnava Tantra* says, 'The body is the temple of God. Jiva is Sadasiva. Let him give up his ignorance as the offering which is thrown away and worship with the thought and feeling 'He am I'.[11]

Thus in Sakta Upasana, the Karma is the ritualistic expression of the teaching of Jnana-kanda and is calculated to lead to it. There is nothing in it which contradicts Brahma-jnana. This doctrine became very popular in Bengal, and in fact most of the upper class people of Bengal are Saktas. Advaita-vada, of course, is a little adapted according to the Sakta definition. Thus to a Sakta, Soham is actually Saaham.

---

9 एवं ध्यात्वा ततो देवीं सोऽहमात्मानमर्चयेत् ।
10 तथा सहितमात्मानं एकीभूतं विचिन्तयेत् ।
11 देहो देवालयः प्रोक्तः जीवो देवः सदाशिवः ।
त्यजेत् अज्ञाननिर्माल्यं सोऽहंभावेन पूजयेत् ॥ (IX.41)

The Saktas claim the highest place for their method of Sadhana in the Kaliyuga. According to the *Kularnava Tantra*, religious practices are to be done according to Sruti in Krita-yuga, Smriti in Treta, Purana in Dwapara and Agama in Kali. *Nigama Kalpataru* says, 'As among castes the Brahmanas are foremost, so amongst Sadhakas are the Saktas.' *Niruttara Tantra* says that salvation does not come without the know-ledge of Sakti. Amongst the Saktas again the foremost are said to be the worshippers of the Kali Mantra.

Saktas have four Sampradayas, viz.: Kerala, Kashmira, Gauda and Vilasa. Each Sampradaya has separate systems— Suddha, Gupta and Ugra—according to the preponderance of Sattva, Rajas and Tamas. Sadhakas vary according to moods which are mainly three, viz.: Divya, Vira and Pasu. As a result there are different Acharas or rituals which are mainly seven, viz.: Vaidika, Vaishnava, Saiva, Dakshina, Vama, Siddhanta and Kaula. These are the successive stages in the ascending order. In Siddhanta stage the Sadhaka has realisation, but he is fully established in that in the Kaula stage, which is the highest stage as the *Kularnava* (II. 8) says, 'There is none higher than a Kaula.'[12] A Kaula is verily Siva. In the *Nitya Tantra* the description that is given of a Kaula is exactly similar to that of Brahmajnani.[13] This Kaulachara is the essence of the Vedas and Agamas[14] and is called the fifth Ashrama by the Saktas. To a Kaula all action is the play or Lila of Siva-Sakti. In this realization

---

12 कौलात् परतरं नहि (*Kulārnava* II.8.)
13 कर्दमे चन्दनेऽभिन्नः पुत्रौ रात्रौ प्रियाप्रिये ।
   श्मशाने भवने देवि तथैव काञ्चने तृणे ।
   न भेदो यस्य देवेशि स कौलः परिकीर्तितः ॥
14 मथित्वा ज्ञानदण्डेन वेदागममहार्णवम् (*Kulārnava* II.10.)

nothing remains secular; everything is spiritual and the expression of the Mother.

The first three stages form an introduction to the fourth— the Dakshinachara. Vedachara in this series means some Vedic rituals as modified by the Tantra. The Vaishnavachara is the path of devotion and the Saivachara, the path of know- ledge. After completing the three preliminaries of Karma, Bhakti and Jnana, the Sadhaka goes to Dakshinachara which is believed to have been started by Dakshinamurti. These four stages belong to Pravritti-marga. Now the Sadhaka takes an opposite turn and enters Nivritti-Marga, the first stage of which is Vamachara (Vama means opposite). At this stage with the help of a Guru he undergoes special initia- tion called Abhisheka and tries to conquer his desires—not by renunciation—Neti, Neti—but by means of sublimation and consecration. He has to rise by the very things by which the ordinary man falls.[15]

We now come to a delicate and much criticised aspect of the Vamachara known as Panchamakara, viz., Madya, Mamsa, Matsya, Mudra, Maithuna. These are the symbols of different Yogic processes. It has different meanings accord- ing as the Sadhaka belongs to the mood of Pasu, Vira or Divya. Thus for the highest aspirant Madya means the bliss of the Union of Siva-Sakti in the Sahasrara. Mamsa means controlling the tongue. Matsya means controlling the breath. Mudra is the knowledge of the soul residing on the thousand-petalled lotus. Maithuna is the unity which is behind all this duality (Mithuna—couple—double idea). By the offering of this fifth item to the chosen Deity is meant the offering of the sense of duality so that the underlying oneness

---

15 यैरेव पतनं द्रव्यैः सिद्धिः तैरेव चोदिता (*Kulārnava* V. 48.)

may be realized. It is to be noted that what is to be offered is the Tattva. the essence, the principle, and the Vira worships internally with the five mental Tattvas and externally with substitutes. Thus in the place of wine, milk, ghee, honey, cocoanut water, etc., are taken.

Even if ordinary meanings are taken, this is nothing bad in itself, as there are people who will anyhow take fish or flesh or wine. But if it is linked with his spiritual Sadhana, slowly his mind will take a turn and go from Pravritti to Nivritti. This is the method of sublimation where progress may be slow but sure. The ideal method of using Pancha-makara can be seen in the life of Sri Ramakrishna who is considered to be a Kaula by the Saktas. As soon as he heard of Karana (wine) he would think of Jagatkarana (Cause of the Universe). If he heard of union, he would not think of physical union but would immediately enter into Samadhi thinking of the union of Siva-Sakti.

Like Panchamakara, Pancha-tattva forms an essential compound of the Tantrika form of worship. These are Guru-tattva, Mantra-tattva, Manasa-tattva, Deva-tattva and Dhyana-tattva. Tattva means essence. The conception of the Guru is peculiarly Tantrika. Guru is not to be thought of as a human being. Mother Herself out of grace for the Sadhaka initiates him through the Guru with the Mantra of the chosen Deity. A Sadhaka is first to meditate on Guru and then on Mantra. Mantra is that in which the Deity has revealed Herself before. As Swamiji puts it, 'These gods are not merely symbols! They are the forms that the Bhaktas have seen.' Mantra is not simple prayer but actually the form of the Mother. Mantras are the combinations of Varnas (letters). Varnas are Matrikas. Matrika is Sakti and Sakti is Siva. This is the connection that is shown. With the uttering of the Mantra the mind (Manas) is concentrated on the Ishta who is the chosen Deity. This idea of having a chosen Ideal according to one's taste prescribed by an experienced Guru is unique. Swami Vivekananda believed that this theory of Ishta can solve all the quarrels between the opposing sects. The particular aspect of the Mother is taken as the Ishta and the Sadhaka thinks and meditates on Her according to prescribed method till he is merged in Her. These are the five tattvas. 'In fact to pass a Tattva is to become it, for each represents a stage of actual realization.'

Tantra accepts Yoga in all its forms, Mantra, Hatha, Laya, Jnana and is in particular distinguished by its practice of Laya or Kundalini Yoga and other Hatha processes. Physical, vital, and mental energy in kinetic and potential forms put together is called Kundalini or the coiled-up Power. Mother Herself in the form of Kundalini sleeps in the lowest chakra. Through devotion, knowledge, Pranayama, etc., She is roused and taken step by step to the highest Chakra, and the Sadhaka then is blessed with the realization of the Supreme. This awakening of Kundalini is the aim of all Sadhana. The peculiar process that is employed is called Shat-chakra-bheda.

Symbols are an essential necessity for all religions. This is specially true of the Tantras. In fact the major portions of the Tantra books are busy in giving the details of Sadhana through symbols. Symbols are of different kinds including the images and the diagrams called the Yantras. But it must be remembered that symbols are not merely symbols; to a sadhaka they are the forms of the Mother Herself.[16]

For imparting the highest conceptions Tantra has formulated a methodical system of worship which is the synthesis of

---

16 चक्रस्यापि महेश्या न भेदलेशोऽपि भाव्यते विबुधैः
(*Kāmakalāvilāsa*)

Pratikopasana and Yoga method, resting on Vedantic basis. 'It is customary nowadays to decry external worship, but those who do so presume too much,' rightly observes Sir John Woodroffe, the great authority on Tantra. Most people require these external helps to go to finer aspects. Tantra admits that Dhyana is better than external worship, but we must proceed step by step. Thus *Saktirahasya* summarises the stages: 'A mortal who worships by ceremonies, by images, by mind, by identification, by knowing the Self, attains Kaivalya.' Puja is based on the psychological fact that repeated suggestion to the mind with proper physical movements affects the mind profoundly and slowly purifies it which is the aim of all Sadhana. Puja has three parts: (1) Stopping the wastage of energy by different external processes (2) Meditation on the Mother, (3) Sacrifice of oneself to the Mother. Thus the Sadhaka forgets his separate ego and gets merged in the Mother.

No discussion is complete without an estimate of the social influence and affect of the principle and its practice. In Bengal it produced a unique literature on Mother. Ramprasad, Kamalakanta and a good many Sadhakas composed soul-enchanting songs which are famous as 'Sakta-padavalis'. Mother is viewed not only as mother but as daughter also as in the Agamani songs which are very human and very appealing.

The glorious feature of the Sakta doctrine is the honour it pays to women. 'Women are gods, women are vital breaths' says the *Sarvollasa Tantra*, 'You are the women, you are the men' says the *Chandi*. Tantra allows women to be Gurus, which is denied by others and asks all its followers to bow to women without distinction as Mother. This worship of women as the Devi Herself had a tremendous social effect. In the West the status of women was raised

after the introduction of the Christian worship of Mary the
Mother. But the predominant note is worship of youth
and beauty. India through the ages established the worship
of the Mother in the family and in the society, which evidently
is the result of the worship of God as the Mother. The new
world order is coming. The barriers of country and culture
and race are slowly being obliterated. Swami Vivekananda
believed that the contact of the Eastern Motherhood and the
Western Wifehood will be harmoniously developed to the
advantage of both. Tantra accepts both the Motherhood
and the Wifehood of women, which must be the total attitude
of a balanced culture.

Another important feature of Tantra is its sympathy for
all. There may be classes and castes in social relation, but
there is no such thing in religious pursuits. It is open to all.[17]

With the Mother, as mother to all, how can there be
difference among Her children? So it is found that though
Tantra could not bring complete equality in society, it
succeeded in bringing equality in religious relations.

'No nation can rise without the worship of Sakti', Swamiji
used to say. Saints like Sri Ramprasad and Sri Ramakrishna,
heroes like Sivaji and Gurugovinda Singh, poets and writers
like Bankimchandra and Bharati and saint-philosophers
like Sri Sankara and Swami Vivekananda were all worshippers
of Sakti. Our country is Matrubhumi; we worship her with
the mantra, 'Vande Mataram.' The whole atmosphere is
saturated with this Mother-idea. And this is the contribution
of the Tantrikas, the Mother-worshippers of our Mother
country.

---

17 सर्ववर्णाधिकारश्च नारीणां योग्य एव च
(*Gautamiya Tantra*)

THE WORSHIP OF MOTHER DURGA

NAVARATRI is an important festival in India, observed with fast, feast and festivals. Sri Rama's performance of the worship of Mother Durga described in the Bengali Ramayana is not mentioned by Valmiki. It is described in the *Devi Bhagavata, Kalika Purana, Brihaddharma Purana,* and *Mahabhagavata.* The Puranas describe the various aspects of the Goddess. The sage Narada advised Rama to obtain the grace of Durga to kill Ravana and to rescue Sita. So Rama worshipped the Goddess in autumn, and thenceforward Durga Puja has been celebrated in this season.

Durga has been described as the Divine Mother possessing the most beautiful figure, bedecked with jewels and dresses. She is the great Queen of the universe as well as the loving Mother. She is very tender, gentle and sweet to those who approach Her with childlike simplicity and surrender. She is terrible and indomitable to those who tyrannise over others. She comes from Kailasa every autumn accompanied by Lakshmi and Saraswati, the goddesses of wealth and learning. They are very handsome and possess all the virtues men aspire after. When pleased, they confer on devotees the blessings of beauty, harmony, riches, learning and all artistic abilities. Mother brings Her son Ganesa also, who confers intelligence, wisdom and success. Durga comes to the earth to Her mother Menaka and father Himalaya. The season is Sarat, the autumn, when fields are full of bumper crops, rivers are full of crystal water and the sky, free from clouds, becomes bright in the day with sunshine and smiles at

night with the milk-white moon. To devotees She is the real
Mother; to them these incidents are spiritual facts not fictions.
Their forms are not idols but ideals.

The Goddess Durga has been worshipped by notable
Devas and incarnations. The *Brahmavaivarta Purana* says
that Sri Krishna once worshipped Durga in Goloka, Siva
also did so when confronted by the demon Tripura, and
Brahma worshipped Her when attacked by Madhu and
Kaitabha, and Indra when cursed by Durvasa. The *Bhagavata*
says that Rukmini and the Gopis worshipped the Great
Goddess for getting Krishna as their husband. The *Tulasi
Ramayana* says that Sita worshipped Her for getting Rama.
In the *Mahabharata* Sri Krishna exhorts Arjuna to sing the
Hymn of Durga before the Kurukshetra war.

In the *Rigveda, Taittiriya Aranyaka, Devi Upanishad*
and *Devi Purana,* the significance of the name Durga has been
explained as the One who rescues Her devotees in times of
danger, despondency and difficulties. The *Mahanarayana
Upanishad* (2.2.) prays to Her saying:

I take refuge in Her, the Goddess Durga, who is fiery
in lustre and radiant with ardency, who is the Power belonging to the Supreme who manifests Himself manifoldly,
who is the Power residing in actions and their fruits, rendering them efficacious (or the Power that is supplicated to
by the devotees for the fruition of their work). O Thou
Goddess skilled in saving, Thou takest us across difficulties
excellently well. Our salutations to Thee.

Sri Ramakrishna looked upon the highest Reality as
the Divine Mother. She is Its Sakti, Power which is not
different from the substance. He says:

One must propitiate the Divine Mother, the Primal
Energy in order to obtain God's grace. God Himself is

Mahamaya. It is His will that we should run about a little. Then it is great fun. God has created the world in play, as it were. This is called Mahamaya, the Great Illusion. Therefore one must take refuge in the Divine Mother, the Cosmic Power Itself. It is She who has bound us with the shackles of illusion. The realization of God is possible only when those shackles are severed.

The Sakti worshippers have produced an independent philosophy of their own. Abhinava Gupta of Kashmir and Panchanan Tarkaratna of recent days in Bengal have written Sakti-bhashyas, commentaries on the Brahmasutras to establish their claim on scriptural authority. We worship Sakti with the age-old Gayatri or Savitri mantra, recited by every twice-born from Kanyakumari to Kashmir.

Every king and kingdom had as their presiding Deity an aspect of Sakti. Many of the villages and towns of Bharat have such presiding Deities. The Buddhists, and Jains too, worshipped the different aspects of Sakti. The Navaratri festival is observed throughout India. In North India Devi is worshipped often in Vasanta or spring. But during Navaratri in autumn, Ramlila is a very important function which stands for the traditional worship of Sakti through the enacting of Rama's victory over Ravana, of Goodness over Evil. In South India the Navaratri festival is dedicated to the Goddess. The festival of victory observed by princely families has the worship of weapons as an important function. Kumari puja or worship of the virgins who are considered to have a special manifestation of the Goddess is common throughout India during Navaratri. The worship of a woman having a husband and children (Sumangali) is also in vogue in some areas. The Vaishnavas celebrate the Navaratri with dramatic presentation of the lives of Rama and Krishna through Ramlila and Raslila.

The worship of the world-cause as Mother has developed into looking upon Her as a daughter. These attitudes have been expressed with great feeling in the literature and folk songs of India in different languages. Even Acharya Sankara, the great Advaita philosopher, wrote two well-known hymns called the *Ananda-lahari* and the *Saundarya-lahari*. Various images and festivals of the Mother have popularized the Sakti-vada through the length and breadth of the land. The *Saptasati* or *Chandi* is recited throughout the country for propitiating Mother and attaining success in any endeavour. The *Lalita-sahasra-nama,* a hymn giving the thousand names of the Divine Mother, is incomparable in its composition and the mood it creates.

References of earliest Sakti worship are available in Tamil literature. Gradually it spread to other parts of India too. The Mohenjodaro people worshipped the images of Pasupati and the Mother Goddess who were known in later days to the Aryans as Isana or Lord Siva and Mother Uma or Parvati. The earliest Mahisha-mardini form of the fourth century has been discovered in Udayagiri. Scholars have tried to find out a blending in Her of various deities of old. She has been identified with Mother Earth or the Vegetation Deity, and that is why so many plants are used in Her worship. Nowadays Navapatrika made of nine plants is worshipped as representing the Goddess. She is identified with Haridra because She is yellow, Jayanti for giving victory (Jaya), Mana for confering fame (Mana), Vilva for being equally liked by Siva, Ashoka for being free from grief (Shoka), Dhanya for giving of life like corn (Dhanya), Dadimba for Her teeth were red like it during the war with the Asuras. Durga Devi is first mentioned in the *Yajnika Upanishad* of the *Taittiriya Aranyaka*. Durga has originated from sacrificial fire, according to some; also by the blending of various deities, viz., Aditi, Ambika, Parvati (mountain goddess), Uma, Sati, Chandika and the like. The Rigvedic *Devi-sukta* and *Ratri-sukta* are the earliest references to Her exalted position. Uma Haimavati of the *Kena Upanishad* represents Her as Brahma-vidya. Ten Mahavidyas and fifty-one holy places related to Her show the tremendous harmonizing power of Hinduism. Devi thus has acquired three types of status: (1) She is looked upon as dependent on Siva, (2) She is equally as powerful as Siva, and (3) She is the Supreme.

Though the Saktas have given the supreme position to the Goddess, other sects also have not given less stress on the worship of the female aspects of their supreme Deity. Sankara introduced the worship of Srividya, Ramanuja of Sridevi, Madhva of Mahalakshmi, Nimbarka of Rukmini, Ramananda of Sita and Chaitanya of Radhika. The most suitable worship of this age (Yuga-dharma) is the worship of God as Mother, as Sri Ramakrishna has shown by worshipping the Mother Goddess.

DURGA PUJA AND ITS SOCIO-PHILOSOPHICAL IMPORTANCE

Swami Vivekananda says:

'Mother worship is a distinct philosophy in itself. Power is the first of our ideas. It impinges upon man, at every step. Power felt within is the Soul, without, nature. And the battle between the two makes human life. All that we know or feel is but the resultant of these two forces. Man saw that the sun shines on the good and the evil alike. Here was a new idea of God as the Universal Power behind all. The Mother-idea was born.'

The worship of the ultimate Reality as Mother is very old. The Rigvedic *Devisukta* refers to Her as the Empress of the universe. Various forms of the Divine Mother are worshipped in different parts of India. The worship of Her as Durga is very popular in Bengal. She is worshipped with great pomp in autumn in an eartheran image which is characteristic of the image worship in Bengal. The Durga puja is done in the image during the Navaratri or Dusserah. On the Shashti in the evening She is invoked in a vilva tree. Next morning, and on two following days elaborate worship is done with innumerable ingredients and ceremonial bath is given with varieties of waters and juices. On the Dasami day the image is immersed in the river or pond and the ceremony of Santijal or sprinkling of water on all present for all-round peace and blessedness takes place terminating this grand and pompous ceremony which is a relic, according to some, of the Rajasuya sacrifice performed by Kings in olden days. This particular form of worship in image of Durga along with other deities is at least a thousand years old, though popular notion puts it later.

Why Image worship?

The highest Reality, according to the Vedanta, is without forms and attributes. But it can, however, assume various forms of the deities of different faiths. The Hindu tradition accepts many other gods and goddesses also as manifestations of the Absolute. Though each of the deities represents one dominant aspect of God, generally the evolutionary process of creation is also symbolized in the images. Images are forms of God visualized by saints and seers in their hours of communion. Art has also contributed to their beauty and richness. Different images have been portrayed by later artists, and they are part of the priceless treasures of our heritage. Images being the focal point of all devotional expressions, have satisfied devotees of varied temperaments. But images are not mere naturalistic representations of artists. They are symbols of the Divine, meant primarily to orient our thoughts and feelings, and not merely for gratifying the aesthetic sense. As the image is the production of the saintly artist, every single detail of the forms is expressive of the deeper universal truth. And this truth presented in artistic forms is more lovable. The images give tangible forms to the abstract concepts of philosophy and mystic realization. They are the link between the Infinite and the finite, the Eternal and the transient, the Formless and the form. If we know the significance of the images, we can easily reach the deeper truth, for meditation becomes easier. To the devotee the human representations of God become so palpable that he sees Him as his near and dear one. Hundreds of instances are there in mystical literature where the devotees have seen God in tangible forms as Mother, Child and the like.

The image of Durga is not alone. There are a number of images of deities worshipped along with the Devi. Lakshmi and Saraswati are represented as standing and Kartika and Ganesha as sitting on their mounts on Her two sides. The Devi is represented as fighting with the demon Mahishasura mentioned in the *Durga Saptasati* which is the most important book of the Devi worshippers. She stands on a lion and fights with Her ten hands bedecked with different weapons.

Symbolism in Durga-puja

The images of Durga and Her associates are symbolic in nature. Symbolism has played a great part in every religion. Hinduism specialized in this art of symbology. It worshipped God through sound, diagram, image, etc. In yogic lore the body itself has been accepted as a temple and various bodily functions as worship of the deity. With this background of richness in symbology, Hinduism naturally has given various spiritual, philosophical and natural interpretations to the group of deities worshipped during the Durga puja. This variety of interpretations is a sign of richness of imagination and profundity of thought. The typical explanation is as follows: Durga, the highest Reality, is realized with great difficulty; She also removes all misery. She fights Mahishasura the demon standing for lower propensities. Durga is born of the collected powers of the Devas. So also all powers come through cooperative effort of many. Her ten hands cover all directions and all aspects of life. The Bodhana worship or awakening of the Goddess is nothing but the awakening of the 'sleeping' Divinity within the worshipper or the Coiled Power of the Yogis. The vilva tree, where She is prayed to dwell, is nothing but a symbol of the Sushumna

canal, the path of Kundalini. Navapatrika made of various
plants, represents Her presence in everything. In her worship
water from various rivers of India, signifying the unity of the
land, is used. Various articles, good or bad, are used, showing
Her evensightedness, for all things and creatures issue from
Her. The deity Ganesa stands for success, Kartika for
strength, Lakshmi for wealth and grace and Saraswati for
knowledge. Their mounts are also meaningful. The Lion is
the vehicle of the Great Power. The Jiva becomes powerful
through complete dedication. The rat is the vehicle of
Ganesa; success comes through snapping the bonds with
sharp intelligence. The peacock is the vehicle of Kartika
the Commander-in-chief of the Devas; this national bird
with variegated plume stands for variegated efforts for the
full manifestation of strength. The dayblind owl of Lakshmi
is like a mammon-worshipper; but it also stands for an
aspirant blind to the worldly affairs. Saraswati's vehicle is
a swan which has the capacity of separating milk from water,
substance from non-substance. Generally Lakshmi and
Saraswati stand on lotuses which stands for self-surrender
through which the world issues; the wheel represents the
wheel of the world. The burning lamp represents the light
of the soul. The five articles with which the Arati or waving
before the deity is done, represent the five basic elements of
the universe. Light stands for fire, water in conchshell for
water, cloth for ether, flower for earth and chamara or fan
for air. In this way the different images and articles in
the Durga-puja are given a symbolic interpretation.

Social Impact

This worship of the Mother or Sakti has had a tremendous social influence. In Bengal it produced a unique literature
on the Divine Mother. Ramprasad, Kamalakanta and a good

many Sadhakas composed soul-enchanting songs which are famous as 'Sakta-padavalis.' Mother is viewed not only as mother but as daughter also, as in the Agamani songs which are very human and very appealing.

The glorious feature of the Shakta doctrine is the honour it pays to women. 'Women are gods, women are vital breaths,' says the *Sarvollasa Tantra.* 'You are the women, you are the men', says the *Chandi.* Tantra allows women to be Gurus which is denied by others and asks all its followers to bow to women without any distinction as Mother. This worship of women as the Devi Herself had a tremendous social impact. In the West the status of women was raised after the introduction of the Christian worship of Mary the Mother. But the predominant note there is the worship of youth and beauty. India through the ages established the worship of the mother in the family which evidently is the result of the worship of God as Mother. The new world order is coming. The barriers of country and culture and race are slowly being obliterated. Swami Vivekananda believed that Eastern Motherhood and Western Wifehood will be harmoniously developed to the advantage of both. The Tantra accepts both the Motherhood and the Wifehood of women which must be the total attitude of a balanced culture. Another important feature of Tantra is its sympathy for all. There may be classes and castes in social relation but there is no such thing in religious pursuits. It is open to all. With the Mother, as mother to all, how can there be difference among Her children? So it is found that though Tantra could not bring complete equality in society it succeeded in bringing equality in religious relationships.

The Mother Goddess is one of the three important deities worshipped through the length and breadth of India. Over and above developing devotion, providing joy and

sharpening artistic sensibilities, the Durga puja makes us
aware of the infinite power hidden in us. 'No nation can
rise without the worship of Sakti', Swami Vivekananda used
to say. Saints like Ramprasad and Ramakrishna, heroes
like Shivaji and Gurugovinda Singh, poets and writers like
Bankimchandra and Bharati and saint-philosophers like
Sankara, Vivekananda and Aurobindo, were all worshippers
of Sakti. Our country is Matṛbhumi;, we worship her
with the mantra 'Vande Mataram'. The whole atmosphere
is saturated with this Mother-idea. And this is the contribution
of the Mother-worshippers of our Mother country.

ON READING THE CHANDI

या देवी सर्वंभूतेषु मातृरूपेण संस्थिता ।
नमस्तस्यै नमस्तस्यै नमस्तस्यै नमो नमः ॥

**Salutations again and again to the Goddess
who abides in all beings in the form of mother.**

Chanting of holy texts has an important place in the scheme of spiritual discipline practised in different religious sects. Meditation and Japa are generally given a higher place, for they help the mind to be merged in the direct thought of the chosen Deity. But it is necessary to keep the mind in the thought of the Deity as long as possible. In that, recitation of hymns and then external worship with various ingredients are prescribed. A verse places stotra in the third place in order of importance.[1]

Moreover, varieties of spiritual disciplines have been evolved, for there are varieties of temperaments. To each according to his needs, is the plan. Chanting is common in almost every system. After ceremonial Puja too this is taken recourse to. The idea is to revolve in the mind the thought of the Ideal. This becomes facilitated if the devotee thinks of the Deity in as many situations as possible. These situations may be connected with his own life or with the lives of earlier devotees who had the vision of the Deity and received the blessings of the Divine. Recitation of the glories

---

1 प्रथमा प्रतिमापूजा जपस्तोत्रादि मध्यमा ।
उत्तमा मानसी पूजा सोऽहंपूजोत्तमोत्तमा ॥ (*Tantrasarah*)

and exploits of the Deity narrated in different holy texts is thus a great help in spiritual progress. If it is done with attention, devotion and proper understanding of the texts selected, it results in clarification of ideas and unbroken memory of sacred scenes and thoughts. It is said that even after realization, a saint, while living in this body, spends his time in practising devotions among devotees. A devotee too follows this exercise of chanting, irrespective of his standard of growth.

Chanting assumes greater importance on special occasions when ceremonially holy texts are recited. Navaratri is one such important occasion when the holy texts of the Devi are recited by all devotees, specially by the Mother-worshippers. Among the Saktas the most popular book for this purpose is the *Chandi*. It is also known as *Durga Saptasati* and *Devi-Mahatmya*. Two other important books are the *Devi-Bhagavata* and the *Lalita-sahasranama*. The first one is a voluminous book, and being a Purana, it includes various other anecdotes. The *Lalita-sahasranama* enumerates the thousand names of the Goddess. There are different Sakta Upanishads as well as often-chanted hymns of Acharya Sankara and others. The *Chandi* is a narrative of different battles fought by the Goddess in keeping with the purpose of Her incarnation, as She Herself assured:

'Whenever there will be trouble from irreligion, I shall incarnate Myself and destroy the enemy.'[2]

The *Chandi* describes different battles fought by the Goddess with the Asuras who were tyrannizing the world. First

---

2 इत्थं यदा यदा बाधा दानवोत्था भविष्यति ।
तदा तदा अवतीर्याहं करिष्याम्यरिसंक्षयम् ॥   (XI.55)

She destroyed Madhu and Kaitabha, then Mahishasura and his retinue and last of all Sumbha and Nisumbha. The whole setting is given as a narration to Suratha and Samadhi by the Sage Medhas.

Sometimes the objection is raised that the *Devi Mahatmya* is full of fights and battles with appropriate descriptions so it cannot generate the mood of devotion. It may be true that it does not do so in the uninitiated, but those who enter into the spirit of the book experience it. What is life? Is it not struggles against opposing forces? What is the condition of the world at large? Is it not full of battles of opposing interests? The fight between the good and the evil is an eternal one. The Gita describes it. Acharya Sankara speaks of *deva-asura-samgrama,* battle between the good and the bad forces in a man's life. It is true in the cosmic field too. So there is nothing abnormal. It is only a realistic description of the world situation. What makes it unique and of ethical and religious value is the fact that ultimately it is the forces of goodness that win over those of evil. Because of this stress it acquires a great value in rendering hope, courage and faith in mortal man in his seemingly hopeless struggle against evil. Had it not been so, wherefrom would man get courage to fight against his fate, reformers against social evils, national leaders against international disharmony? So this description of battles is not meaningless.

As for the creation of an instant mood of devotion by reading holy books, we must remember the Tantrika view of the world and the Deity. It is in the struggles, even in the lost battles, that a Sadhaka is to see the hands of the Mother. Then only is he established in steadfast devotion. Swami Vivekananda beautifully describes the mood of an ordinary devotee in a poem, 'And let Shyama dance there'; and suggests the worship of the Terrible also in the following lines:

The flesh hankers for contacts of pleasure,
The senses for enchanting strains of song,
The mind hungers for peals of laughter sweet,
The heart pants to reach realms beyond sorrow;
Say, who cares exchange the soothing moonlight
For the burning rays of the noontide sun?
The wretch whose heart is like the scorching sun,
—Even he fondly loves the balmy moon;
Indeed, all thirst for joy.

    Breathes there the wretch
Who hugs pain and sorrow to his bosom?
Misery in his cup of happiness,
Deadly venom in his drink of nectar,
Poison in his throat,—yet he clings to hope.
Lo! how are all scared by the Terrific,
None seek Elokeshi whose form is Death.
The deadly frightful sword, reeking with blood,
They take from Her hand, and put a lute instead!
Thou dreaded Kali, the All-destroyer,
Thou alone art True; Thy shadow's shadow
Is indeed the pleasant Vanamali.
O Terrible Mother, cut quick the core,
Illusion dispel—the dream of happiness,
Rend asunder the fondness for the flesh,

      *   *   *

Free thyself from the mighty attraction—
The maddening wine of love, the charm of sex.
Break the harp!   Forward, with the ocean's cry!
Drink tears, pledge ev'n life,—let the body fall.
Awake, O hero!   Shake off thy vain dreams.
Death stands at thy head,—does fear become thee?
A load of misery, true though it is,—
This Becoming,—know this to be thy God!
His temple—the Smasan among corpses
And funeral pyres; unending battle,—
That verily is His sacred worship;
Constant defeat,—let that not unnerve thee;
Shattered be little self, hope, name and fame;
Set up a pyre of them, and make thy heart
A burning-ground—And let Shyama dance there.

So we see that a Sakti-worshipper believes in Sakti, strength. He is to steel himself against all fears and weaknesses and the worship of the Mother as Power prepares him for it. Somehow or other the idea is current that devotion must make a man mellow and soft; and then the opponents of religion charge that it is devitalizing, effeminating, weakening. The Saktas have counteracted this notion about devotion. Their idea is, when with the Mother it is surely soft and mellow, but when dealing with the aggressions of evil forces, this same devotion must give him the courage of a lion, and giving up all fear, hesitation and selfishness, he must overcome all obstacles, evil forces or distractions and go straight to the Mother. When we appreciate this idea of devotion held by the Sakti-worshippers we shall understand the value of this book.

Moreover, is it a mere chance that other great books of Hinduism also contain much of these wars and battles? The message of the Gita was given in the battlefield. The Mahabharata centres round the fight between the Pandavas and the Kauravas, and the Ramayana between Rama and Ravana. A spiritual aspirant is a man of the world. He is to face the struggles of life and at the same time must strive for reaching the highest goal, acquiring on the way all the noble virtues that make life sweet and noble too.

It may be admitted that a book like the Gita giving wonderful truths in every other line is more attractive, for it does not spend much time in describing the background. But we must remember that the Gita forms part of the Mahabharata and thus all the background is supplied by the epic. Moreover, a collection of terse, good sayings is good only for advanced students who have already heard or can themselves supply the necessary background for each saying to make it appealing, realistic, convincing.

When we plead so much against the charges, we shall
fail in our duty if we do not draw the attention of the critics
that even for general devotional temperament, there are four
suitable hymns addressed to the Devi, satisfying their temperament. In between the descriptions of fights, these hymns
were chanted by the Devas whenever they were in difficulty.
The first one is spoken by Brahma (I, 70-87), the second
by Sakra and other Devas (IV, 2-27), the third by Devas
again (V, 9-82) and the fourth is also by them (XI, 2-35).
The first one is known as the Tantrika Ratri-sukta, addressed
to Mother in the form of Yoga-nidra to Vishnu. Mahakali
with the predominant quality of Tamas is Yoga-nidra and is
the deity of the first part of the *Chandi*. The three deities
with three predominant qualities are three aspects of Mahamaya. As the *Devi Bhagavata* says:

'Her three powers of Sattva, Rajas and Tamas are
Mahasarasvati, Mahalakshmi and Mahakali respectively[3]'

The chanting of the second one, the *Sakradikrita-stuti,* is
often spoken of as equivalent to the reading of the whole
Chandi. The third Stotra is called the Tantrika Devi-sukta
or *Aparajita-stava.* The fourth is known as the *Narayani
Stuti.* Narayani means the Refuge of the Jivas or Tattvas
(*Nārasya ayani*).

These hymns show that the goddess is the very essence
of the deities including Brahma, Vishnu and Siva and is the
ruler of the world. She has two sets of forms, gentle and
terrible. In the gentle forms She is surpassingly beautiful
and in the terrible forms She is surpassingly fearful. Mother

---

3 तस्यास्तु सात्त्विकी शक्ती राजसी तामसी तथा ।
महालक्ष्मी सरस्वती महाकाळीति ताः स्त्रियः ॥ (I. 2. 19-20.)

Durga is not only one who rescues man from dangers and difficulties, but also one who helps man to cross the ocean of Samsara. She is the giver of both Abhyudaya and Nihsreyasa, the coveted goals of man. Her immanence is greatly stressed in the third hymn saying that She is present in all creatures as consciousness, power, intellect and so on. Moreover these hymns connect Her with all the great deities worshipped by different sects. Thus She is the Vishnumaya, and Narayani as well as Mahamaya, Gauri, Sivani and Kali, also all the powers behind Brahma, Indra, Kumara and others. This is not all. The Divine Mother is Brahman Itself. She is also the supreme deity. It is She who creates, maintains and destroys the entire universe. Therefore it is She who has both the good and the evil. As we said before, the devotees generally try to look upon God as the repository of good qualities only. It is the speciality of the Tantra that it accepts both the Saumya as well as the Raudra (calm and terrible) aspects as belonging to the Mother. It is because of this that in Her terrible aspect also Mother is worshipped in various parts of India. The *Chandi* says:

'We prostrate before Her who is at once most gentle and most terrible; we salute Her again and again. Salutation to Her who is the support of the world. Salutation to the Devi who is of the form of volition.'[4]

Remembering this background we may very well appreciate the four hymns. The different epithets used in the hymns appeal deeply to the devotees. Take for instance, the third hymn where the Devas repeatedly offer their salutations to Her with the words: *Namah tasyai*. The depth of feeling

---

4 अतिसौम्यातिरौद्रायै नतास्तस्यै नमो नमः ।
नमो जगत् प्रतिष्ठायै देव्यै कृत्यै नमो नमः ॥ (V. 13.)

created by the act of Pranama, reciting rhythmically the 23
couplets with the same form throughout, is simply marvellous.
While reciting this the devotee is reminded that the Goddess
has three aspects, viz. Sattvika, Rajasika and Tamasika
(serene, active and dull). The sustaining, creating and destroy-
ing are the three functions of Her powers in these three
aspects. And salutations are offered three times indicating
that they are done with the body, speech and mind. It
is not for nothing that the *Lakshmi Tantra* says:

> 'This Devisukta is the giver of all fruits. By chanting
> to the Devi everyday with this Sukta the devotee goes
> beyond all sufferings and achieves all wealth, noble and
> great.'[5]

On knowing this, who will not like to offer with the devas
his respects to the Mother repeatedly saying: *Namastasyai,
namastasyai, namastasyai, namonamah*—Salutations, salutations, salutations to Her.

---

5 नमो देव्यादिकं देवीसूक्तं सर्वफलप्रदम् ।
   इमां देवीं स्तुवन्नित्यं स्तोत्रेणानेन मामिह ॥
   क्लेशानतीत्य सकलानैश्वर्यं महदश्नुते ॥

LESSONS FROM AN ANECDOTE

दुर्गेषु नित्यं भवसङ्कटेषु दुरन्तचिन्ताहिनिगीर्यमाणान् ।
शरण्यहीनान् शरणागतार्तिनिवारिणी त्वं परिपाहि दुर्गे ॥

Goddess Durga! You who remove the distress of those who take refuge in you and have no other saviour, protect us who are eternally being swallowed by the python of endless anxiety, in the insurmountable difficulties of life.

—Tripurarahasya

The annual worship of the Divine Mother is celebrated in autumn. Throughout the country She is worshipped during the Navaratri in Her different forms by thousands of people. In accordance with their faith and devotion they will derive benefit. It is often questioned how the common man, burdened with the worries and anxieties of life as he is, can derive the maximum benefit. Is worship of the Mother Goddess, or for that matter any worship, capable of bestowing some tangible result on the ordinary votary? The answer can be gathered from the scriptures. One of the most important books of the Devi cult is the *Devi-māhātmyam,* also known as the *Chandi* and the *Durgāsaptasati*. In thirteen chapters and seven hundred verses, it deals with the glory of the Devi and Her exploits in killing tyrannous demons, interspersed with fine hymns to Her. Instead of going into the philosophy or teachings in the body of the book let us see some of the practical hints given for spiritual benefit, which are woven round the story preparing for the delineation of the glory of the Goddess.

The book begins with a description of the sufferings of a king and a merchant. King Suratha had been defeated by his enemies, troubled by his subjects and ignored by his employees and relatives. So he repaired to the forest, being fed up with the world and its ways. The merchant Samadhi had a similar fate. He had been cast out by his wife and sons. So he also came to the forest. But their present trouble was not so much the old suffering as the meaningless attachment they felt for their old relatives and property. As the *Chandi* graphically describes: 'There then, overcome with attachment, the king fell into the thought; "I do not know whether the capital which was well guarded by my ancestors and recently deserted by me is being guarded righteously or not by my servants of evil conduct. I do not know what enjoyment my chief elephant, heroic and always elated, and now fallen into the hands of my foes, will get. Those who were my constant followers and received favour, riches and food from me, now certainly pay homage to other kings. The treasure which I gathered with great care will be squandered by those chronic spendthrifts, who are addicted to improper expenditures." The king was continually thinking of these and other things.'

The merchant also was worrying: 'Dwelling here, I do not know anything as regards the good or bad of my sons, kinsmen and wife. At present is welfare or ill-luck theirs at home? How are they? Are my sons living good or evil lives?'

When the king asked, why his mind was affectionately attached to those ungrateful folk, the merchant replied that he did not know why it was being drawn to them. Then they went to the sage Medhas and narrated their sorrow and the problem. The king said: 'Sir, I wish to ask you one thing. Be pleased to reply to it. Without the control of my intellect, my mind is afflicted with sorrow. Though I have lost the kingdom, like an ignorant man—though I know it—I have an attachment to all the paraphernalia of my kingdom. How is this, O best of sages? And this merchant has been disowned by his children, wife and servants, and forsaken by his own people; still he is inordinately affectionate towards them. Thus both he and I, drawn by attachment towards objects whose defects we do know, are exceedingly unhappy. How does this happen, then, sir, that though we are aware of it, this delusion comes? This delusion besets me as well as him, blinded as we are in respect of discrimination.'

The great sage informed them that it was by the illusive power of Mahamaya that the entire world is deluded, but it is She who, when propitious, becomes a giver of worldly and heavenly enjoyment as well as final liberation to human beings. The sage then told them about the exploits and glory of the Goddess, which engendered respect and faith in the two devotees. At the end the sage advised: 'O great King, take refuge in Her, the supreme Goddess. She indeed when worshipped bestows on men enjoyment, heaven and final release from transmigration.'

Both the king and the merchant practised hard penance to please the Goddess. She then offered two boons to them according to their wishes, one boon granting sovereignty of the universe and the other final realization. Thus the Devi according to the *Chandi* grants both material and spiritual fruits—bhukti and mukti.

Now when we study the cases of Suratha and Samadhi, we find that both of them were well-placed in life but met with reverses of fortune. They were let down even by their near and dear ones. Yet the property, the pet animals which they lost, as well as their unkind relatives were still in their mind, which was being drawn to those very objects. We can take some lessons from this anecdote, for similar is the case with most of us. Grief over the past and worry for the future take away most of our energy and time. It has been pointed out by a psychologist that 40 per cent of our worries centre round the past, 50% round the future and only 10% round present problems. We know it is futile to weep over the past or meaningless to think disproportionately about the future. But worrying becomes a habit in spite of ourselves, often for unworthy causes. The same thing happened to the king and the merchant. They knew it was fruitless to grieve or worry; still the mind was moving in the old groove.

Worry is the greatest problem of modern times. The primitive man was satisfied to live for himself and only one day at a time, but with the growth of a complex society, we worry for the future of ourselves, our family, our country, even the whole world. Any incident anywhere in the world is enough to scare us. This worry may be real or imaginary. It is a matter of habit, formed through years of unconscious practice. Like any other habit it may be broken. The method for it is to realize that it is an enemy and has a devastating effect on us, and then to forget it, to practise poise. To do that one must empty the mind of all anxieties and fears and suffuse it with the Divine and cultivate positive thoughts regarding the world where He resides. The modern psychiatrists use definite techniques to free the mind from tension and fill it with positive thoughts. The cause of worry is attachment, and so the religious method is to practise non-attachment and fill the mind with thoughts of God and surrender oneself completely to Him. The conception of the Divine Mother as the supreme Reality brings God very near to us, for mother is so near to one who is a child. So the Sastras prescribe surrender at Her feet, which will free man from all attachment and the resulting worry, anxiety and tension.

The king and the merchant were introspective, and so they discovered by themselves that the real root of trouble was their lack of control over the mind. If they were the masters of their mind, they could be free from meaningless attachment. Self-control is the only means to gain mastery over all reactions when unpalatable experience inevitably comes to a man. So he discovers the urgent need for it. But alas, one cannot achieve it overnight. Specially when he knocks the bottom of life, he painfully realizes that it is impossible for him to gain mastery over himself. So he looks for a guide, a person of mature wisdom, who could help him to achieve the requisite mastery.

When a man is really anxious, and a piteous cry goes from his agonized soul in supplication to the Great Lord, He sends a proper guide who directs his way towards self-realization. This very thing happened in the case of the above two. With utter helplessness and agony of soul they went to the forest and found the great sage Medhas who became their teacher.

What was the path he showed them? Medhas informed them that the cause of uncontrollable attachment was the deluding aspect of the Divine Mother. She keeps attachment, which is vigorous and blind, so that the world process might go on. But when after different experiences, sweet and sour, the bound soul feels tired and tries to go out of it, the releasing aspect of the same Divine Mother comes forward and helps it break the shackles of delusion. The pre-requisite for this release from limitations is the grace of the Mother, and that can be achieved when one surrenders his all to Her and fervently prays to Her. To do that he must have enough faith and love for Her. This the sage implanted in his disciples by narrating in the eleven chapters of the *Chandi*, the exploits of the Goddess.

Hearing the Lila of the Supreme Goddess, contemplating on it, meditating on Her form and repetition of Her name are the methods through which the mind is prepared for total surrender. When a man progresses through this discipline, all his mental worries, sufferings, grief, etc., drop away, and with total surrender the grace of the Mother descends and he achieves the *summum bonum* of life. Here the two supplicants had their wishes fulfilled, one material and the other spiritual.

The Divine Mother granted enjoyment of his kingdom as well as the heavenly kingdom to King Suratha. How is that? Will he not attain the highest goal, the final release? In answer it may be pointed out that Suratha had desire, and he must work out his Karma by experience and enjoyment before he could have liberation. But now he knew where to place the worldly pleasure. It was no more the primary objective of life, and so there was no chance of any attachment, conflict or tension.   With firm faith dawning on him, he knew that the goal of life is the final release. So bad experience in the world would no more upset him. While allowing the normal joys of life to the king, the *Chandi* first gives proper emphasis to the supreme objective of life and relegates the other enjoyments to the secondary position. Thereby the devotee will enjoy the fruits of his Karma but will not be affected by them. As Sri Ramakrishna said, if milk is kept with water, it cannot be separated, but if it is churned and butter is brought out, it floats on water and does not mix with it. Similarly if the mind also is kept in the world after the attainment of knowledge, it remains untainted.

The Holy Mother Sarada Devi pointed out that there were two types of Karma, one that binds and the other that releases. We see only the middle of the chain of Karma and know not whether it is the one or the other, whether it is winding or unwinding. But the progress in spiritual life seen later convinces us that it was of the second type, as in the case of the king.

By allowing worldly enjoyment while the supreme goal is not lost sight of, religion frees itself from the charges of some psycho-therapists who hold that it is the cause of tension. It is not necessary for religion to stress guilt and sin; its primary emphasis is on love of God. For ordinary devotees harping on sin is not at all necessary; for serious spiritual aspirants too it is useless. As Sri Ramakrishna once said to the Brahmo devotees:

> Will you tell me one thing? Why do you harp so much on sin? By repeating a hundred times, 'I am a sinner', one verily becomes a sinner. One should have such faith as to be able to say, 'What? I have taken the name of God; how can I be a sinner?'

So the anecdote of Suratha and Samadhi gives us interesting clues to our life. First of all, we need not consider our sufferings in life as meaningless. They have a divine purpose. Through them we learn the true lessons of life and become aware of a higher Presence. With the awareness of a Presence and a purpose, much of our suffering will lose their sting. We will be able to face the darker side of life squarely. With a stable anchor, the imaginary worries will drop away, and the mind will be fit for contemplation and faith. Faith is of two types—the faith of realization and the faith of preparation. The former is unshakable and is the fruit of illumination. **Preparatory faith also** can be developed gradually into it. The method generally sought is through intellectual conviction. But the way of the heart is more

potent, specially for despondent souls.   Assert faith right now
and you have it.   By repeating assertion of it in every under-
taking of the day, faith becomes stronger and stronger and
possesses the entire soul.   This facilitates meditation.   The
mind habituated in the application of faith naturally enters
into meditation of the Lord.   Moreover, feeling the presence
of the Lord is itself contemplation.   When the mind is thus
directed purposively to a divine object, control of it is achieved.
That is the goal of all Sadhana.   Wherever the concentrated
mind is directed, success is achieved.   When it is directed to
God, the highest illumination is obtained.   Devotion, worship,
faith or religion help a man to have a rich, healthy and peaceful
life, which is so much coveted by an ordinary man of the world.
But they become significant only when they hold to the supreme
ideal of life; religion is religion when it leads a bound soul to
the final liberation.   The *Chandi* gives us these grand lessons
through the fine anecdote of Suratha and Samadhi.

THE WAY OF THE MOTHER

REALITY is one and is of the nature of Satchidananda, existence, knowledge and bliss absolute. The absolute and the relative (Nitya and Lila) are the two aspects of the Divine. Sri Ramakrishna, who realized both the aspects through different spiritual disciplines, says:

'It is true that He is with forms and it is as well true that He is without forms.'

'Water has no particular form but ice has. The indivisible Satchidananda, likewise, gets condensed, as it were, through devotion and assumes various forms like ice.'

'He whom you call Brahman, I call Mother.'

The devotees have intuited Her in manifold ways in accordance with their attitude. In the following pages are narrated a few anecdotes describing how the Divine Mother revealed Herself to Her votaries.

Mother in Everything

A great saint that he was, Sri Totapuri had the highest spiritual wisdom through discrimination and mental absorption propounded in the path of knowledge. Equipped with a strong physique, brought up in a holy atmosphere away from the meshes that Maya weaves round the worldly life, he had no occasion to recognize the Divine Power or the necessity of surrendering to Her. While staying at Dakshineswar, attracted by the sweet personality of his disciple Ramakrishna, the child of the Divine Mother, he cut jokes at the latter's

taking the name of God while clapping his hands, 'What,
are you fashioning chapatis?' With such an abstracted mind
Totapuri was attacked by dysentery. The excruciating pain
in the stomach did not allow him to keep his mind in the
highest regions. He got disgusted with the body and wanted
to give it up in the Ganga. He waded through the river at
dead of night. Swami Saradananda writes:

'But was the deep Bhagirathi dry tonight? Or was
it only the external projection of his mental picture?
Who could say? Tota almost reached the other bank
but could not get water, deep enough for drowning
himself in. When, gradually, the trees and houses on
the other bank began to be visible like shadows in the
deep darkness of the night, Tota was surprised and
thought, "What strange divine Maya is this? Tonight
there is not sufficient water in the river even to drown
oneself! What strange unheard-of play of God?"
And immediately some one as it were from within pulled
off the veil over his intellect. Tota's mind was dazzled
by a bright light and he saw "Mother, Mother, Mother;
Mother, the origin of the universe; Mother, the unthinkable Power; Mother in land and Mother in water;
the body is Mother, and the mind is Mother; illness is
Mother, and health is Mother; knowledge is Mother,
and ignorance is Mother; life is Mother, and death is
Mother; everything I see, hear, think or imagine is
Mother! She makes nay of yea and yea of nay! As
long as one is in the body one has no power to be free
from Her influence, no, not even to die, till She wills!
It is that Mother again who is also beyond body, mind
and intellect—the Mother, the supreme "fourth", devoid
of all attributes. That one whom Tota had so long been
worshipping as Brahman and to whom he offered his
heartfelt love and devotion was this very Mother!
Siva and Sakti are, One, ever existing in the form of
Hara-Gauri! Brahman and Brahma-Sakti are one and
the same!'

Such was the realization of a great Jnanayogin.

Mother as Sat-Chit-Ananda

Sri Ramakrishna was a master of various moods. He enjoyed in countless ways the bliss flowing from the visions of the Mother. A grand realization similar to the above he had as is clear from his description:

> 'The Divine Mother revealed to me that She had become everything. She showed me that everything was full of consciousness. The image was consciousness, the altar was consciousness, the water was consciousness, the doorsill was consciousness, the marble floor was consciousness—all was consciousness. I found every-thing inside the room soaked, as it were, in bliss—the bliss of Sat-Chit-Ananda.'

Mother as Power

There is a story current about Sri Sankara. One day he was passing through a street in Varanasi. A dead body was lying on the road and a young woman, presumably the wife of the dead man, was sitting by its side, weeping. Sankara asked the people to remove the dead body. The woman replied, 'Why, you may ask the body to move away.' 'What', said Sankara, 'has the dead body any power to move of itself?' The woman retorted, 'If it is not possible for a tiny body to move without power, how do you hold the view that this whole universe moves without a power behind it?' Another vista, as it were, opened before Sankara, that there is such a thing as Divine Power and the world is Her sport. This knowledge was necessary, for unless the man of realization is on the threshold of reality and has at least the partial realization of the reality of the world, he cannot do any work even for the spiritual regeneration of the society. After this vision Sri Sankara sang in the first verse of the famous *Saundarya Lahari*:

> 'If Siva is joined to Sakti, He is able to create. If not so, God is not even capable of movement.'[1]

As Sri Ramakrishna puts it:

> 'Brahman is actionless. When It is engaged in creation, preservation, and dissolution It is called the Primal Power, Adyasakti. This Power must be propitiated.'

Mother as The Giver of Boons

Swami Vivekananda, then Narendranath, did not believe in the Divine Mother. As a follower of the Brahmo Samaj, he did not accept the forms of Brahman. After the death of his father he could not fully engage himself in spiritual Sadhana, for the family became very poor. So he thought of removing the poverty with providential help and importunately requested Sri Ramakrishna for this. The Master replied affectionately, 'My child, I cannot say such words, you know. Why don't you yourself pray? You don't accept Mother; that is why you suffer so much.... Go to the temple tonight and bowing down to Her, pray for a boon. My affectionate Mother is the Power of Brahman. She is pure Consciousness embodied. She has given birth to the universe merely by Her will. What can She not do, if She wills?' Narendranath describes:

> 'As I was going, a sort of profound inebriation possessed me; I was reeling. A firm conviction gripped

---

। शिवः शक्त्या युक्तो यदि भवति शक्तः प्रभवितुं ।
न चेदेवं देवो न खलु कुशलः स्पन्दितुमपि ॥

me that I should actually see Mother and hear Her words.
I forgot all other things, and became completely merged
in that thought alone. Coming into the temple, I saw that
Mother was actually pure Consciousness, was actually
living and was really the fountainhead of infinite love
and beauty. My heart swelled with loving devotion;
and, beside myself with bliss, I made repeated salutations
to Her, praying, "Mother, grant me discrimination, grant
me detachment, grant me divine knowledge and devotion;
ordain that I may always have unobstructed vision of
You." My heart was flooded with peace. The whole
universe completely disappeared and Mother alone
remained filling my heart.'

Though he went thrice for earthly goods, he was ashamed
to ask Mother for them and prayed to Her for spiritual
qualities. He came out of the shrine and sang the song
'Thou art the saviour, O Mother', throughout the night.
Sri Ramakrishna expressed his joy saying, 'Narendra has
accepted Mother; it is very good.'

Mother as The Terrible

Henceforward, through a series of realizations Narendranath came to see Mother in everything, even in the
seemingly destructive aspects of the Divine manifestation.
Destruction is no destruction when it leads to a fresh mode
of existence. This is a unique conception in Hinduism
and is specially recognized by the Saktas. Powers of destruction are not delegated to an extraneous Satan. The gentle
and the terrible are both Her manifestations. As the beautiful
Tripurasundari She creates, and as the terrific Kali She
destroys. Swami Vivekananda records his realization of
the Terrible in the famous poem 'Kali the Mother':

> 'For Terror is Thy name,
>   Death is in Thy breath,

And every shaking step
  Destroys a world for ev'r.

Thou "Time" the All-Destroyer!
  Come, O Mother Come!'

'Who dares misery love,
  And hug the form of Death,

Dance in Destruction's dance,
  To Him the Mother comes.'

This emphatically answers the charge made by some critics of Tantra that it is meant for 'suffragette monists'. Moreover, from the empirical point of view, both the principles, static and dynamic, male and female, are necessary for explaining the world-creation. Even in ordinary life, the mother's part is more abiding and intimate and God can be both Mother and Father according to the attitude of the devotee. From the transcendental stand-point, however, the distinctions of sex have no application to the Absolute. Even the Sanksrit word Matri (mother) is both feminine and masculine.

There are interesting anecdotes in the lives of mystics illustrating how Mother bestowed Her grace on them by granting Her vision in the forms of affectionate relations.

Mother Helps as a Daughter

Ramprasad was a Sakta mystic of the eighteenth century. He had composed hundreds of songs about the Divine Mother. In feeling, depth and intuition his lyrics are unique. The devotional attitude, the spiritual discipline and the realization of the Divine in the form of the Mother delineated in them, have endowed them with special strength and appeal. Because of his deep love, the Divine Mother blessed him with Her visions. One day Ramprasad was mending the bamboo fencing around his house. It required the help of an assistant to turn back the thin rope from the other side of the fencing. He was engaged in singing about the Mother and was expecting his daughter to come and do the job for him. When he began the work he was helped from the other side in tying the knots of the fencing. Joyful like a child in the thought of the Mother, Ramprasad carried on. After some time his daughter came and was astonished to see the progress of the work. On inquiry the father found out that the daughter was inside the house till then, engaged in some other household duty. He understood that it was the play of his chosen Deity to bless Her child in this way. With great emotion he composed and sang a song immortalizing the event:

'O mind, why are you away from the lotus feet of Mother?

Think of Mother, O mind, bind Her with the rope of devotion; you will have liberation.

You could not see Her, O mind, in spite of the eyes, how unlucky are you!

To play with Her devotee Mother came in the form of his daughter and tied the fencing of his house!

Whoever meditates on You with concentration will realize You, O Mother Divine.

In his last moments come once as his daughter and tie the fencing of Ramprasad.'

Mother Accompanies as a Daughter

To Veerai Kavi Rajendra, a Tamil mystic of Ramnad, Mother revealed Herself as his daughter. The pious Kavi once desired to go on a pilgrimage to Kasi to visit Viswanath and Annapurna. While he was making all preparations, his only daughter approached and requested him to take her along with him. The father, of course, dissuaded her, for the journey was difficult and risky and he had to travel the whole distance on foot. The girl, who was grown-up and intelligent enough to see the difficulty, desisted. The Kavi then took leave of all the people in the family and the little hamlet and started on his journey.

Hardly had he gone a mile away from the house when he heard behind him the rustling sound of footsteps on dry leaves. He looked back and was astonished to see his daughter. She explained, 'Father, when you had started I felt a great urge to accompany you, so I informed mother, had her permission and came away by the backdoor of the house.' The father was perplexed but, 'Possibly this is the will of the Divine Mother', he thought and took her with him. For nearly a year the Kavi travelled in Kasi and other places of pilgrimage. All this time the daughter served her father in all possible ways, cooking for him, and washing his clothes. On their return journey when they were about a mile away from the house, the daughter said, 'Father, when you reach the house all people of the village will come to receive you, they do not know that I accompanied you; so it is better that I go in advance and enter the house through the door behind it.' The simple father agreed.

When he reached home, all the people of the locality came to meet him. He was joyful and inquired about the welfare of all. After some time his wife came and asked, 'You are inquiring about all the people of the locality but don't you remember that we have a daughter also, and that too an only daughter? The girl is so sorry that she is weeping, retiring to a corner of the house.' 'What is the matter?' said the husband. 'She was with me throughout the year, still you say I neglect her!' The wife was flabbergasted and protested saying, 'There must be something wrong with you. Why, the girl was all the time with me here.'

Then it dawned on the Kavi that it was the Divine Mother who had accompanied him as his daughter and served him for a year.

Another incident is mentioned about him. While he was doing the worship in the shrine a man came to sell bangles. As is common in villages, women and girls from different houses came out and selected their bangles. But when the Kavi's wife wanted to pay, the man demanded money for two sets taken by two girls of the house. Naturally she protested, other ladies joining her. Veerai Kavi, who was engaged in worship, felt disturbed by the noise and called out to the man that he had only one daughter. Just then he saw two hands bedecked with the bangles coming out with jingling sound above the worship jar painted with the Mother's face and he heard a voice: 'Why, father, I lived with you all the year round and served you according to my capacity. Do you grudge paying a few annas for me?' The devotee was overwhelmed to have the vision of the Mother. The bangle-seller, of course, was immediately paid. The Mother then endowed him with the capacity to translate as an offering to Her the famous *Saundarya Lahari* of Sri Sankaracharya into beautiful Tamil verses, which won for him the title of Kavi, the poet.

A later poet, Pichu Aiyar of Vembathur, Ramnad, who was the court poet of Setupati, composed a poem in which he refers to the two divine sports (Lila) of Devi which show to what extent the poet Kaviraja Pandita was blessed with Her grace. A free translation of the poem is as follows:

'O Queen of Madura, you, in the guise of the daughter of the majestic Kaviraja Pandita accomapnied him on his pilgrimage up to the famous Kasi, washed his clothes, cooked for him, and even decked your hands (with bangles)!'

Kaviraja Panditar or Veerai Kaviraja Panditar hailed from Veerai or Veerachalapuram in Ramnad district. He became a monk in later life and has his Samadhi (burial place) there.

Mother Gives Milk to a Weeping Boy

Sri Sankara's *Saundarya Lahari*[2] mentions "the Dravida child' who drank milk from the breast of the Divine Mother:

> 'The milk of your breast, I feel in my heart O daughter of the Mountain,
> is an ocean of milk flowing like the waters of Sarasvati,
> Having tasted which the Dravida Child became the graceful poet among great poets.'

The child was the great Saivite saint Tiru Jnana Sambandar. As a boy of three he was taken by his father to the river where the latter got down to take his bath. Not seeing the father, the little thing became afraid and began to cry, 'Mother, father.' Then Mother Parvati appeared and gave him the milk of her breast in a cup. The child drank the milk, and as is common with children, some portion of it was flowing down the edges of his mouth. His father came and asked him who it was that gave him milk. Then the little child burst forth in beautiful Tamil verse, describing Siva and Parvati to his father, who was a devout Saivite: 'He it is

---

2   तव स्तन्यं मन्ये धरणिधरकन्ये हृदयतः
पयःपारावारः परिवहति सारस्वतमिव ।
दयावत्या दत्तं द्रविडशिशुरास्वाद्य तव या
कवीनां प्रौढानामजनि कमनीयः कवयिता ॥ 75

whose ear is adorned with a ring, who rides on the bull, who wears the moon on his head, who has a body besmeared with the ashes of the cremation ground, the thief who steals my heart.'

God Becomes Mother and Midwife

There is an interesting account of how the great God Siva took the form of an earthly mother to cater to the needs of an ailing daughter. Near Trichi there was an old lady who gave her daughter in marriage in a village a few miles off, on the other side of the river Kaveri. When the time was ripe for the daughter to give birth to a child, her mother was requested to be present, as there was nobody else in the house. But, alas, the river was in floods, there was no bridge and it would not be possible for country boats to cross the ferocious river even for the next few days. The anxious mother kept on praying to the Lord of the hill and the daughter also must have done the same because of ailment.

After a few days when the mother was actually able to cross the river, she hurried to the daughter's house. And on reaching she found her quite safe having already given birth to a child. She made anxious inquiries but the daughter could not understand her. 'Why', she replied, 'from the time of the labour pain you were here, and all these days you were serving me even up to a few minutes earlier, and now you ask, how I am doing!' The mother was taken aback. Then on further discussion it dawned on the devout mother and daughter that the Lord of the hill, out of sympathy for them, had come to their rescue. Henceforward the Deity of the temple was called 'Thayumanavar', the God who became also the mother. Even now there exists a big temple dedicated to Him in Trichi where the great mystic Thayumanavar bearing the Lord's name sang beautiful songs on Him.

Mother as Sister

Sarada Devi, the Holy Mother, had many intimate visions of the Mother. While going to Dakshineswar from Jayrambati to see her husband, she had an attack of high fever on the way. How she was relieved of this suffering is depicted in her own words:

'I lost all consciousness on account of high temperature and was lying unable even to look to the propriety of my dress, when I saw a girl come and sit beside me. The girl was black in complexion, but I never saw such beauty before. She sat and began to pass her hand over my head and body. Her hand was so soft and cool that the heat and the burning sensation of my body began to subside. I asked her affectionately, "May I know where you come from?" The girl replied, "I come from Dakshineswar." Astonished to hear it, I said, "From Dakshineswar? I thought of going there to see him (Sri Ramakrishna) and serve him, but as I have got this fever on my way, I shall not have the good fortune of fulfilling these desires." "Why not?" said the girl. "You will surely go to Dakshineswar. Come round and go there and see him. It is for you that I have detained him there." I said, "Is that so? Pray, tell me, are you related to us?" "I am your sister," said she. I said, "Indeed? That is why you have come!" I had this conversation with her when I fell asleep.'

Mother Gives Speech and Wisdom

There are many interesting anecdotes about the grace of the Mother to the devotees suffering from some permanent ailments. That God makes the dumb eloquent is exemplified in the case of Muka, the dumb man. Through the grace of Mother Kamakshi of Kanchi he was not only endowed with the power of speech but also with an incomparable capacity of composing hymns full of fervour, devotion and beauty

of cadence and diction. He mentions about this gaining by
him of the power of speech in the famous *Muka Panchasati:*

'O Kamakshi! The creature which contemplates
on you even for a fraction of a second, even should it be
dumb and immersed in sorrow's depths born of ignorance,
will become one of unequalled fame in this world.'[3]
Arya Satakam (57)

'That which will please even mute persons with
speech as pellucid and purifying as the flow of Ganga's
waters.'[4]   *Stuti Satakam* (11)

'O Kamakshi, at the very start of the procession of
your glances, rising wave on wave in sheer play, the
dumb man becomes articulate enough to chant the four
Vedas, the ugly one turns into a very Manmatha (Love-
God) and the poverty-stricken is transformed into the
very Indra.'[5]   *Kataksha Satakam* (74)

Conclusion

Infinite are the ways in which the Divine Mother plays.
It is not possible for limited beings to fully comprehend
the unlimited, much less to describe It. As Pushpadanta
puts it:

---

3 मूकोऽपि जटिलदुर्गंति शोकोऽपि स्मरति यः क्षणं भवती ।
एको भवति स जन्तुः लोकोत्तरकीर्तिरेव कामाक्षि ॥

4 मूकानामपि कुर्वंती सुरधुनी नीकाश-वाग्वैभवम् ।

5 मूको विरिञ्चति परं पुरुषः कुरूपः
कंदर्पति त्रिदशराजति किंपचानः ।
कामाक्षि केवलमुपक्रमकाल एव
लीलातरङ्गितकटाक्षरुचः क्षणं ते ॥

'O Lord, if the blue mountain be the ink-pill, the
bed of the ocean the ink-stand, the branch of the large
heavenly tree be the pen, the earth the writing leaf, and
by taking these if the Goddess of Learning writes for
eternity, even then the limit of Thy virtues will not be
reached.'[6]

Siva-mahimnah Stotram (32).

An embodied, limited man can at best take shelter at the
lotus feet of the Divine Mother. He must surrender his all,
even himself, to Her, and bow down to Her, who is ever
ready to shower Her grace, who is always intent on removing
the sufferings of those who take refuge in Her.

---

6 असितगिरिसमं स्यात् कज्जलं सिन्धुपात्रं
   सुरतरुवरशाखा लेखनी पत्रमुर्वी ।
   लिखति यदि गृहीत्वा शारदा सर्वकालं
   तदपि तव गुणानामीश पारं न याति ॥

Siva-mahimnah Stotram (32)

SIVA WE WORSHIP

Salutation to Siva!

From whom the entire universe with its creation, preservation and dissolution shoots forth,

To whom uncountable glories are attributed, who resembles the sky in clearness, who while being the Lord of all, transcends the Lord Himself,

To that Siva may I have burning devotion.

—SWAMI VIVEKANANDA

Siva embodies eternal India, whose message is two-fold—activistic and meditative. By one the sons of her soil traversed the old world with the message of goodwill and a Godward view of life. Spiritual and cultural ideas were the motive force for those missionaries. Siva used them as His carriers in the conquest of the hearts of the people. Thus many of the South East Asian people, accepted Siva as their Chosen Ideal. Campa and Cambodia accepted Saivism as their state religion.

But the meditative India was at the back of this activistic aspect. And this is represented by the conceptions of her ideals. Don't we see Siva always in the meditative posture? Is not Buddha too meditating perpetually? This dual aspect is the message of life too. Life comprises both contemplation and action. And both are symbolised in the conception of Siva.

Siva immersed in contemplation is the ideal of Sattva, of poise, calmness and reflection. Every meditation is transformed into an action. Even a scientist meditates

first, formulates a law and then experiments and if it is sub-
stantiated he accepts it as a truth. Of all the sciences Mathe-
matics is able to approach nearest to truth for it is nearer to
contemplation. Reflection again is the root of all creation.
As the Upanishads[1] say, the Great One reflected and the
five basic constituents of the gross universe came into existence. Whatever flashed in that Cosmic Mind had its counterpart in the gross world. That is the process of creation, in all
fields, in all climes. First idea, then representation; first
feeling, then tears, poems, painting, sculpture and so on.
Thought, contemplation, reflection, is at the root of all action.
So the former must be kept at the back of all activity. Is it
not Sri Krishna's message too? Does not the Gita recommend
'intense activity amidst intense rest and intense rest amidst
intense activity'? An image of Siva in your shrine or His
picture in your parlour will remind you that life is not all
activity, movement, race; it is contemplation, poise, absorption too. If the controlling apparatus is not operative, life
in the true sense will be lost, like the misguided missile, in the
meshes of purposeless, meaningless activity. Many people
nowadays like to live in excitement. They want to escape
from their thoughts. They are anxious to drown their
minds in the busy programme of the day. Siva in contemplation will save them from this unrest; only let them look
at His picture now and then, reflect on Him and the mind
will be at peace. What makes a man worried or restless?
Is it the immediate crisis? What was the problem before
that, and still earlier? It is in the mind of man that the
abode of peace must be established. Meditation, retiring to
one's inner self at least for the time being, is the solution.
Siva is the perfect ideal of that. Him we worship.

---

1 *Chandogya Upanishad* VI. 2-3.

Is life all growth, is all progress evolution? Is it not spiral or cyclical? Is construction possible without destruction? The trees of an age-old forest are hewed down to make a village. The huts of a village are broken down to construct the buildings of a town. The buildings of a town are demolished to make way for the sky-scrapers of a city. Then one day everything topples down. Today's caravan route becomes tomorrow's Steppes. So in Hindu conception, creation, sustentation and dissolution are in the natural order of things. Brahman or Sadasiva is the root of all these three functions which are represented by His trident. See Him in every creation and destruction; be calm and worship Him.[2] In the form of Kala, Time, with His Power Kali, He destroys the universe. Nataraja's dance symbolizes pralaya. But is it all destruction? No. Pralaya is the gathering back of the seeds of creation which will be projected again in the beginning of another cycle.

Nataraja is a first-rate dancer. No other god is so expert in this art. But dance here is not a means of self-expression but rather of self-forgetfulness. It liberates one from the ego and leads to self-effacement. Self-immersion renders the full unfoldment of creative power. Siva in the dancing pose is a veritable example of aesthetic and divine perfection in carriage, gesture and movement. Naturalness and rhythm are the watchwords. Siva in meditation expresses the flow of inner joy and perennial bliss. Out of that static meditative posture He flashes into the most dynamic action. Schools of Eastern art follow Nataraja's dance of self-forgetfulness. They appeal to us, for they transport us to a haven of bliss where the deadweight of ego is lifted up and we are at peace.

---

2 शान्त उपासीत *Ch. Up.* III, 14. 1.

Nataraja is the repository of all dances, though He
Himself is a specialist in the Tandava dance.[2*] In fact, both
creation and destruction have been conceived as the dance
of the Divine. Of all the temples of India, it is Nataraja's
temple at Chidambaram that has preserved the mudras of
Bharata Muni, the founder of Natya sastra. The temple
walls that bear the impress of those poses are a sight for the
rasikas to enjoy. This is because Siva is a real connoisseur
of art. Does not Kali dance continually on His breast?
Is it not in the Purusha's presence and with the sole object of
pleasing Him that Prakriti dances?[3] If Siva plays truant,
all artistic talents of Maya evaporate just as the multi-coloured
panorama created by the evening sun melts away in the
absence of the vast expanse of the sky. Siva is the substratum
on which the pleasant play of creation is reflected. He is
the white paper on which the exquisite poem of life is written.
He is the canvas on which the variegated painting of human
joys and sorrows is represented. He is also the sandalwood
that is carved out and given manifold shapes. He is the
master of self-immolation. The world is fashioned out of
Him. But is He exhausted thereby? No. He is both
immanent and transcendent. He abides to enjoy the Lila, the
divine cosmic sport.

Siva is Nilakantha, the blue-throated one. And He
became so by drinking the poison arising out of the ocean-
churning, wealth-searching expedition of the gods and demons.
Are all poisons already drunk? What about the constant
fight between the chastened and unregenerate senses? What
about the outer conflict? Do we not see every morning the

2* *Cf Siva-tandava-stotram, verse* 11.

3 मायान्तु प्रकृतिं विद्याद् मायिनन्तु महेश्वरम् ।
                                        Svetasvatara Up.

newspaper bringing reports of the production of more fresh poison? We want more and more of Nilakanthas to make the world habitable. By meditating on Siva the self-immolator, we get the proper inspiration, the relevant virtue, so urgent, so important, so imperative in the modern context. Why run to world or even social context? Every family, every home, requires one or two miniature Nilakanthas to keep it functioning. Every co-operative effort requires Him.

But is this role not a painful one, it may be asked. Look at the calm face of Siva. Is it not beaming? Is it not refuge-conferring? Does it express pain? Does it betray the suppression of a concealed suffering? The benign look, the serene face, the body without movement. all radiate calmness, coolness, peace, Santi. Siva takes away all pangs of pain and suffering, the fatigue of toiling and moiling. Restlessness is the evil of modern living. It is the reversal of life, this not living in harmony and poise. One made in the mould of Siva can transmit peace and calmness all around. Have you not seen a man of calm, composed nature radiating peace and benediction? Have you not noticed under a way-side tree a half-naked fakir a follower of Siva in grim literality, but still who is much maligned by some ultra-moderns as burdens to society—giving solace and consolation to a bereaved father, a wailing mother, or a disconsolate wife? Siva is India's eternal ideal. Did not Swami Vivekananda recognise this and say: 'Oh, India! forget not that the God thou worshippest is the Great Ascetic of ascetics, the all-renouncing Sankara'?

Siva is the pattern for all sacrificing people. The monks of the ten Sankarite Orders accept Him as their Lord. Why? It is because He is all-renouncing, non-possessing, completely detached. Did He not burn Manmatha, the symbolised

7

desire, with His third eye, the eye of Knowledge? He lives in
the burning ground, wears a tiger skin, eats fruits and roots
and whatever chance may bring. In a world mad after lust
and lucre, name and fame, power and position, luxury and
leisure, He stands as a challenging example that in voluntary
renunciation of men's rights alone lies the solution of the
problems of a competitive society. But Siva is the ideal of
householders too; for are not He and Parvati the original
parents of the world as the great poet Kalidasa has sung?[4]

Siva is white, because He is pure Sattva. He is Tamas too,
but that is during the dissolution of the universe. He stands
for purity. He is sometimes colourless due to the happy
blending of all colours.

Siva means Mangala, auspiciousness. He is ever ready
to do good to the bound souls whose Lord He is. He bestows
knowledge and vision, both Apara and Para, secular and
spiritual. He who desires knowledge must supplicate to
Sankara.[5] Devotees following the path of Jnana are especially
attracted to Him. People with more inclination to knowledge
are considered to be born with the attributes of Siva. Philo-
sophically speaking, Siva Himself becomes the bound soul,
so service to Him is service to humanity and vice versa.
This has a tremendous social implication. Wherever there
is Jiva, there is Siva too.[6] Siva permeating the entire universe

---

4 जगतः पितरौ वन्दे पार्वती-परमेश्वरौ *Raghuvamsam* 1. 1.
   Cf. माता मे पार्वती देवी पिता देवोमहेश्वरः । बान्धवाः
   शिवभक्ताश्च स्वदेशो भुवनत्रयम् ॥ *Annapurna-stotram*

5 ज्ञानमिच्छेच्च शंकरात् । *Tantrasarah, Saivacara-*
                                      prakaranam

6 जीवः शिवः शिवो जीवः स जीवः केवलः शिवः ॥
                                      Skanda Purana 6

confers value to all efforts. He is thus the ground of all ethics. For Sadhakas aware of the separateness of the world, a special discipline is to look upon all created beings as the manifestations of Siva, just as the orders of the King's men are considered as the King's commands.[7]

Siva is Asutosh. He is easily satisfied. Did He not accept the unknowing worship of a born hunter? Therein lies our hope. Otherwise, is it possible for ordinary people to come out of the meshes of illusion after performing all the difficult practices? He is grace personified. His grace descends upon the foiled and the forlorn. Every one is fit to do His worship. Devotion to Siva is a rare thing. It comes through the merit accrued in millions of lives.[8] Of all sacrifices for God, repetition of His name is the best.[9] Meditation on Siva in silence again is the best form of Japa.[10] While worshipping Him, one must first identify oneself with Him and then do the services.[11] The Ahamgrahopasana based upon the Advaitic outlook is the best form of His worship So'ham, Sivo'ham—He am I, Siva am I—are the formulae

---

7 शिवदृष्टिस्तु सर्वत्र कर्तव्या सर्वजन्तुभिः ।
  राजदृष्टिः यथामात्ये क्रियते सर्वजन्तुभिः ॥

                              Vedasara-sahasranama-tika

8 कोटिजन्मार्जितैः पुण्यैः शिवे भक्तिः प्रजायते ।

                              Siva-gita I. 16

9 यज्ञानां जपयज्ञोऽस्मि । *Gita* X 25

10 मौन एव परो जपः । *Kularnava Tantra* [Quoted in *Sri Sivajingopagasana* (*Marathi*) by Dr Sadasiva Krishna Phadke]

11 शिवो भूत्वा शिवं भजेत् Quoted by Dr Phadke.

of His meditation.[12]   A devotee looks upon all his activities
in imitation of a liberated soul as worship to Siva and thus
spiritualises his whole life.[13]

The worship of Siva has a close alliance with Yoga.
The whole concept and practices of Tantric discipline are
pressed into the service of His votaries. Saivism in fact is
a federation of cults.[14] Whatever good was found in any of
the sects, it has embraced it as its own. Siva is Mahadeva, the
Great God, His conception is concrete and His relation with
the devotees is of an intensely personal nature. His austere
life has given rise among His followers to the extremes of
ascetic fervour. Among them the Nathayogis are specially
famous for austerity and miraculous powers.

Historically speaking, Siva is a very old Deity. He is
known as 'propitious' in the Rigveda. His counterpart
Rudra was a terrible god and the supplicants prayed to Him
to show His benign face.[15] *Svetasvatara Upanishad* exalts
Maheswara, and prescribes devotion to Him for realization.[16]
Satarudriya prays to Him as the Lord of all creatures.[17]
He is represented in Yogic posture even by the Mohenjodaro
sculptors. He was worshipped in the days of Megasthenes

---

12 चिदानन्दरूपः शिवोऽहं शिवोऽहम् । *Nirvanasatkam*
शिवः केवलोऽहम् *Nirvanadasaka*

13 यद्यत्कर्म करोमि तत्तदखिलं शम्भो तवाराधनम् ।
Siva-manasa-pujana-stotram 4

14 *The Cultural Heritage of India*, Vol. IV. p. 63.

15 रुद्र यत्ते दक्षिणं मुखं तेन मां पाहि नित्यम् ।
Sve. Up. IV. 21.

16 *Sve. Up.* IV. 7, 23.

17 पशूनां पतिः Quoted in *C.H.I.* IV. p. 68.

too. But the efflorescence of Saivism was in the days of the Gupta kings. Greater India got a fresh lease of life at that time. In South India the expansion of the Siva-cult took place during the reign of the Cholas.

Three main religio-philosophical schools have sprung up centring on Siva. The Trika School flourished in Kashmir in the 9th century but its beginning must have been in earlier days. Its philosophical branch is called Pratyabhijna-sastra. It is monistic and idealistic in view. The tradition is that Saivism spread from Kashmir. The Southern School is also very ancient. The Saiva Siddhanta philosophy is more or less Visishtadvaitic in view. In the Tamil area the four great Saints, the Samayacharas—Appar, Sundarar, Sambandhar and Manikkavachagar—popularised Saivism. The Siddhars specialised in having powers like Siva. *Tevaram* records the mystic and religious outpourings of the great souls. The *Periapuranam* gives the lives of the 63 Nayanmars, the Saivite saints. *Tiruvachakam* abounds in devotional fervour and ecstasy. Meykandar's *Siva-jnanabodham,* the first systematic philosophical treatise says that *Siva* is One, *jnana* is the knowledge of its true nature, and *bodham* is the realization of such knowledge.[18]

The Virasaiva school or the Lingayat system was started by Basava in the 12th century. Allama Prabhu, Akka Mahadevi, Chenna Basava are some of the noted teachers of this system. Mala or impurity, according to it, can be washed off by triple Diksha (initiation), by carrying Siva's emblem on the breast, and by Yoga and five Acharas. In its scheme, Guru, Linga and Jangama (monks) have a crucial place. Sacred ashes, holy water and Rudraksha beads are

---

18 *C.H.I.* IV. p. 68

the purifying agents. The Mantra meaning 'salutation to Siva' is liberating. Monday is a specially holy day for the Saivites. Kasi and Ganga are specially holy because of their connection with Him. Saivism accepts 36 principles. It takes the universe as a play of the Lord. Many of the Tantras are mentioned as the veritable words of Mahadeva.

Siva in His absolute aspect has no attributes. The same Brahman became the Trimurti.[19] Though the Pauranikas assigned to Him the Tamas aspect of destruction, in His real nature He is the abode of all auspiciousness.[20] For the welfare of the devotees, He has taken this beautiful form. He is even in the heart of Vishnu.[21] He is the embodiment and source of all gods. They are satisfied through His worship, just as the branches put forth flowers through the watering of the root of the tree.[22] In this Iron age He is the Lord, say the Pauranikas.[23]

Siva resides in Kailasa. But His most favourite place of residence is the heart of the devotees. Is it not for this that His Lingayat devotees keep His emblem even physically near their heart?

Siva and His emblem are identical. Though we say Siva's Linga, it is like the head of the mythological Rahu

---

19 स ब्रह्मा स शिवः स हरिः । *Nrsimhāpurvatapani* I. 4

20 *Tantrasarah*

21 यथा शिवमयो विष्णुः ।
    शिवस्य हृदयं विष्णुर्विष्णोश्च हृदयं शिवः   *Skanda* 8. 9

22 वृक्षस्य मूलसेकेन शाखाः पुष्यन्ति वै यथा ।
    शिवार्चनेन देवाश्च तथा तृप्ता भवन्ति हि ॥

                                        Quoted from *Tantrasarah*

23 कलौ देवो महेश्वरः । *Kurmapurana* 18

which is his whole being. Linga means emblem, symbol.
It is the refuge or repository of the entire universe. In it all
inauspicious things get merged and transmuted.[24] Of the
different Sivalingas, Banalinga and Swayambhulinga are the
best. While the former was created by the Lord to please
His devotee Bana, the latter came out of itself and its source
is not known.[25] The lingas found in the Narmada river are
most suitable. The Linga is the nearest and barest symbol. As
meditation is the nearest approach to the state of perfection,
Sivalinga is the most immediate symbol of the Absolute
Brahman.[26] Worship of Siva in the Linga is the best. In
its absence images are made use of.[27]

Siva is infinite even in qualities. However much we may
try, we cannot exhaust them. Pushpadanta in his famous
verse[28] narrates how even the Goddess of Learning recording
for all times with all the huge paraphernalia of writing—
the mountain as the ink-pill, the sea as the ink-pot, the branch
of the mighty heavenly tree as the pen, the wide earth as the
paper—finds it impossible to complete the description of His
qualities. And then he says, 'I do not know the truth
about you, how you are, O Maheswara; of whatever form

---

24 आलयः सर्वदेवानां लयनाल्लिंगमुच्यते । *Skanda* (Phadke)

25 *Tantrasarah*

26 Cf. 'Of all the representations of the deity which India
    has imagined', observes Barth 'these (lingas) are perhaps
    the least offensive to look at. Anyhow, they are the
    least materialistic' *C.H.I.* IV. p. 67.

27 लिंग-संपूजनं मुख्यमलाभे प्रतिमादिषु ।

                              Padma Purana 101. 114

28 *Sivamahimnah-stotra* 32.

you are, O Great Lord, I bow down to you again and
again.'29

    If it is impossible to know His nature fully, and if we
suffer the pain of the tightening bond of Maya and feel we
are lost in this ocean of transmigratory existence, our only
hope lies in taking refuge in Him, making Him the helmsman
of our life and praying to Him, 'O Lord, take our boat now
across this ocean of Samsara.'30

---

29 तव तत्त्वं न जानामि कीदृशोऽसि महेश्वर ।
     यादृशोऽसि महादेव तादृशाय नमोनमः ॥   *Ibid* 41

30 अब शिव पार कर मेरे नेइया ।   From *Devisahaya's* song.

SRI KRISHNA
THE ETERNAL CHARIOTEER

Fear-Complex is the Root of All Our Problems

PEACE is a contemporary slogan though the desire for peace is an eternal, universal yearning of the human heart. Nowadays one hears often about peace in the international field and that there should be no war which disturbs it. As a corollary, violence also is considered to be an unethical, brutal force. When one analyses the mental background of this clamour for collective peace and non-violence, one finds a fear-complex dogging the modern leaders. Not that all of them do not like war or forced peace of the Pax Romana brand, for the first thing that strikes them to solve any international problem is an armed intervention. But the modern weapons are so perfected at present with the invention of the Atom, Hydrogen and other bombs that the existence of both the belligerent and the attacked nations is at stake. In fact a future war may not merely be a global one; it has the potentiality of totally wiping out the whole human race. So the statesmen of both camps are anxious to maintain peace.

In the national field also the fear-complex and the consequent distrust arise. The totality of humanity is not taken notice of, for the fictitious boundaries created by accidents of history are maintained, and the leaders feel that it is their responsibility to look after the needs of their own group or people. Out of this selfish feeling one group or country exploits another, and naturally its relation with the exploited group or country is much strained. While the last two centuries saw the growth of colonialism and imperialism, the present century shows the progress of the people in the colonies and the so-called backward countries. Though efforts are being made to keep all sections of people within the country satisfied, feuds between nations continue, for issues of national self-interest are often made international ones, and thus the difficulty thickens. It is because of the selfishness of each nation or group that this tension is mounting. Even within the country different groups are at enmity with one another. Racial, linguistic and other parochial feelings vitiate the peaceful atmosphere and breed jealousy, intolerence, distrust and mutual fear.

In the case of individuals also the want of peace is keenly felt because of insecurity and fear. The modern civilization is a complex one. With the growth of industry, technology and science people are gradually migrating to the thickly populated cities. Want of accommodation, keen competition for employment and lack of intimate feeling among men—for they no more live only with their blood-relations—are creating great stress and strain in contemporary minds. Because of the phenomenal increase of the population of the world in the last two hundred years, people can no longer rest content with the agricultural structure of society, which by its very nature was more congenial to the growth of fellow-feeling and lessening of the competitive spirit. The economics of the modern times is a global one. No one can remain cut off from or untouched by the constantly changing economic forces. The sense of individuality in contrast to the ancient group-sense is also contributing much to this whirlpool of confusion and unrest. Moreover, modern man is at war with himself for he is losing his spiritual moorings. Dr. Jung bears testimony to this fact when he comes to the conclusion after years of research in mental health that in the majority of cases of men above 35 or 40, the problem is a spiritual one, of finding a faith that could sustain them from the ever-growing sense of frustration, the feeling of insecurity of occupation, anxiety to know the purpose of life and the fear of decrepitude and death.

Solution

So we find that the mental climate behind all these talks of peace at the individual, national and international levels is mainly fear, the ethical or spiritual consideration being secondary. This is similar to the mental state of Arjuna before the famous Kurukshetra war. On seeing the great generals like Bhishma and Drona in the opposite camp and almost all the near and dear ones, the soldiers of the then India, ready to kill one another, he was overtaken by a mixed feeling of fear and ethical indecision. Sri Krishna's message embodied in the *Song Celestial* invigorated him and helped him to shake off fear, indecision and unmanliness. This point of similarity shows that Sri Krishna's teachings can serve a distinct purpose in guiding men even in modern times.

Unity of Existence

Man's innate fear-complex was recognized by the ancient scriptures. So they tried to root it out by removing the wrong notions about the ultimate truths of life, for this complex is a mental one. The *Brihadaranyaka Upanishad* points out that fear is generated when there is the existence of another.[1]

As there is one Brahman existing in the universe,[2] there

---

1 द्वितीयाद्वै भयं भवति । *Brihadaranyaka Upanishad* I. 4. 2.

2 सर्वं खल्विदं ब्रह्म ।   *Chandogya Upanishad* III. 14. 1.

is really no cause of fear. This unity of existence can neither be proved nor disproved through reason alone. It is a statement of fact intuited by saints and seers of all ages and nations. Its vague, indistinct presence is felt in the hearts of men, in their avowedly cherished aspiration of one world. Sri Krishna, quite in line with the ancient masters, emphasizes this unity of existence or ultimate reality while revealing his true nature to Arjuna. In his universal aspect he is Brahman Himself and not merely the son of a cowherd woman.[3] He is God Himself,[4] and as the *Bhagavata* points out, the Reality designated by the words Brahman, Paramatman and Bhagavan is one and the same.[5] In Him are all the created beings strung together as gems of a necklace on a string.[6] He holds the whole universe in a part of Himself.[7] Taking refuge in Him[8] man goes beyond fear and conflict and attains peace. This is the secret of secrets.[9]

Now, this is a metaphysical truth. The truth of it may not be accepted by materialists as a fact logically proved, dialectically incontrovertible and scientifically arrived at. But the vast practical utility of it cannot be doubted. The proof of the pudding is in the eating. We cannot clearly express the nature of electricity but we can use it to our best

---

3 न खलु गोपिकानन्दनः । *Bhagavata* X. 31. 4.

4 कृष्णस्तु भगवान् खयम् । *ibid.* 1. 3. 28

5 ब्रह्मेति परमात्मेति भगवानिति शब्द्यते । *ibid.* I. 2. 1. 1.

6 सूत्रे मणिगणा इव । *Gita* VII. 7.

7 एकांशेन स्थितो जगत् । *ibid.* X. 42.

8 तमेव शरणं गच्छ । *ibid.* XVIII. 62

9 गुह्याद्गुह्यतरम् । *bid.* XVIII. 63.

advantage. The really intelligent man is he who goes to a mango grove, makes friends with the owner and begins to eat mangoes, and not the man who goes on counting the leaves— as a parable of Sri Ramakrishna has it.

Non-attachment and Dedication

Faith in the ultimate reality is necessary, for it can sustain a man in moments of doubt and despair. But Sri Krishna is not dogmatic about it. He has solutions for all types of people. So we have his grand philosophy of non-attached action.[10] In this no faith is necessary. Only a man must be determined not to be carried away by futile worries before and after the work. Every day is a fresh start for him. He has the right to action—in fact he is compelled to do it by his very nature[11]—but he has no right to the fruits thereof.[12] The success in a work depends on various factors. Sri Krishna enumerates them as five: the seat of action, the agent, the various implements, the manifold efforts and the higher forces.[13] The cause and effect sequence is not entirely under man's control and the unseen causes, the past Samskara, fate, heredity or the society play a decisive role in his life. While he should have initiative and effort, he must be resigned to the higher forces or practise strict detachment as to the result. Otherwise frustration is inevitable. That is why we see that hundreds of people begin

---

10 असक्तो ह्याचरन्कर्मं परमाप्नोति पूरुषः ।   *ibid.* III. 19.
11 करिष्यस्यवश्योऽपि तत् ।   *ibid.* XVIII. 60.
    नहि कश्चित्क्षणमपि जातु तिष्ठत्यकर्मकृत् ।   *ibid.* III. 5.
12 कर्मण्येवाधिकारस्ते मा फलेषु कदाचन ।   *ibid.* II. 47.
13 *ibid.* XVIII, 14.

their lives in youth with great enthusiasm but after a few years of struggle they turn cynics if not misanthropes.

There are two aspects in suffering—physical or real and mental. While the health of relatives, education of children, security of employment, group-feuds, national calamities international cold war are all grim realities, the worry and tension that follow them are the futile creations of our own mind. No useful purpose is served by them. Sri Krishna exhorts man to give up this meaningless concomitants of objective experience. While the suffering that is physical or real must be gone through, may be fighting all the time, the mental suffering can be disowned. This equanimity of mind is described by Sri Krishna as Yoga.[14] This is the secret of real work.[15] Men of faith, however, can have the free play of all their emotions by connecting them to the Lord. Whatever they do—eat, offer, or give—they do as a dedicated service.[16] This supplies them with a refuge wherein they can take shelter whenever they are in danger of being cowed by the weight of adverse circumstances.

Preparedness

This frame of mind has got the preparedness for all situations. 'Ripeness is all', said Shakespeare.[17] His Macbeth strove hard to push himself up and did it also. But at the end he discovered that he was digging his own grave all the time. 'They have tied me to a stake; I cannot fly. But,

---

14 समत्वं योग उच्यते ।   *ibid.* II. 48.

15 योगः कर्मसु कौशलम् ।   *ibid.* II. 50.

16 *ibid.* IX. 27,

17 *King Lear* V. 2.

bear-like, I must fight the course.'[18] As a result of this
discovery and resignation a complete catharsis takes place
which is immensely beneficial psychologically. But this is the
readiness of a desperate man given to hopelessness and despair.
This is not Krishna's readiness. He exhorts Arjuna to see
through the nature of things, that all creation abides in the
Universal form of God and all creatures move according
to the Divine Will. Man's duty is to attune himself to
the Divine Will and work unattached to the fruits thereof.
Whichever station of life he is put in, whatever may be the
nature of work he is expected to do, he must do it with all
enthusiasm, all vigour, but all the time completely unattached.
While desires and passions are normally considered to be the
springs of action. Sri Krishna raises humanity to a higher level
and asks man to perform his duties according to his Swadharma.[19] This attitude towards work will prepare the mind for
any eventuality and supply the courage to face life with perfect
equanimity. Sri Krishna's life itself is a grand example of
this truth. 'Intense activity amidst intense rest and intense
rest amidst intense activity' has been pointed out by Swami
Vivekananda as the Gita ideal of work. And this can be
properly done when one is established in the conception of
Swadharma and then goes to fulfil his duty unattached, not
only to himself and his fellow-beings, but extends his service
to other creatures also.

Divert the Energy to Higher Channels

Even in times of peace and plenty man is gradually facing
another difficulty, especially in the materially advanced

---

18   *Macbeth* V. 7

19   सहजं कर्म कौन्तेय ।   *Gita* XVIII. 48.

स्वधर्मे निधनं श्रेयः ।   *ibid.* III. 35.

countries. In the absence of war, when hectic, feverish activity is no more necessary, he finds it difficult to pass his leisure due to lack of occupation and so is in search of new excitements. Because of the invention of numerous, time-saving machines, he is, happily, free from hard soul-killing labour. But as the higher aspirations are absent in him because of his materialistic view of life, he is left in a mental vacuum. This feeling of emptiness urges him to climb mountains, dive into deep oceans and live the life of cave-dwellers in the forests. In this there is a good deal of the spirit of adventure, no doubt, but it is more the result of mental and spiritual dryness. There is a soul in man which is not satisfied with the small, with the finite.[20] The lure of the Infinite, though unconscious, prompts him to build the tallest building, the biggest mansion, the longest road and to do a hundred other things in big dimensions. This hunger for the Infinite points the way in which man should go to fill up his mental vacuum. While there is no objection to these adventures even in the material field, there is positive danger of their being overstressed. Such a social climate is a favourable ground for political adventurers also. So in the interest of the vast humanity it is imperative that we divert our energies to a different channel. Future adventures should be in the fields of culture and spirituality. It was Parnell who said that there is no limit to the progress of a nation. And this progress is not circumscribed merely in the field of material possession where keen competition is inevitable. After all, progress is a relative term, and it keeps alive the bitter strife for possession if not shifted to a higher

---

20. नाल्पे सुखमस्ति भूमैव सुखम् ।
Chandogya Upanishad VII. 23. 1.

level. Hence it is the duty of the real leaders to divert the
mind of man in that direction. Sri Krishna, the eternal guide
of humanity, does precisely that. He exhorts man to look
to the empyrean heights of thought he could climb, the incomparable depths of emotion he could plunge into and the
deep caves of the heart he could take shelter in. This man
can do by his search for reality and the manifestation of his
higher nature. He commands man to live in tune with the
Infinite, to move and have his being in unison with the infinite
spirit. The search for God or the ultimate truth is the eternal
quest of the human soul. He should intensify this adventure
of his, instead of frittering away all his energies for lesser
things pregnant with problems. Sri Krishna shows Arjuna
his universal form to convince him about the ultimate truth
before he could guide him to action. Then he asks him to
surrender his all to him and do his duty while remembering him.[21] On having the knowledge of truth and insight
into the nature of things Arjuna was free from egoism, fear
and delusion[22] and became a ready instrument in the hands
of the Divine. As soon as a man orients his life to the
universal law, he becomes the fittest vehicle for working out
the Divine plan.

Conclusion

The *Gita* has been considered by Swami Vivekananda
as 'a great mine of strength'. He thought that 'the one word
that comes out from the Upanishads like a bombshell is
Abhih, fearlessness'. This fearlessness is to be achieved
through unattached action, belief in the ultimate reality

---

21 मामनुस्मर युध्य च । *Gita* VIII. 7.

22 नष्टो मोहः । *ibid*. XVIII. 73.

and working out one's duties according to the Divine plan.

When the fear of total extinction hovers round the mind of man today, this teaching of fearlessness will serve as a tonic to his depressed soul. When all his efforts and ingenuities fail and the situation goes out of his control, he can face death boldly with the hope that he will have a fresh start from that evolved state of being in his next birth. The sum total of his efforts in this life plus his residual Karma will give birth to a new psycho-physical entity to give him another chance to strive for perfection. No effort goes in vain. 'The flower that has dropped down on earth before blossoming, the river that has lost its course in the desert, I know is not lost, yea, I know,' as Tagore puts it. Sri Krishna repeatedly assures us in the *Gita* that even a little practice of righteousness will save a man from great dangers,[23] that a doer of beneficent deeds will not enter into the meshes of evil.[24] He promises with all seriousness and sympathy,'He soon becomes righteous-minded and attains eternal peace. O son of Kunti, proclaim boldly that my devotee never perishes'.[25] Let these soul-stirring words engender firm faith in us, so that we can surrender our all to Him and accept Him as our Charioteer even as Arjuna did.

---

23 स्वल्पमप्यस्य धर्मस्य त्रायते महतो भयात् । *ibid.* II. 40

24 नहि कल्याणकृत्कश्चित् दुर्गतिं तात गच्छति । *ibid.* VI. 40.

25 *ibid.* IX. 31.

SRI KRISHNA
THE GUIDE AND GOAL DIVINE

SRI KRISHNA has been looked upon for a number of centuries from various points of view. Some have worshipped him as an ideal man, some as a complete, all-round incarnation, some as God. While all these are true, his life on earth may broadly be classified into two aspects. Swami Ramakrishnananda in his book *Sri Krishna the Pastoral and Kingmaker* has narrated them in detail. One is the aspect of his younger days and is depicted elaborately in the *Bhagavata, Vishnupurana* and *Harivamsa,* and the other is his life as a teacher of humanity described mainly in the *Gita* and the *Mahabharata.* The earlier life of Sri Krishna has appealed to devotees down the ages, and different religious sects have developed round the child or younger Krishna considering him as the goal of life. The latter part of his life where he manifests himself as a teacher *par excellence* has always attracted rational and intellectual minds. Thus Sri Krishna's personality has a charm for all varieties of people. Like the facets of a diamond there were many sides to his brilliance. Even the earlier part of his life was multiform.

The sylvan surroundings of Vraja far from the madding crowd, the idyllic setting of Yamuna and the Nidhu, and other groves, the love of the simple-hearted Gopas and Gopis, the maddening music of Krishna's flute—all these have a great emotional appeal. His life at Vrindavana transports us to a haven of pure, unalloy-

ed, spiritual joy. It is all sweetness too as a saintly poet
puts it:

> Sweet His lips, sweet His face,
> Sweet His heart, sweet His gaze,
> Sweet His smile, sweet His gait,
> Sweet's ev'rything of Madhura's
>
> > Lord great!
>
> Sweet His words, sweet His deeds,
> Sweet His lilts, sweet His words,
> Sweet His moves, sweet His turns,
> Sweet's ev'rything of Madhura's
>
> > Lord great!
>
> Sweet His singing, sweet His drinking,
> Sweet His eating, sweet His sleeping,
> Sweet His person, sweet His head-mark,
> Sweet's ev'rything of Madhura's
>
> > Lord great! [1]
>
> > (A.S.P. Ayyar's translation)

Lilasuka goes further and says:

> Sweeter than sweetness, livelier than liveliness, the
> childhood of Krishna, the Father of Love, carries away
> my heart. What shall I do?

---

[1] अधरं मधुरं वदनं मधुरं नयनं मधुरं हसितं मधुरम् ।
हृदयं मधुरं गमनं मधुरं मधुराधिपतेरखिलं मधुरम् ॥
वचनं मधुरं चरितं मधुरं वसनं मधुरं वलितं मधुरम् ।
चलितं मधुरं भ्रमितं मधुरं मधुराधिपतेरखिलं मधुरम् ॥
गीतं मधुरं पीतं मधुरं भुक्तं मधुरं सुप्तं मधुरम् ।
रूपं मधुरं तिलकं मधुरं मधुराधिपतेरखिलं मधुरम् ॥

> (Sri Vallabhacharya—Madhurashtaka)

Sweet, sweet is the body of the Lord; sweet, sweet is His face, sweet; Oh, sweet it is smelling, sweet it is smiling; it is sweet, sweet, sweet, sweet.[2]

Sri Krishna has attracted great souls like Chaitanya, Vallabha, Nimbarka and others who have formed different sects round Him. His message of overflowing and self-effacing love has a transforming power. It cleanses the baser passions of their dross and makes people God-conscious. The *Bhagavata* accepts even the passions as a spiritual discipline, if directed to God. Thus were saved Sisupala, Kamsa and others. In the *Bhagavata*[3] Narada says to Yudhishthira:

Through the passion of love, hatred, fear or affection as through loving devotion, many concentrated their mind on the Supreme Being and, having thereby got rid of their sin resulting from the passions of love, hatred, etc., attained to Him.

The women of Gopas through love, Kamsa through fear, Sisupala and other kings through hatred, the people of the Vrishni clan through their relationship and you through affection and friendship, and we through devotion, O king, (have attained His grace).

Sri Ramakrishna explained that even if Radha were not a real character we could very easily imbibe her deep, passionate

---

2 माधुर्यादपि मधुरं मन्मथतातस्य किमपि कैशोरम् ।
चापल्यादपि चपलं चेतो मम हरति किं कुर्मः ॥
मधुरं मधुरं वपुरस्य विभोर्मधुरं मधुरं वदनं मधुरम् ।
मधुगन्धि मृदुस्मितमेतदहो मधुरं मधुरं मधुरं मधुरम् ।

(*Krishnakarnamrita* I.65. 91)

3 VII. I. 29-30

attachment to the Lord; that will assure the achievement of the *summum bonum* of life. He said:

> It is immaterial whether one believes or not that Radha and Krishna were Incarnations of God. One may believe (like the Hindu or the Christian) in God's Incarnations. Or one may not believe (like the modern Brahmos) in His assuming form, human or otherwise. But let all have a yearning for this Anuraga or intense love for the Lord. This intense Love is the one needful thing.

In the renunciation of the self by whatever method, lies the realization of the Self. The love of the Gopis, however, was of the earth but not earthy, as is evident from the fact that some Gopis unable to go to Venugopala on hearing his flute left the mortal coil and joined him in spirit.[4]

His relation with the people of Vraja exemplifies the different approaches to the Divine. The calm devotional attitude of the cowherds in general, the servitude of Raktaka, the friendly love of Sridama and Sudama, the parental affection of Nanda and Yasoda, and the bridal love of Radha and the Gopis are recognised as the five valid attitudes in spiritual disciplines.

There are many facets of devotion. And 'as is one's attitude such indeed is one's success'. There is a conception of eternal Krishna playing in eternal Vrindavana. This personality is a matter of direct spiritual experience. To have this Krishna-consciousness intense longing is essential, as Sri Chaitanya reveals in stating his own condition:

> In the state of separation from the Lord (Govinda), even the twinkling of the eye seems to me a cycle, copious

---

4 X. 29. 9-11.

tears flow from my eyes like unto the rainy season, and
all the world appears to me a void.[5]

Alwar Kulasekhara wanted to be a step leading to the sanc-
tuary of the Lord.   Nammalwar was satisfied to be 'the
servant of the servant of the servant of the Lord'.   Such
was the fascination of Sri Krishna's rich and varied personality.
This is the mystery of an incarnation.   The unique conception
of Godhead as an incarnation visualizes Him to be ever
anxious for the redemption of the suffering souls.   Sri Parasara
Bhatta beautifully describes how Lord Ranganatha is ready
to swear to establish His claim that the Jivas really belong
to Him.   The poem runs thus:

> (God   says:)   'Thou   art   Mine.'   (Jiva:)   'I   am
> mine.'   'How   is   that?'   'What   is   your point?'   'My
> contention   has   Veda   for   its   authority'.   'I   claim   it   on
> account   of   the   splendour   of   the   long   enjoyment   of   the
> same.'   'But   that   has   ever   been   disputed.'   'When   did
> you   dispute   it?'   'I   have   mentioned   this   point   in   the
> Gita   and   other   works.'   'Who   will   bear   witness?'   'Men
> of   divine   wisdom.'   'Alas,   they   are   your   partisans   (favou-
> rites).'   Thus   in   this   quarrel   of   the   individual   soul   as
> though   there   can   be   no   mediator,   (so)   Thou   (Lord,
> art   ready   to   swear).[6]

5 युगायितं निमेषेण चक्षुषा प्रावृषायितम् ।
  शून्यायितं जगत् सर्वं गोविन्दविरहेण मे ॥

                                        (Sikshashtaka. 7)

6 त्वं मेऽहं मे कुतस्तत् तदपि कुतः एवं वेदमूलप्रमाणात् ।
  एतच्चानादिसिद्धादनुभवविभवात् सोऽप्यसाक्रोश एव ॥
  क्वाक्रोशः कस्य गीतादिषु मम विदितः कोऽत्र साक्षी
                                           सुधीः स्यात् ।
  हन्त त्वत्पक्षपाती स इति नकलहे मृग्य मध्यस्थवत् त्वाम् ।

The poet concludes his poem on the bathing ceremony of Ranganatha thus: 'Dost Thou, sweet Lord, in the impossibility of getting an arbitrator, thinkest it advisable to establish Thy claim by going to the length of swearing, and thereby redeeming and reclaiming Thy lost child, man? Verily, Thy dripping waistcloth and Thy garland make Thee appear as one prepared to swear on behalf of one's claims'. This superb lyric of the 'Disputant Divine' far surpasses the 'Hound of Heaven' in its unique conception of the soul-hunger of the Lord.[7]

The personality of Sri Krishna has yet another manifestation in the vision of the devotees. The intense faith stirs the devotee to his inmost depth and as Sri Ramakrishna says, he develops the especial eye of love by which he sees visions. 'Today's imagination becomes tomorrow's realization', said Swami Turiyananda. Thus the devotee meditates on Sri Krishna's purifying form with intense love and becomes a saint. This saint-making personality of his takes different forms even in recent times according to aspirations of devotees. So we have the Giridharilal of Mirabai, the Ranganatha of Andal and the Bala Gopala of Gopaler Ma. Thus has Sri Krishna been regarded by devotees as the goal of all beings.

The later life of Sri Krishna reveals him as a great teacher which appeals more to intellectuals. The *Bhagavata* describes him as the Supreme God who descended on the earth as a fullfledged incarnation to protect the good and destroy the evil. The modern age is an age of aggressive evil. Evil there was in every age, but it could be distinguished from the good. The seers of the Upanishads were much concerned about the play of good and evil in life. That is why they

---

7 c.f., The *Disputant Divine* by A. Srinivasachariar in *Vedanta Kesari*, 1929.

analysed the nature of sreyas and preyas (the good and the pleasant). The pursuit of pleasure is by itself not bad. But when it becomes the be-all and end-all of one's life or the life of a nation, it becomes a positive evil. For such a man or a nation any method is acceptable if it could serve the purpose. The purity of the ends and means is of no consideration. Even those who value much the ethical perfection in their lives, do not hesitate to transgress it when their countries are involved. They hold a higher standard of ethics before the people of the land, for in its absence the social order will crumble, and follow a different standard in their dealing with other nations. This double standard has a disastrous effect on the national mind. The result in the language of psychology is a split personality. What a tremendous stress it creates on the sensitive, susceptible minds, especially of the youths of a nation! Its effect is incalculably extensive but too subtle to be easily detected. Many thinkers have warned about the startling increase of half-witted, dull and delinquent children. And they find a connection between this phenomenon and the ever-increasing stress and strain the contemporary minds are subjected to, due to the ideological conflict, intellectual confusion and ethical uncertainty. The result is a spiritual crisis and a nervous breakdown. Still, spurious systems of philosophy are built up and the confusion is made worse confounded. Of course to remedy this, psychological therapy grows, psychiatrists flourish. But the malady of the modern people of today is too deep for surface solutions. The modern society has lost all sense of direction. It has no purpose, no goal. But the solution is deeply felt to be in having a goal of life. Hence develop life's philosophies. But alas, they are too numerous. Every man has his own philosophy of life. The outlook of men as a unified whole, springing from the same source, sporting in the same social

milieu and marching towards the same goal, has been forgotten.
In such a confusing intellectual climate it is difficult for an
ordinary individual to seek the truth and find it. The necessity
in such circumstances of a guide, of a principle, of a goal that
never fails is imperative. Sri Krishna satisfies all these
demands. He is the friend, philosopher and guide of
humanity. His teachings represent a principle and point
out to us an eternal goal.

The setting in which Sri Krishna delivers his message of
the Gita is very significant and bears close similarity to the
tension and uncertainty prevailing in the contemporary world.
The occasion was the great Kurukshetra war. The whole of
existing India divided itself into two warring camps. The
dark clouds were not merely hovering on the horizon. The
huge conflagration was about to start in which thousands
of able-bodied men would be offered as fodder. Arjuna,
the great hero, was in a dilemma. He was overawed by the
sight of a sea of soldiers ready to shoot arrows at one
another. The fear of losing the battle against the great
generals like Bhishma and Drona and the ethical consideration of being the cause of the death of near and dear ones
confused him. He could not find out the way. As Nehru
says in his *Discovery of India,* 'Arjuna becomes the tortured
spirit of man, which from age to age has been torn by conflict-
ing obligations and moralities'. And as is common with all
confusion, it resulted in indecision and the accompanying
depression of the mind. He lost all calmness of the mind,
and out of sheer despair surrendered to Sri Krishna. It
has been described as 'the confused mind surrendering to
calm philosophy.' Sri Krishna observed his condition and
was filled with compassion. But he was a great teacher and
wanted to create a great disciple out of his own mould.
He first encouraged Arjuna to regain the calmness of his

mind before he himself could solve his problems. It is our day-to-day experience that clarity of vision and free play of reason are possible only when we are tranquil and free from agitation and flurry. The solution of a problem of great dimension demands the full play of all our intellectual and spiritual faculties. At the outset we must feel a want, an urge, a hunger and then with a calm mind we must solve it. And at the end we must translate our conclusions into action, for a real problem demands a real solution which has a practical bearing on life. And the whole process must be undergone by the disciple himself. The teacher's part is to help manifest the inner potentialities of the student. All knowledge is in the soul; the teacher's part is to help make it manifest, as Swami Vivekananda puts it.

Arjuna with all humility approached Sri Krishna for a solution. His humility was born of the strength and purity of his character. As his character was strong, his doubt also was deep. The question raised by Arjuna was a vital one. And the answer it solicited was equally vigorous. Even now the doubts raised by Arjuna are hovering round the mental climate of the thinking men of the world. How various are the interpretations from different points of view that have been given to the Gita by eminent modern men like Vivekananda, Tilak, Gandhi and Aurobindo. The creative doubt of Arjuna brought forth such a body of enduring, classical truth of a universal character, that it defies all attempts to exhaust its significance and its meaning to men. Life raises problems at every step and Sri Krishna's teachings help men to solve their own problems. The conflict, both inner and outer, and its solution gives the ethical character to the Gita. It gives an insight into the nature of things and suggests a solution for the threefold sufferings—natural or social, individual or personal and supernatural or divine.

In the Gita Sri Krishna shows Arjuna the ultimate Truth
and the way to realize it through performance of one's duty,
being non-attached, practising equality and surrendering
one's all to God. The teachings of the Gita represent the
best he gave to the world. It is no wonder Sri Krishna
says in the *Mahabharata:*

'The Gita is my heart, O Partha. It is my very essence.'[8]

It is always ennobling to dive deep into the teachings of
the Gita. But no spiritual teaching acquires validity and
strength unless practised by the propounder. Sri Krishna
is superb in this aspect. He practised his message to such
perfection that he remains the incomparable ideal in this
field. The cowherd boy of Gokula playing on his divine
flute, spending his time in boyish pranks, protecting the
dwellers of Vrindavana from the onslaught of Kamsa's
retinue, Indra's wrath, Brahma's tricks and teaching the
Gopas the highest truths, helping the Gopis to overcome
the eight bonds, changed overnight to a king-maker and
killed the tyrant Kamsa, put Ugrasena on the throne and
brought peace to Mathura. When it was being repeatedly
troubled by Jarasandha, he removed the capital to the walled
city of Dwaraka to avoid meaningless bloodshed. The hero
of a hundred battles tried to avert the conflagration of the
Kurukshetra war, going himself to the Kauravas as a messenger of peace. But when all efforts failed, he accepted calmly
the relentless divine decree. He was so free from egotism
that he became the mere charioteer of Arjuna.

Thus the life of Sri Krishna as the king, king-maker and
charioteer presents the superb ideal conduct before men of

---

8 गीता मे हृदयं पार्थं गीता मे सारमुत्तमम् ।

all times, to imitate, to follow, to emulate.   He is ever the
eternal guide of humanity.   His life as a pastoral presents
him as the destination, the refuge, the goal of man.   Visualizing him in such a mood may we bow down to him saying:

> Thou art my mother, Thou my father; Thou art
> my kinsman, Thou my friend (or guide); Thou art know-
> ledge, Thou wealth; Thou art my all, O God of gods.[9]

---

9 त्वमेव माता च पिता त्वमेव
    त्वमेव बन्धुश्च सखा त्वमेव ।
    त्वमेव विद्या द्रविणं त्वमेव
    त्वमेव सर्वं मम देवदेव ॥

SRI CHAITANYA
THE PROPHET OF THE DIVINE NAME

RELIGIOUS life in Bengal has followed two main channels, viz. Vaishnavism and Saktaism. But they have some common characteristics peculiar to the soil. Bengal is full of rivers including the Mother Ganga. In fact, the land is called Nadimatrika, 'mothered by the rivers'. In olden days the poetic atmosphere, the easy-going life of the society based on agriculture which allowed ample time to think, and the continuous advent of the teachers of emotional cults made the mind of the people peculiarly soft, devotional and imaginative. This emotional temperament found its expression in poetry, drama, art and in devotional songs and mystic realisation. In fact, love which stirs the emotions of all people was chastened and found expression in their religious life. The cult of Sakti worship was already familiar. The Siva-Sakti conception contributed a good deal in giving the peculiar doctrine of Radha-Krishna in Bengal of which Sri Chaitanya is the best exponent. Radha is accepted by two other Vaishnava teachers, viz. Vallabha and Nimbarka, but She is not mentioned by name in the *Harivamsa, Vishnu-purana,* and *Bhagavata,.* According to scholars, no woman conception was connected at first with the Krishna worship, as we see in the pure Pancharatra or Bhagavata system. Then came Radha to be associated with Him in the system of these three saints, while Rukmini, the lawful wife, was united with Him in the Maratha area. Among the predecessors of Sri Chaitanya there were three famous Vaishnava mystics who have immortalised themselves by writing on the divine Sport of Radha-Krishna. They are Jayadeva, Vidyapati and Chandidas.

There is controversy regarding the place and time of these holy men. Jayadeva was an Oriya poet of the 12th century domiciled in Birbhum, a district in Bengal. His *Gitagovinda* in Sanskrit verse has become a classic and is the property of the whole country. It is said that before marriage Jayadeva was practising severe austerity, but on receiving an order from God in his inmost heart, he married Padmavati who was to be given in marriage to the Lord Himself because of a vow made by her parents. The union proved to be very beneficial. Jayadeva's songs about the Sport of Sri Krishna are masterpieces of poetry in subject matter, imagination, and diction, and they show clearly that the poet wrote them in a mood of higher mystic inspiration. His famous hymn on the ten Incarnations of God is chanted everwhere in India.

Vidyapati belonged to the 14th century. He was also an old devotional composer and dealt with the cult of love and devotion in his superb poems. In a famous line he says:

> Vidyapati takes shelter at the feet of the Lord and prays imploringly for a little grace to cross this ocean of transmigration.

Chandidas wrote his *Sri Krishnakirtana* in the 14th century. He also popularised the Krishnalila, the Sport of Krishna in Vrindavana.

Thus before the advent of Sri Krishna Chaitanya, the field was ready for the Radhakrishna cult of love and devotion.

Chaitanya was born in the 15th century (in 1484 or 1485 A.D.), in the holy Phalguni Purnima in Navadwipa in West Bengal, amidst the constant Sankirtana and the sound of the name of Hari. The present Navadwipa, according to some scholars, was a part of the original Navadwipa but the actual place of birth was washed away by the Ganga. Chaitanya's parents, Jagannatha Misra and Sachi Devi, hailed from the district of Sylhet, now in Bangladesh. His life shows three periods, viz. (1) the first twenty-four years from his birth to the time of his entering the monastic order; (2) the next six years of pilgrimage to South and North India; and (3) the last eighteen years which were spent in Puri.

Chaitanya was known as Viswambhara, and also as Gauranga because he was of fair complexion, and Nimai because he was born under a Nim tree. The saying, 'The child is father of the man,' was perfectly corroborated in his case. One day a Brahmin came to their house as a guest, cooked his own food and offered it to his Chosen Deity. But strangely enough, as soon as he offered, the boy went stealthily and began to eat! It happened thrice like this. Then the Brahmin had a vision and understood that it was his Chosen Deity who had incarnated in this form. This phenomenon was seen in the case of some other great souls also. About the divine status of Sri Chaitanya his followers believe that Sri Krishna wanted to taste and enjoy His own sweetness as Radha did. But this could not be done to the fullest extent unless Krishna were infatuated with Himself as Radha had been. Accordingly He assumed a form in which all the aspects of the Krishna of Vrindavana and those of Radha co-existed; and in this aspect Krishna enjoyed His own charm and sweetness. This form is known as Sri Gauranga, who was a blending of Radha and Krishna. About his divine qualities, it is said that as an energetic boy when Nimai would grow boisterous and uncontrollable, the embarrassed mother would chant the name of Hari, and the boy would be silent like the boy Vivekananda with the name of Shiva.

As a student Gauranga was exceptionally brilliant and in a short time became a great scholar in different branches of

Sanskrit studies. He had his schooling under the famous Raghunatha Shiromani. He started a Sanskrit school and began to teach different subjects. During this time a great scholar named Keshava Mishra came from Kashmir and though hitherto undefeated he was defeated in debate by Gauranga. When his elder brother Vishvarupa renounced the world, Gauranga married Lakshmi Devi to console his mother. At her death he married the devotional Vishnupriya. To perform the ceremonies after the death of his father he went at his twenty-second year to Gaya. There he met Isvara Puri, a disciple of the great Madhavendra Puri. Gauranga returned to Nadia but he was a changed man. Tears rolled down his eyes every now and then, and the name of Hari always was on his lips. He closed his Sanskrit school and began to spread the name of Lord Hari through the length and breadth of the land. He visited East Bengal to see his relatives and made thousands mad with the name of Krishna. In the Navadwipa city he conquered the heart of all, even the hostile, rich ruffians like Jagai and Madhai. The Kazi, the Muslim Governor, could not tolerate this movement where even the Muslims would join. So he passed an order that there must not be any sound of the drum any where in his area. All the devotees were sorry and did not know what they should do. Gauranga went to the house of the Kazi with his Sankirtana party and transformed him into a devotee.

At this time Gauranga found that he could no longer continue in an ordinary life. So he renounced his family and entered the monastic life initiated by Keshava Bharati, another disciple of Madhavendra Puri. In his twenty-fourth year, Gauranga became Sri Krishna Chaitanya. But he had a great love for his mother, so partly because of her direction and partly because of his love for his devotees in Bengal, he decided to stay at Nilachala (Puri), the place of Lord Jagannatha. Every year the devotees would go there to meet him. He, however, went out on an extensive tour in South and North India. In the South, he visited Vidyanagar, Srisaila, Tirupati, Kanchi, Srirangam (staying there for four months), Sethubandha, Cape Comorin, Udipi, and returned via Maharashtra and Vidyanagar. In the North, he visited Kasi, Allahabad, and Vrindavana. Everywhere he went, he sang the Hari Sankirtana. There was a great effect of his preaching; so much so that in U.P. there is still a village called the Pathan-Vaishnava grama, full of Vaishnavas who were Muslims. Till his passing away in 1533, possibly in the waters of the sea, many disciples came to him at Puri and were blessed with divine realisation.

Of the associates of Chaitanya, Nityananda the Avadhuta, Advaita the old Vaishnava, Vasudeva Sarvabhauma the great scholar, Ramananda Ray the exponent of Vaishnava mysticism, were already very famous. The Vaishnava philosophy was developed later by Rupa, Sanatana, Jiva Goswami, Baladeva Vidyabhushana, Viswanatha Chakravarti and others. The anecdotes of Chaitanya's life were recorded by Krishnadasa Kaviraja, Vrindavanadasa, Lochanadasa and others. Of these Krishnadasa's *Chaitanya charitamrita* is not only a life but a handbook of practical mysticism and is a great authority with the Bengal Vaishnavas.

Sri Chaitanya himself did not compose much excepting the *Sikshashtakam* and also the *Sri Jagannathastotram* in Sanskrit. In the latter he prayed fervently, 'O Lord Jagannatha, kindly let me have Thy vision'. In his *Sikshashtaka*, he gives the cardinal virtues of a Vaishnava thus:

> Humbler than the grass, more tolerant than the tree, giving up all egotism and paying respects to all, a man should sing of Hari.

This is the ideal which still rules all the Vaishnavas and which they still try to maintain even through unfavourable circumstances. In another verse he prays:

> Oh Lord, I do not hanker after wealth, men, beautiful wife, nor even the all-knowingness. Oh Lord, see that I get the motiveless devotion in every life of mine.

Two of the great contributions of Sri Chaitanya are the discovery through mystic vision of many of the places of interest in Vrindavana, connected with Sri Krishna and the recognition of the singing of Divine Name alone as a valid sadhana. As a result, he may be described as the prophet of Divine Name. His disciple Haridasa was a great examplar of the efficacy of the Divine Name. Sri Chaitanya's philosophical system is known as *Achintya-bhedābheda–vāda.*

Sri Chaitanya teaches us that the rational attributes of men are not capable of approaching the Divine sphere of spirits. Yukti, as he styles reason, is quite incompetent in such a matter. Ruchi, the religious sentiment in men, even in very small quantity, has the power to comprehend God. It is the mystic inspiration that can give light in spiritual matters. Inspirations exhibited themselves in the Vedas, which with the explanatory Puranas are the only evidence in matters of spirit and are eternal in nature. Reason only helps the growth of faith. 'Krishna can be reached through faith and not by logic', is the opinion of Chaitanya. The Shastras according to Chaitanya teach nine principal doctrines:

(1) Hari is one without a second. (2) He is always vested with infinite power. (3) He is the ocean of Rasa or enjoyable spiritual feelings. (4) The soul is His separated part. (5) Certain souls are engrossed by Prakriti or His illusory energy. (6) Certain souls are released from the grasp of Prakriti. (7) Devotion is the only means of attaining the final object of spiritual

existence. (8) Overflowing love for Krishna is alone the final object of spiritual significance. (9) All spiritual and material phenomena are manifestations of Hari, the manifestations which can neither be said to be different from nor identical with the Almighty. The Vedas go sometimes to establish that Jiva is distinct from the Deity, and sometimes that Jiva is the same as the Deity. The Vedas always reveal the truth. The Jiva is simultaneously distinct from and identical with God.

According to the *Bhāgavata,* devotion is of two kinds, *Vaidhi* and *Rāgānugā*. In a sloka (3.1.5) it says that man without a natural desire for Krishna adores him in obedience to the bidding of the Shastras. Such Bhakti is called *Vaidhi*. In 3.25.35., it says that in the path of inclination (raga) he takes Krishna as the object of his chief emotion, viz. as master, comrade, child or lover. From the sprout of love (prema) issue two things, addiction (rati) and emotion (bhava).

Cultivation of an intimate feeling for Krishna is performed in nine different ways: (1) To hear of the spiritual name, form, attribute and sport of Krishna, (2) to utter His name and sing about Krishna with an especial stress on Kirtana, (3) to meditate on and reiterate all the exploits of Krishna, (4) service of His Holy Feet, (5) worship, (6) bowing down, (7) doing everything that pleases Him, (8) friendship, (9) surrender.

Devotion can be practised having different attitudes towards Krishna. These attitudes are of five different types possessing different elements of love in an ascending order. The attitudes are: (1) Shanta or calm attitude, as was seen in the cases of Rishis worshipping Rama. In this attitude there is devotion to God as well as conquest of desire. (2) Dasya or the attitude of a servant, as was in Hanuman. In it the above elements as well as service to Him were manifest. (3) Sakhya or the attitude of a friend, as was in the cases of

Subala, Sudama and Arjuna. The extra factor of reliance on Him was there. (4) Vatsalya or the attitude of a parent, as was in the cases of Yasoda and Nanda. In it over and above the preceding elements, tenderness for God developed. (5) Madhura or the attitude of a lover, as was seen in the cases of Radha and the Gopis. It has the sixth element of love and forgetting of one's self. These attitudes are taken from the analogy of worldly relations though they are all spiritual and have no body idea.

Devotion in its highest stage is higher than Mukti or liberation from the world. As Sri Ramakrishna would quote a Vaishnava dictum:

> I am not stringent in giving liberation, but I am so in the case of devotion.

To achieve this devotion the devotee undergoes severe anguish from the separation of the Lord. This is described as 'pain of God' in mystical literature. Sri Chaitanya underwent different stages of realisation and suffered or enjoyed the corresponding suffering or bliss. Sri Ramakrishna described the God-intoxicated state of Sri Chaitanya in the following words:

> What is this divine intoxication? In this state a man forgets the world. He also forgets his own body, which is so dear to all. Chaitanya had this intoxication. He plunged into the ocean not knowing that it was the ocean. He dashed himself again and again on the ground. He was not aware of hunger, of thirst, or of sleep. He was not at all conscious of any such thing as his body.

> Chaitanyadeva used to experience three moods. In the inmost mood he would be absorbed in śamadhi, unconscious of the outer world. In the semi-conscious mood he would dance in ecstasy but could not talk. In the conscious mood he would sing the glories of God.

Sri Chaitanya believed in teaching by the example of his own life. His personal life was very rigid and his followers also practised hard austerity. He became a spiritual dynamo, so much so that even by an indirect touch he could change a man's life, as was evident in the cases of the fishermen and Prataparudra. Once, in an ecstatic mood Chaitanya fell in the sea and was caught in the net of some fishermen. Even this indirect touch created such an upsurge of divine emotion in them that their whole lives were changed. King Prataparudra was anxious to see Chaitanya, but the latter would not meet the king. His devotees wanted to help the king. They sent his son, a small boy, who was embraced by Chaitanya, making him divinely mad with the name of Krishna. The king embraced his son and got the same results.

Merely by seeing Sri Chaitanya's fervour of devotion, the truths of the scriptures became real to his followers. Even if there was no Radha, here was a soul which underwent all the realisations written in the Sastras. In some mood he would dance, sometimes sing, sometimes weep, and with him danced, sang and wept for God the whole of Bengal, Orissa and Assam for a pretty long time. Even now in these provinces villagers assemble together and have the Nama-sankirtana, the singing of the name of the Lord in groups, which is a special contribution of his. His life and message had a tremendous impact on the society. As a result it became liberal and escaped the danger of total conversion to an alien faith. Sri Chaitanya thus was a great social reformer and he is remembered, followed and worshipped by thousands of people as a great devotee, a founder of the Bhakti cult, a prophet of the Divine Name, nay, as an Incarnation of the Lord Himself.

ACHARYA SANKARA

Swami Vivekananda would often advocate the necessity of the blending of knowledge and devotion and would say that we require 'the brain of Sankara and the heart of Ramanuja'. While expounding the Vedanta philosophy he would take the stand of Sankara giving here and there the views of Ramanuja. He, in fact, was the best exponent of Sankara's philosophy in modern times. Hearing his lecture in America, Professor William James remarked that Sankara's philosophy was 'the paragon of all monistic systems'. Even Thibaut said that it was 'the most important and interesting philosophy on the Indian soil.' Jacob remarked that 'in the impossible task of reconciling the contradictions of the Upanishads his system is the best'. In the words of Dr. Radhakrishnan his philosophy is 'complete—needing neither a before nor an after.'

Sri Sankara himself announced that he was born to regenerate the religious faith.[1] He is, in fact, considered to be the incarnation of Siva on earth.[2] The greatest tribute, however, consists in the fact that all the philosophers of India after him were so either by supporting him or by contradicting him. This is true of Ramanuja and Madhva and

---

1 कृते विश्वगुरुर्ब्रह्मा त्रेतायां ऋषिसत्तमः ।
  द्वापरे व्यास एव स्यात् कलावत्रभवाम्यहम् ॥

Quoted from *Mathamnaya* by Rajendra Nath Ghosh in his Bengali book '*Acharya Sankara and Ramanuja*' p. 300.

2 शम्भोर्मूर्तिश्चरति भुवने शङ्कराचार्यरूपा ।

also of Vidyaranya and Madhusudana.   Naturally, therefore, such a great soul compels our attention.

There is a saying that every man, especially a great man, is the product of the necessities of his age. When we look at the times of Sankara we find that the degeneration of Buddhism had already set in, a general weakening of the religious ideals came in, and a preponderance of the fallen cults began in the name of religion.

At such a time Sankara was born as the son of a pious Brahmin couple of Kaladi in South India.   There is a variety of opinions about his time.   The source book for his life is the *Sankara-Digvijaya* of Madhava, as also the *Sankara-Vijaya* of Anandagiri.   The generally accepted time is A.D. 788 to 820.   This is more or less supported by Max Muller and Macdonell as well as by Keith and Bhandarkar.

It is recorded that in a few years he became proficient in all the scriptures, showed his spiritual powers by getting wealth for a poor lady and changing the course of the river, both by sheer prayer, renounced the world by promising to his mother that he would be by her bedside in her last days and went to Guru Govindacharya for spiritual training. He had the realization of the Absolute and was merged in it. Then came the incident of the corpse and the young lady which made him accept the Power of Brahman, the incident of the Chandala which gave him the realization of Brahman in all the created beings.   These made him fit for the work of amelioration of the sufferings of humanity for which task the constant absorption in the Absolute was not quite congenial. So God kept his ego, or rather the semblance of it, the 'ego of knowledge' as Sri Ramakrishna would put it. He then wrote the commentaries which are the classics of Indian philosophical systems. He toured round the whole of India even in those days and established his views by defeating the scholars of rival theories, the defeat of Mandana being the most famous. He defeated the fallen Buddhists and the Tantrics and the Kapalikas and eliminated their supremacy as major religious sects. By this time he had a band of disciples—four of them, namely, Padmapada, Hastamalaka, Totaka and Sureswara being very prominent—who propagated his message after him. He passed away in A.D. 820, after the fulfilment of his mission, at the age of thirty-two.

Though Sankara lived for a very short time he did a lot of work. He restored the Vedic tradition and propagated the Upanishadic thoughts. He re-established God and soul in a way suited to rational thinking and did away with futile rituals and purged the various sects of the accretions of fallen days. Among the other concrete works, mention may be made of the four Maths that he established in the four corners of the country. He established the sect of the pious Brahmins to preserve the religious culture and the scriptures, and for preaching the religious ideas he founded the monastic orders. To fight against speculation regarding religious matters he wrote the commentaries. He went to various places of pilgrimage and revived their ancient glory by renovating the temples and instituting worship.

He was an aspirant and became a realized man and recorded his realizations himself. Thus the three characteristics which make a good religious teacher were present in him. And that is why he was universally acclaimed as a world-teacher.

He produced a vast literature of which his commentaries on the Upanishads, the Gita and the Brahmasutras are very famous. They have sustained the religious and philosophical life of India for the last one thousand years. He was a writer of sparkling prose and wrote many moving hymns to different

gods and goddesses in beautiful diction, full of ennobling
ideas and heart-felt devotion.

He himself summarized his whole philosophy in half a
sloka that Brahman is the only reality, the world is an illusion
and the soul is nothing but Brahman.[3]

He establishes this proposition by examining the theories
presented by the different contemporary philosophical schools
and rejecting the invalid portions. He does not reject them
in toto but accepts as much of them as is possible for him to
accept. To the Sankhya philosophers he showed that their
Prakriti is unconscious and Purusha is inactive and the harmo-
nious world requires consciousness for its existence. The
views of Vaisheshikas, who hold that the world is a combination of atoms which are unconscious, are also not acceptable.
Their Adrishta is also unconscious. So the first movement
cannot be thought of. If it were always in movement, then
Pralaya is denied. Souls, they say, come after creation. So
the same difficulty arises. The different Buddhistic theories
he meets with different arguments. To the Kshanikavadins,
who hold that the objects of the world are the aggregates of
different momentary elements, he answers that momentary
things cannot possess any causality which requires duration
of time, for a cause must arise and then act. Even if it is
possible, the aggregate cannot be formed without substances
which can bring together the elements. Consciousness, according to them, is itself the aggregate. So the same difficulty of
unconscious cause comes in. The Vijnanavadins who deny
the external world are also not acceptable because the world
is perceived by all, and if the immediate experience is disbelieved, even the reality of mental states can be disbelieved.

---

3 ब्रह्म सत्यं जगन्मिथ्या जीवो ब्रह्मैव नापरः ।

The ideas of mind cannot illusorily appear as external objects unless something external is admitted as real. Unless different perceived objects like pot and cloth are admitted, the idea of a pot cannot be distinguished from that of a cloth since as consciousness they are identical. The dream objects and the perceived objects vitally differ. The former are contradicted by the waking experience, while the latter, according to them, are not. So Subjective Idealism as well as Nihilism fail to explain the world. The Deistic theories of creation (held by the Saivas, the Pasupatas, the Kapalikas and the Kalamukhas) which hold that God is the efficient cause and matter, the material cause are not accepted as they are non-Vedic, and against experience, for spirit cannot work without a body. God has neither body, nor any motive. Thus with superb skill Sankara refutes the views of the rival schools of thought. That does not mean that his philosophy is absolutely free from all inconsistencies and is accepted by all dialecticians. But as Dr. Radhakrishnana puts it,

'The inconsistencies and the incompleteness in which Sankara's theory of knowledge is content to remain are not due to any defects in his reasoning but are the inevitable imperfections of a philosophy which tries to go to the depth of things.'

Sankara was not a mere dialectician free from any allegiance. His problem was how to reconcile the Upanishadic accounts of creation with the denial of plurality. This he does by taking the creation as a magic show. He gives here his famous theory of the three levels of experience and the three kinds of realities. (1) The Pratibhasika (apparent or illusory)—the objects possessing it exist only so long as they appear to some mind. (2) The Vyavaharika (phenomenal or practical), which is experienced in the normal waking state. (3) The Paramarthika (noumenal or absolute), which exists in all times. The first has the transiency of illusion, the second, of the ever changing finite which is contradicted by the supreme experience; but the third has the permanence of a changeless Infinite.

This division is similar to the Pure Reason and the Practical Reason of Kant. Basing on this standpoint, Prof. P. N. Srinivasachari has divided Advaita into 'pure' and 'practical' in his book *The Aspects of Advaita*. According to Sankara the world is not a dream but unreal like a dream which is contradicted by the waking experience. The world is unreal in the sense that it is contradicted by the experience of one who realizes that Brahman is the only reality. The world is not a groundless illusion but has Brahman as its ground—a well-grounded phenomenon—in Leibnitz's expression. So it will be more true to Sankara's ideas to call his system as the Brahmavada, as the theory of Maya is the means of establishing Brahman, the only Reality.

This world is Maya. It is neither real nor unreal. 'Sat' means absolutely real and 'Asat' means absolutely unreal. As the world is perceived it is not 'Asat' and as it is stultified through knowledge it is not 'Sat'. Therefore, it is other than real and unreal (*Sadasadbhinna*) but that cannot be explained in language. 'Maya from the standpoint of Sruti is negligible, from the logical standpoint it is inexplicable and from the empirical standpoint it is real,'[4] The world as Brahman is always real.[5]

---

4 *Sutra Bhashya*, I. 4. 2.

5 यथा कारणं ब्रह्मत्रिषु कालेषु सत्वं न व्यभिचरति, तथा कार्यमपि जगत् त्रिषु कालेषु सत्वं न व्यभिचरति ।

S. B., II. 1. 16

Like Descartes, Sankara finds the basis of truth in the
immediate self-certainty. Nobody doubts his own existence
so no proof is necessary. Atman is the essential nature of
him who denies it.[6] It cannot be known by thought, which
is a part of the not-self. It is only intuited—*Pratibodha-
viditam* as the Kena Upanishad (II.4.) puts it. It is the basis
of all proof[7] and so logically it is a postulate. But as different
opposing views are given about its nature the Vedanta Sastra
is promulgated[8] which is based on the Sruti that gives the
truth that the Atman is Brahman[9]. The Atman is neither
the individual self nor a collection of such selves. They
depend on the Atman, the Universal Self. Even the Nirguna
description is a limitation of the Atman but it leads towards
that realization. God is both immanent and transcendent.
From the transcendental standpoint He is Existence, Knowledge and Bliss Absolute, and from the empirical view-point
He is omniscient and omnipotent. The Jiva is absolutely
identical with Brahman. 'That thou art' (*Tattvamasi*)
reveals that truth. It is not tautological or superfluous but it
reminds us of the eternal truth. Bondage is to forget this
truth and identify oneself with the body through ignorance.
Liberation is thus the realization of the identity of the self
and Brahman. It is not a new product; only the illusion
is removed. 'It is de-hypnotization'[10] And this is possible
even while one is in this body[11].

6 य एव हि निराकर्ता तदेव तस्य स्वरूपम् । *S. B.*, II. 3. 7.
7 *S. B.*, II. 3. 7.
8 अस्यानर्थहेतोः प्रहाणायात्मैकविद्याप्रतिपत्तये सर्वे वेदान्ता
   आरभ्यन्ते । *Adhyasa Bhashya.*
9 *S. B.*, I. *Mandukya Up.* 2.
10 *The Complete Works of Swami Vivekananda* Vol. V p. 227.
11 सिद्धं जीवतोऽपि विदुषोऽशरीरत्वम् । *S. B.*, I. 1. 4.

Though Sankara shows his superb dialectical skill, he is not impractical. He is a prophet who shows a way of life. Though work does not give knowledge directly, it purifies the mind and in the purified mind knowledge dawns. So there is every necessity of work for a man in bondage. A man of realization is, however, not bound by duties, but he works out of sympathy for the people in bondage and leads an ideal life to be followed by the lesser people. Sankara himself did tremendous work in a short time. In a *sloka* he encourages men of his times 'to be enthusiastic and fight against the fall of religious standard.' [12]

Sankara's philosophy is neither pessimistic nor optimistic. 'It is a simple statement of fact.'[13] Browning is optimistic when he ignores the sufferings of the world and thinks that 'all is right with the world.' T.S. Eliot is pessimistic when he forgets the joys of life and considers this world as 'a waste land'. Sankara's theory only exposes the contradictions of the world. But in one sense it can be said to be optimistic as it believes in the cessation of ignorance and shows the way to that goal.

Sankara's life and philosophy have a great message to the modern world. He upholds the supremacy of Vairagya. There is competition in possession, but no such thing in renouncing one's claims. So renunciation must be the social ideal to wipe out all competition from society.

He was a great harmoniser blending all the faiths, establishing the six prevalent faiths on firm ground. He supplied

---

12 यतो विनष्टिमंहती धर्मंस्यात्र प्रजायते ।
    मान्द्यं संत्यज्य एवात्र दाक्ष्यमेव समाश्रयेत् ॥
Quoted by Durga Chaitanya Bharati in his Bengali book 'Sannyasa O Sannyasi' p. 241.

13 The Complete Works of Swami Vivekananda Vol. II. p. 80.

the basis of all the faiths of the world. He was an incomparable unifier. Even in those remote days he had the vision of the unity of India. So we find that Pandit Nehru, the great messenger of unity, pays tribute to the great unifying and organizing capacity of Sankara. It was Sankara who wrote, 'All the three worlds are my homeland'.[14] His philosophy revealed his vision of the unity of all beings. The unity of existence he propounded has a great possibility in the service of men. In fact, herein lies the basic reason of all ethics—why a man should be moral and not otherwise. The conception of the divinity of man has a great message to the modern man who is confronted with the theories of 'the insectification of man'. The ideal of immortality gives solace and strength in these days of uncertainty and international suspicion. Rightly does William James appreciate its value: 'An Absolute One, and I that one —surely we have here a religion, which, emotionally considered, has a high pragmatic value; it imparts a perfect sumptuosity of security.'

---

14. स्वदेशो भुवनत्रयम्—*Annapurna Stotram.*

THE IDEA OF TAPAS IN THE
UPANISHADS

THE Sanskrit word *tapas* normally means austerity or penance. Asceticism too refers to the same idea. It has been derived from the root *tap* meaning, to heat. Because of this, one Upanishad identifies it with fire. In the Upanishads the idea of Tapas had a variety of developments; so much so that some scholars have tried to find out a sort of evolution of the meanings attached to Tapas. What originally meant warmth, then knowledge, next came to mean meditation or concentration of the mind and the senses and finally the action or practice that purifies the mind. And this is perfectly understandable, for to acquire knowledge concentration is essential, which is possible when the mind is purified by a course of righteous conduct. At this stage it became identified with Varna and Ashrama, the station and stage of life. Thence followed the Gita idea of various types of Tapas. Nowadays Tapas presupposes contemplation along with isolation, renunciation of desires and pleasures and self-inflicted sufferings and pains.

The idea of Tapas, though it underwent a change, is found in all the ancient books including the Rigveda Samhita. The Rigveda (10.190.1) says that 'From Tapas, kindled to its height, truth and eternal law, Satya and Rita, were born'. Again, it (10.183) considers Tapas as the germ of everything.

'I saw thee meditating in thy spirit what sprang from Tapas (ardent devotion) and hath hence developed. In plants and herbs, in all existing beings I have deposited the germ of increase.'

Tapas has been hailed as the ally of Manyu (10.83), where it stands for fervour or heat of emotion or righteous indignation. It again (10.154) speaks of persons being 'invincible through Tapas'. The Taittiriya Aranyaka also says that the devas triumphed over the Asuras by Brahmacharya and Tapas, self-control and concentration.

The various ideas regarding Tapas can be had from the Upanishadic texts. The Chhandogya Upanishad considers Tapas as conferring meritorious worlds, but for attaining immortality, it says that one must be firmly established in Brahman.

> 'Three are the branches of religious duty. Sacrifice, study and gifts—these are the first. *Austerity* alone is the second, and the celibate student of sacred knowledge, who lives in the house of the teacher throughout his life mortifying his body in the teacher's house, is the third. All these become possessors of meritorious worlds; but he who is established firmly in Brahman, attains immortality' (2.23.1).[1]

Acharya Sankara explains that here 'austerity' stands for Krcchra, Candrayana and other forms of mortification. In 3.17.4, the Upanishad considers austerity as a largess[2] of the Purusha sacrifice where the life of a man is looked upon as a Yajna.

The Brihadaranyaka Upanishad says (in 1.2.6) that by Tapas[3] Prajapati created vigour, etc., and (in 1.5.1.) that he created food with it. This and other Upanishads speak

---

1 तप एव द्वितीयः...एते पुण्यलोका भवन्ति ।
2 अथ यत्तपो दानमाजंवमहिंसा सत्यत्रचनमिति ता अस्य दक्षिणाः ।
3 स तपोऽतप्यत ।
10

about the creation of the entire world through Tapas. The Upanishad is particular to point out that mere austeriy, sacrifices and worship are of little use without the knowledge of the Imperishable.

'Verily, O Gargi, if one performs sacrifices and worship and undergoes austerity in this world for many thousands of years, but without knowing that Imperishable, limited indeed is that work of his' (3.8.10).

Here austerity, etc., help the beings 'to conquer the worlds'[4] (6.2.16). But it again points out that the Soul is sought by wise people 'by repetition of the Vedas, by sacrifices, by offerings, by penance, by fasting'[5] (4.4.22). Another beautiful idea this Upanishad speaks of (in 5.11.1) describing as 'supreme austerity' what a sick man suffers before death. Acharya Sankara explains that this suffering should be looked upon with the eye of worship; thereby sins are destroyed and the fruits of Tapasya are obtained. The physical sufferings and fear of death are terrifying and disheartening but much consolation may be derived from this assurance of the scriptures in such dire needs.

The Taittiriya Upanishad too speaks of Tapas in different contexts. In 1.9.1 it asks us to perform austerity.[6] It also says that according to Taponitya, performance of austerity is a duty and that Naka considers study and teaching to be so, for they are the real Tapas.[7] The importance of austerity

---

4 अथ ये यज्ञेन दानेन तपसा लोकान् जयन्ति ।

5 तमेतं वेदानुवचनेन ब्राह्मणा विविदिषन्ति यज्ञेन दानेन तपसाऽनाशकेन एतमेव विदित्वा मुनिर्भवति ।

6 तपश्च स्वाध्यायप्रवचने च ।

7 तप इति तपोनित्यः पौरुशिष्टिः । स्वाध्यायप्रवचने एवेति नाको मौद्गल्यः । तद्धि तपस्तद्धि तपः ।

and effort has been well recognized in this Upanishad. In fact, for every goal, spiritual or material, the means set forth is Tapas. And in one place Brahman Itself has been identified with it. When Bhrigu repeated his visit to his father Varuna for instruction about Brahman, the latter said, 'Desire to understand Brahman by austerity. Brahman is austerity.'[8] Then by performing austerity Bhrigu came to know of further aspects of truth (3.2.1). The commentator points out that till realization of the truth of Tattvamasi is attained, Tapas consists in the repeated thinking of the meanings of the two terms 'Thou' and 'That'. Elsewhere it has been said that the supreme Tapas is nothing but 'concentration of the mind and the senses'.[9]

In the Katha Upanishad (2.15) the supreme goal has been identified with the Pranava, *Aum,* the realization of which all austerities aim at.

> 'The word which all the Vedas rehearse, and which all austerities proclaim, desiring which men live the life of religious studentship, that word to thee I briefly declare. That is Om!'

The Svetasvatara Upanishad too recognizes the importance of austerity for realizing the Atman, for the latter, it says, is rooted in austerity and self-knowledge.

> 'As oil in sesame seeds, as butter in cream, as water in river-beds, and as fire in the friction-sticks, so is the Atman apprehended in one's own soul, if one looks for Him with true austerity.[10]

---

8 तपसा ब्रह्म विजिज्ञासस्व ।   तपो ब्रह्मेति ।

9 मनसश्च इन्द्रियाणां च ऐकाग्र्यं परमं तपः ।

10 सत्येनैनं तपसा योऽनुपश्यति ॥

'The Soul, which pervades all things as butter is contained in cream, which is rooted in self-knowledge and[11] austerity —this is Brahman, the highest mystic doctrine! This is Brahman, the highest mystic doctrine!' (1. 15-16).

The Mundaka Upanishad declares that Brahman swells for creation by Tapas and His Tapas consists of knowledge.

'By austerity Brahman becomes built up. From that, food is produced; from food—life-breath, mind, truth, the worlds, immortality too in works.

He who is all-knowing, all-wise, *whose austerity consists of knowledge*[12]—from Him are produced the Brahma here, name and form, and food' (1. 1. 8-9).

Moreover, it is from that Supreme Being that Tapas too originates.

'From Him, too, gods are manifoldly produced, as also the celestials, men, cattle, birds, the in-breath and the out-breath, rice and barley, *austerity,* faith, truth, chastity, and the law (2.1.7).

In 3.1.5 the Upanishad says that by Tapas etc., one should try to realize the Self.

This Soul is obtainable by truth, by austerity, by proper knowledge, by the student's life of chastity constantly practised.[13]

---

11 आत्मविद्या तपोमूलम् ।

12 यस्य ज्ञानमयं तपः ।

13 सत्येन लभ्यस्तपसा ह्येष आत्मा सम्यग्ज्ञानेन ब्रह्मचर्येण नित्यम् ।

Here the commentator reminds us that it is not so much the physical austerity that is directly useful but the concentration of the mind and the senses. Then by meditation with the purified mind Brahman is realized.

'That subtle Soul is to be known by thought wherein the senses fivefoldly have entered. The whole of men's thinking is interwoven with the senses. When that is purified, the Soul shines forth' (3.1.9).

In 3.2.4 it again says that the Self cannot be realized through Tapas or knowledge unless Sannyasa (linga)[14] is practised along with it. Acharya Sankara lays much stress on it. Anandagiri explains that complete renunciation is Sannyasa and Indra, Janaka, Gargi and others realized the Self because they were free from attachment though they did not have the external paraphernalia of a recluse.

The Prasna Upanishad too extols austerity. When the sages went to Sage Pippalada, he asked them for preparation to practise for one year faith, celibacy and austerity (1.2).[15] In 1.10 it is said that through these an aspirant reaches the Sun in the Northern Path. Those who observe Prajapati-vrata go to the Moon if they are endowed with austerity and chastity (1.15)

The Mahanarayana Upanishad speaks of Tapas as fire; it is practised by strength and it gives rise to faith. In a passage (10.1) it eulogizes various categories as Tapas, by repetition of which the enumerated qualities are attained.

'Right is austerity. Truth is auserity. Understanding of the scriptures is austerity. Subduing of

---

14 नायमात्मा बलहीनेन लभ्यो न च प्रमादात्तपसो वाप्यलिङ्गात् ।

15 भूय एव तपसा ब्रह्मचर्येण श्रद्धया संवत्सरं संवत्स्यथ ।

one's senses is austerity. Restraint of the body through such means like fasting is austerity. Cultivation of a peaceable disposition is austerity. Giving gifts without selfish motives is austerity. Worship is austerity. The Supreme Brahman has manifested Himself as Bhuh, Bhuvah and Suvah. Meditate upon Him. This is austerity par excellence.'[16]

It will be seen that they practically include all that is required for a complete moral and spiritual discipline. In another passage (78.2) it extols religious fasting as a great Tapas.

'Some hold the opinion that austerity is the means of liberation and that there is no austerity higher than religious fasting. This excellent austerity is hard to be practised. A person who practises it becomes invincible (or such austerity is unthinkable for the commonalty). Therefore seekers of the highest good delight in austerity.'[17]

The commentator, however, points out that this declaration of the superiority of religious fasting does not detract from the value of self-control, pilgrimage, Japa, oblation and the like, which are also considered as different forms of austerity. In 79.3 the Upanishad says:

'By Tapas performed in the beginning gods attained godhood. By Tapas seers attained to heaven gradually. By Tapas we get rid of our enemies who stand in the way of our acquisitions. Everything is founded in Tapas.

---

16 ऋतं तपः सत्यं तपः श्रुतं तपः शान्तं तपो दमस्तपः
शमस्तपो दानं तपो यज्ञं तपो भूमुँवः सुवब्रँह्मैतदुपास्यैतत्तपः ॥
17 तप इति तपो नानशनात्परं यद्धि परं तपस्तद् दुर्धषं तद्
दुराधर्षं तस्मात्तपसि रमन्ते ।

Therefore they say Tapas is the supreme (means of liberation).'18

Thus we see that the idea of Tapas is well developed in the Upanishads, it having different shades of meaning. This fact shows its richness and emotional appeal to the consciousness of the ancients. It has not lost its charm even now. The lure of austerity draws hundreds of spiritual seekers to the hills and dales, to places of solitude and of pilgrimage. It is because of the deep respect for austerity that thousands of people are attracted to leaders even in other fields who have risen only through great sacrifice. Spiritual attainment, wide sympathy and purposeful austerity are the three elements that have drawn people down the ages to the saints and sages, Sadhus and Sannyasins, Yogis and Vairagis and even to other people. True, things of the mundane world also were sought through their probable miraculous powers. But still the fact remains that people are awed at the sight of the complete abandon and the determined effort to get at the goal, throwing to the winds all considerations of personal gain and even of minimum physical comfort. This austerity is the soul of all one-pointed efforts, essential for growth in different fields. Tapas is therefore sure to retain its hold on man even in modern times.

---

18 तपसा देवा देवतामग्र आयन् तपसार्षयः सुवरन्वविन्दन् तपसा सपत्नान्प्रणदामारातीस्तपसि सर्वं प्रतिष्ठितं तस्मात्तपः परमं वदन्ति ।

THE IDEA OF TAPAS IN THE GITA

THE idea of Tapas is cardinal in the ancient scriptures of India. Before creation, it is said, the Creator Himself performed Tapas and brought forth the world. Tapas thus stands for expansion, growth, multiplication. Right from the Rigveda Samhita the idea of Tapas is found in various contexts. Tapas literally means heat. But it has acquired different shades of meaning in different ages. So it is variously translated as heat, contemplation, concentration, penance, austerity, suffering of pain, repentance, self-mortification and the like. In the Gita Tapas naturally gets an important place. It has been described as a Sattvic quality (16.1) and also as Yajna, (4.28) Sri Krishna says that He Himself is the Tapas of the ascetics. (7.9). Yajna, Dana and Tapas are the three main ideas of every spiritual discipline and the Gita takes due note of them when it says:

> The work of sacrifice, gift and austerity should not be relinquished, but it should indeed be performed; (for) sacrifice, gift and austerity are purifying to the wise. (18.5.)

Whatever helps a man to progress towards realization is Tapas. It is specially the effort, physical and mental, to bring the mind under control. Thus study, meditation, etc., also come under this heading. The Gita defines three types of Tapas in the following words:

> The worship of the Devas, the twice-born, the Gurus, and the wise, purity, straightforwardness, continence and non-injury are called the austerity of the body.

Speech which causes no vexation, and is true, as also agreeable and beneficial, and regular study of the Vedas—these are said to form the austerity of speech.

Serenity of mind, kindliness, silence, self-control, honesty of motive—this is called the mental austerity. (17. 14, 15, 16.)

Here the idea of strenuous efforts and suffering of pain for mental purification is stressed. The idea of purification is important. The Gita idea of Tapas is not mere austerity for austerity's sake, but austerity as a means of purifying the mind, which is the goal of all Sadhana. The crucifixion of the flesh is a much discussed idea in the Christian literature. But the Gita does not recognize this as very valuable unless it leads to the desired goal of mental purification. It is because of this idea that the Gita speaks of the barbarous type of Tapas.

Those men who practise severe austerities not enjoined by the Sastras, given to ostentation and egoism, possessed with the power of lust and attachment, torture, senseless as they are, all the organs in the body, and Me dwelling in the body within; know them to be of Asurika resolve. (17. 5, 6.)

That austerity which is practised out of a foolish notion, involving self-torture or for the purpose of ruining another, is declared to be Tamasika. (17. 19.)

The ideal is to perform these actions without any desire of fruit.

Even these works, O Partha, should be performed, leaving attachment and the fruits; such is My best and certain conviction. (18.6.)

Tapas, to be spiritually fruitful, must be Sattvic. It must be spontaneous and motivated by the highest objective. Self-torture has no place in real spiritual life. Sri Krishna quite definitely speaks against all types of extreme practices in various contexts. For this He is said to be the prophet of balanced, spontaneous discipline. Of course, human nature is such that it often goes to excess. Hence we find that this idea of Tapas often degenerated into mere physical suffering. But even in that we may find a beauty when we see that these Tapasvins endured great physical hardship for the sake of God or even for lesser ideals. Men of realization, however, lead a simple, spontaneous life. Fully resigned to God they may even be seen to perform great austerities. But they have no plan of their own. Moreover, as they are singularly free from the body idea, these austerities do not affect them.

Tapas is, in a sense, the most important discipline enjoined. Yajna and Dana, sacrifice and charity, are dependent on external factors other than oneself. It is Tapas alone that fully pertains to the individual himself, both physically and mentally, culminating in mental growth. And spiritual growth is nothing but inner growth. Of course, thereby the other two are not minimized. They too require a great mental effort and growth for accomplishment. In the end they too turn more mental and become identified with Tapas. Tapas, to be fully fruitful, must be properly motivated. It is the spirit in which we undertake a discipline that counts more in spiritual life.

For the Jnanins Tapas is knowledge. So it has also been described as *jnanamaya*, 'being of the nature of knowledge'. It is more internal than external. It is the growth of the mind, making it more reflective, concentrated, purified. The self-concentration and self-mastery thus gained is for individual and social benefit.

Tapas is divine in origin. It has been referred to as Karma with God as its object. As Sri Krishna says:

Knowing Me as the dispenser of Yajnas and asceticisms, as the Great Lord of all worlds, as the friend of all beings, he attains Peace. (5. 29.)

The Gita stresses the ideal of spiritual life, which is Self-realization, union with the Godhead, and not mere self-control, which is only a negation of the lower self.

The Yogi is regarded as superior to those who practise asceticism, also to those who have obtained wisdom (through the Sastras). He is also superior to the performers of action (enjoined in the Vedas). Therefore, be thou a Yogi, O Arjuna! (6. 46.)

Because of this, a Yogi, who is united with Brahman, has a higher place.

Whatever meritorious effect is declared (in the Scriptures) to accrue from (the study of) the Vedas, (the performance of) Yajnas, (the practice of) austerities and gifts —above all this rises the Yogi, having known this, and he attains to the primeval, supreme Abode.(8.28.)

According to Sri Krishna the highest knowledge consists in knowing God as the root. Devotion can lead an aspirant to that realization.

Neither by the study of the Veda and Yajna, nor by gifts, nor by rituals, nor by severe austerities, am I in such Form seen, in the world of men, by any other than thee, O great hero of the Kurus.

Neither by the Vedas, nor by austerity, nor by gifts, nor by sacrifice can I be seen as thou hast seen Me. (11. 48, 53.)

The practice of Tapas much depends upon the conditions of life. It is the natural duty of an evolved soul.

The control of the mind and the senses, austerity, purity, forbearance, and also uprightness, knowledge, realization, belief in a hereafter—these are the duties of the Brahmanas, born of (their own) nature. (18.42.)

The Vanaprasthas, because of their austere life, have specially been known as the **Tapasvins** throughout the times.

How various are the forms of Tapas can be seen from the Gita. In the seventeenth chapter human nature has first been divided into divine and demoniac. Then there is Tapas of body, mind and speech, and each again according to Sattva, Rajas and Tamas. Even Sattvic Tapas must be directed towards God-realization only. The Tapas of body, mind and speech has already been referred to. The Tapas, inspired by Sattva, Rajas and Tamas, has been described thus:

This threefold austerity practised by steadfast men with great Sraddha, desiring no fruit, is said to be Sattvika.

That austerity which is practised with the object of gaining welcome, honour, and worship, and with ostentation, is here said to be Rajasika, unstable, and transitory.

That austerity which is practised out of a foolish notion, with self-torture or for the purpose of ruining another, is declared to be Tamasika. (17. 17, 18, 19.)

The Tamasika and Rajasika Tapas are performed because of mistaken notions of right and wrong, the sense of values being wrong. The desire for fruit is preponderant there.

That which has a distorted apprehension of Dharma and its opposite and also of right action and its opposite, that intellect, O Partha, is Rajasika (18. 31.)

Moreover their objective is often very low.

Saitvika men worship the Devas; Rajasika, the Yakshas and the Rakshasas; the others—the Tamasika men—the Pretas and the hosts of Bhutas. (17.4.)

The scriptures enjoin giving up of all actions, as they are mixed with evil. But it prohibits giving up the action of Yajna, Dana and Tapas.

Some philosophers declare that all actions should be relinquished as an evil, whilst others (say) that the work of Yajna, gift, and auserity should not be relinquished.

The work of Yajna, gift, and austerity should not be relinquished, but it should indeed be performed; (for) sacrifice, gift, and austerity are purifying to the wise. (18. 3, 5.)

Because the distinction between the different types is so subtle, there is every chance of making mistakes in the performance of Tapas, etc. So the Gita prescribes Om, the name of Brahman, should be repeated before the commencement.

Therefore, uttering 'Om', are the acts of sacrifice, gift, and austerity as enjoined in the ordinances, always begun by the followers of the Vedas. (17. 24.)

Uttering 'Tat', without aiming at fruits, are the various acts of sacrifice, austerity, and gift performed by the seekers of Liberation. (17.25.)

Tapas has been described as Sat and Asat.

Steadiness in Yajna, austerity, and gift is also called 'Sat': as also action in connection with these (or, action for the sake of the Lord) is called 'Sat'.

Whatever is sacrificed, given, or performed and whatever austerity is practised without Sraddha, it is called Asat, O Partha; it is naught here or hereafter. (17. 27, 28.)

Tapas, etc., can be purified, as told earlier, by repeating **Om, the name of Brahman.**

Sri Krishna, however, asks the devotees to perform all actions as an offering to God. Then they generate no evil effect and produce the best results.

> Whatever you do, whatever you eat, whatever you offer in sacrifice, whatever you give away, whatever austerity you practise, O son of Kunti, do that as an offering unto Me. (9. 27.)

The importance of Tapas can be well appreciated when we see that Sri Krishna prohibits the holy teachings of the Gita being imparted to one who does not practise Tapas.

> This is never to be spoken by you to one who is devoid of austerities or devotion, nor to one who does not render service, nor to one who cavils at Me. (18.67.)

Tapas is thus a very important item in spiritual discipline. It is to practise penance and austerity, to bring the body and mind under control and to purify them, thus bringing in concentration directed to the Self, which is the goal of all Sadhana. The ideal of Tapas has inspired scores of men down the ages to sacrifice their self-interest, nay even their minimum comforts, so that they might realize it. Men of Tapas have naturally a tremendous influence on the society. It is sure to retain its hold on man in the future too, in spite of the progress of the modern materialistic view of life, which apparently is so opposed to this noble idea.

THE IDEA OF DANA IN THE GITA

THE idea of Dana, charity, is one of the three cardinal ideas in the Gita, viz., Yajna, Dana and Tapas—sacrifice, charity and austerity. In recent days this term has been much used by Sri Vinoba Bhave and his followers. The word Dana is very widely applied. In political treatises Dana has been accepted as one of the means of subduing a foe. But Dana or gift is primarily religious in motive and so is free from any selfishness. It has been technically defined as complete severance of one's influence and interest in, or proprietorship in, any form over the gift given, and making it the property of the donee completely and forever. So Dana is gift, benevolence, charity—giving away something to another without any expectation of return. This important idea has been much extolled in the holy scriptures. In various contexts the Gita speaks of it. Sri Krishna says that along with other virtues Dana springs from God alone.

> Intellect, knowledge, non-delusion, forbearance, truth, restraint of the external senses, calmness of heart, happiness, misery, birth, death, fear, as well as fearlessness, non-injury, evenness, contentment, austerity, *benevolence,* good name, as well as ill-fame;—these different kinds of qualities of beings arise from Me alone. (X. 4-5.).

Dana has been listed as a quality of those who have a divine nature.

> Fearlessness, purity of heart, steadfastness in knowledge and Yoga; *alms giving,* control of the senses, Yajna, reading of the Sastras, austerity, uprightness....—

these belong to one born for a divine state, O descendant
of Bharata. (XVI. 1-3).

Human nature has been divided in the Gita into three types—
Sattvika, Rajasika and Tamasika. Their gifts as well as food,
activity and aspiration are also different.

> The food also which is liked by each of them is three-
> fold, as also Yajna, austerity, and *almsgiving*. (XVII. 7.)

These three qualities again pervade every action of man.
So though Dana is a divine quality, it can be practised in three
ways according to the nature of the attitude of a man.

> 'To give is right'—gift given with this idea, to one
> who does no service in return, in a fit place and to a
> worthy person, that gift is held to be Sattvika.
>
> And what is given with a view to receiving in return,
> or looking for the fruit, or again reluctantly, that gift is
> held to be Rajasika.
>
> The gift that is given at the wrong place or time,
> to unworthy persons, without regard or with disdain,
> that is declared to be Tamasika. (XVII. 20-22.)

Among the four Varnas, Dana is a natural quality of
the Kshatriyas as Tapas is of the Brahmanas.

> Prowess, boldness, fortitude, dexterity, and also
> not flying from battle, *generosity* and sovereignty are the
> duties of the Kshatriyas, born of their own nature.
> (XVIII. 43.)

As every action in a way tends to be tainted by evil, methods
have been shown of purifying it.

> Therefore, uttering 'Om', are the acts of sacrifice,
> *gift,* and austerity as enjoined in the ordinance, always
> begun by the followers of the Vedas.

Uttering 'Tat', without aiming at fruits, are the various acts of Yajna, austerity, and *gift* performed by the seekers of Liberation. (XVII. 24-25.)

Actions may be good or bad. Dana is a good action and it becomes still better when performed for the sake of the Lord.

Steadiness in Yajna, austerity, and *gift* is also called 'Sat': as also action in connection with these (or, action for the sake of the Lord) is called 'Sat'. (XVII. 27.)

If actions must produce bad results also, is it not better then, to give up all actions? The Gita answers:

Some philosophers declare that all actions should be relinquished as an evil, whilst others say that the work of Yajna, *gift,* and austerity should not be relinquished.
The work of Yajna, *gift,* and austerity should not be relinquished, but it should indeed be performed; for Yajna, *gift,* and austerity are purifying to the wise. (XVIII. 3, 5.)

If charity is performed as an offering to God, it produces the best results. Sri Krishna says:

Whatever you do, whatever you eat, whatever you offer in sacrifice, whatever you *give* away, whatever austerity you practise, O son of Kunti, do that as an offering unto Me. (IX. 27.)

Tapas is a very important discipline enjoined in the scriptures. The *Mahanarayana Upanishad* (10.1) identifies Dana as Tapas.[1] It again says:

---

1 दानं तपः ।

11

All creatures praise selfless gift as supreme; for there is nothing more difficult to perform than giving selfless gift. Therefore seekers of the highest good delight in giving selfless gift. (78, 5.)[2]

It accepts gifts as a means of liberation.

Giving of gift in the shape of *dakshinā* is the secure abode of the sacrifices. In the world all creatures subsist on a giver. People remove by gifts those who are envious and malignant towards them. By gift the unfriendly become friendly. Everything is established in gift. Therefore they say that the gift is the supreme means of liberation. (79. 6.)[3]

The *Chhandogya Upanishad* (2. 23.1) speaks of the three branches of religious duty. Of these the first consists of sacrifice, study and gifts. Again the same Upanishad (3.17.4) considers austerity, gifts, uprightness and truthfulness as the largess of the Purusha sacrifice where the life and activities of a man are looked upon as a Yajna.

The *Brihadaranyaka Upanishad* (6.2.16) says that the various worlds in the Arciradi-marga are obtained through the performance of sacrifices, gifts and penance. Again it mentions Dana as one of the means of realising Brahman:

'The seekers of Brahman wish to realise It through

---

2 दानमिति सर्वाणि भूतानि प्रशंसन्ति ।
दानान्नातिदुष्करं तस्माद्दाने रमन्ते ॥

3 दानं यज्ञानां वरूथं दक्षिणा, लोके दातारं सर्वभूतान्युप-
जीवन्ति, दानेनारातीरपानुदन्त, दानेन द्विषन्तो मित्रा भवन्ति,
दाने सर्वं प्रतिष्ठितं तस्माद्दानं परमं वदन्ति ॥

regular reading of the Vedas, sacrifices, *charity* and austerity not leading to death.' (4.4.22.)[4]

These means lead to indirect knowledge and purification of mind which culminate in the realisation of Brahman. The same Upanishad gives the interesting story of gods, men and demons approaching their father Prajapati who taught them with a simple word *Da* and it was the men who understood it as 'Be charitable', for men are very greedy. Devas and the asuras lacking in self-control and mercy understood it to mean those virtues. Then the Upanishad says:

> That very instruction this heavenly voice in the form of the thunder-cloud repeats as 'Da, Da, Da': 'Control yourselves', 'Be charitable', 'Be merciful'. Therefore one should learn these three—self-control, charity and mercy. (5. 2. 3.)[5]

Though Dana is very much praised, the grace of God is essential. As Sri Krishna says in the Gita:

> Neither by the study of the Veda and Yajna, nor by *gifts,* nor by rituals, nor by severe austerities, am I in such Form seen, in the world of men, by any other than you, O great hero of the Kurus.
> Neither by the Vedas, nor by austerity, nor by *gifts,* nor by sacrifice can I be seen as you have seen Me. (XI. 48, 53.)

Again He praises Yoga which gives the highest realization.

---

4 तमेतं वेदानुवचनेन ब्राह्मणा विविदिषन्ति यज्ञेन दानेन तपसाऽनाशकेन ॥

5 तदेतदेवैषा देवी वागनुवदति स्तनयित्नुर्द द द इति—दाम्यत दत्त दयध्वमिति; तदेतत्त्रयं शिक्षेत्—दमं दानं दयामिति ।

Whatever meritorious effect is declared (in the Scriptures) to accrue from (the study of) the Vedas, (the performance of) Yajnas, (the practice of) austerities and *gifts*—above all this rises the Yogi, having known this, and attains to the primeval, supreme Abode. (VIII 28.)

So it is clear that devotion, Yoga and grace are very important. Hence Dana coupled with devotion is necessary for speedy spiritual progress. But what about people who have not enough to give? Holy Mother, Sri Sarada Devi, has given a fine direction—those who have, must give; those who have not, must repeat the name of God. Wealth is so dear to man that giving it away is definitely a way to measure the sincerity of purpose and so the Gita and other scriptures rightly stress it.

THE PRINCIPLE OF SVADHARMA

EVERY culture stands for some noble principles. Especially its religious system enshrines them in their pristine purity. Even if the society changes, there is the urgent need of preserving the basic ideals; otherwise that particular society will die for all practical purposes. As Swami Vivekananda says:

> Each nation has its own part to play, and naturally, each nation has its own peculiarity and individuality, with which it is born. Each represents, as it were, one peculiar note in this harmony of nations, and this is its very life, its vitality. In it is the backbone, the foundation, and the bed-rock of the national life. In one nation political power is its vitality, as in England. Artistic life in another, and so on. I have seen that I cannot preach even religion to Americans without showing them its practical effect on social life. I could not preach religion in England without showing wonderful political changes the Vedanta would bring.

> Here in this blessed land, the foundation, the backbone, the life-centre is religion and religion alone. In India, religious life forms the centre, the keynote of the whole music of national life.

Religion is the repository of some grand ideas, and they are essential in preserving the individuality and morale of the national culture. The principle of Svadharma is one such noble and universal ideal. It has preserved the Hindu society down the ages, even in days when administration was weak and divided and there were frequent political upheavals. The steadying factor was the division of labour according to the Varnas, and efficiency came through the performance of duty with devotion and responsibility. The message of this ideal is very much needed now, when there is a tendency to avoid doing one's duty and expecting economic and other benefits through agitation alone.

Financially backward, India is anxious to make progress that is at once speedy and effective. The raising of the standard of living is the immediate goal. But this standard can be raised only if there is higher production, which, however, requires hard and honest work. The ideal of work as a form of Sadhana will impart the required devotion to work. It is the experience of every society that to generate enthusiasm even for material objectives, it is necessary to rouse the minds of people. This can be properly done with enduring effect only when the society is supplied with a suitable ideal which is not merely a time-serving one, but is itself of enduring value. The idea of Yoga coupled with Svadharma is such an ideal.

Svadharma is applicable to every society. It is the law of one's own individuality. Every one of us is unique in a sense. We have a particular vocation in our life in tune with our inherent nature. The Gita speaks of this also as Svakarma, one's own duty. This duty is determined by one's Svadharma or natural equipment of the body and mind. The best results can come only when a man follows his own nature and not by doing some other more glamorous work. As Vinoba Bhave says in his book on the Gita:

> 'Svadharma comes to one naturally. It can be compared to one's mother. Even if it is unattractive, in it only lies the growth.'

> 'One's Dharma consists in following one's true nature and vocation. The question is not whether it is

high or low, easy or difficult. The growth must be real; the evolution must be a genuine process. Even if someone else's Dharma seems easier, one should not take it up.'

According to Indian philosophy, man's nature depends on the three Gunas—Sattva, Rajas and Tamas. All the three are present in a man at every moment. But there is a preponderance of one Guna in an individual, and the same individual may have the dominance of different Gunas in different situations. The important thing is to find out one's own dominating Guna and then slowly transcend it by the higher Gunas. This can be done by supplying the leaven of the Yoga-idea in every action. This is what is described in the Gita (II.45) as being Sattvastha, established in Sattva or purity. And this is the ideal for all actions. It will, however, be easy to purify and tranquillise oneself if one knows one's predominant tendency.

Dharma varies according to time and place. But the individual Dharma is to be subservient to the general, eternal Dharma, meant for all. This point has been discussed in the Ramayana:

'When Lakshmana proposed to kill Dasaratha who had broken the law of primogeniture, Rama advises him not to follow an Anarya (ignoble) and cruel Kshatriya Dharma but to follow the higher way, i.e. obedience to one's father. (Ayodhya, XX, 43). Similarly when Bharata was asked by Rama if he was doing all his duties as a king aright, Bharata asks Rama how he could follow Raja Dharma when he had fallen away from Dharma itself. (Ayodhya, CI, 1.)'.

(K. S. Ramaswami Sastri: *Studies in Ramayana,* p. 91.)

Hence we see that Svadharma has two parts. One is changeable and the other unchangeable. And a man is

never to go against the eternal Dharma. This conflict can
be resolved by a man if he knows the goal of life and the
purpose of all action. Herein comes the Hindu philosophy,
for a philosophy of life is a prerequisite for a philosophy
of duty.

The Hindu philosophy takes for granted the law of
Karma and rebirth. The goal of life is to realize the true
nature of the Self, for which action and experience are
necessary. This striving can go on from birth to birth.
The action in this life will produce some Samskaras or inherent
tendencies with which a man will be endowed in the next
birth. Hence is the importance of following one's Samskaras
and one's Svadharma. So Svadharma is also related to
one's birth and station in life. It is according to one's guna
and Karma, which are the basis of the Varna. According
to the profession, one's Varna may vary. From this, however,
in later days originated the idea of Varna according to birth,
which hardened into caste irrespective of one's qualities and
profession. Based on the Varna idea are the various duties.
These accord with one's cultural level and spiritual progress. It became popular specially because it gave stability
to the society.

In the modern societies the intellectuals are similar
to the Brahmanas, the administrator and military to Kshatriyas, men of commerce and agriculture to the Vaishyas and
those doing service directed by others to the Sudras. This
division is prevalent in every society. As Swami Vivekananda
says:

The right and correct means (for attaining the four
Purusharthas) is that of the Vedas—the Jati Dharma, that
is the Dharma enjoined according to different castes—the
Svadharma, that is one's own Dharma, or set of duties
prescribed for man according to his capacity and position—

which is the very basis of Vedic religion and Vedic society... This Jati Dharma, this Svadharma, is the path of welfare of all societies in every land, the ladder to ultimate freedom. With the decay of this Jati Dharma, the Svadharma, has come the downfall of our land. But the Jati Dharma or Svadharma, as commonly understood at present by the higher castes, is rather a new evil, which has to be guarded against.

Though the Varna ideal speaks of different duties, it promises the same goal of Release to all who perform Svadharma. As the Gita says:

Devoted each to his own duty, man attains the highest perfection. How, engaged in his own duty, he attains perfection, that I shall explain.

From whom is the evolution of all beings, by whom all this is pervaded, worshipping Him with his own duty, a man attains perfection.

Better is one's own Dharma, though imperfect, than the Dharma of another, well-performed. He who does the duty ordained by his own nature incurs no evil.

(XVIII. 45-47.)

The Varnas turned into castes through the process of history. But modern society demands mobility. For this the basic scientific idea of Varna will be quite suitable. However, the modern problem is a little different, for individualism based on secular democracy ignoring inherent tendencies and preaching equality dominates the field. Has the ideal of Svadharma any message to modern men engaged in various types of activity? What adjustment should it make, if of course it must, to help people find a proper motivation of work and purpose of life? In other words, what will be the method of applying the ideal of Svadharma in the modern context? In the contemporary society the original arrangement of social division of duty is no more. The later division based on birth also is going away. What then will be its application? Obviously, the method will be to apply the ideal based on the original idea of aptitude. But then, it is not possible for the vast majority of the people to choose their vocation according to their temperament. An intellectual young man is often put to a piece of work a 'mechanical' man to tedious work requiring drive and so on. And when securing two square meals is the deciding factor, there is no chance of following one's taste. We are to take the situation as it obtains and see what idealism can do to improve the situation. In this context, the ideal of Karma Yoga has a great part to play. When there will surely be effort to find out a suitable avocation in life, one must accept the situation calmly when it is unavoidable. If we apply the ideal of disinterested action, i.e., not identifying too much with the desire to choose our actions, things may be expected to be smoother. 'Do the duty that lies nearest to thee', says Goethe. 'Can any man or woman choose duties?' asks George Eliot and answers, 'No more than they can choose their father and mother.' Epictetus states more clearly, 'We do not choose our own parts in life, and have nothing to do with selecting those parts. Our simple duty is confined to playing them well.'

The ideal of Svadharma is based on the three basic Gunas which are mingled in us. It is not easy to disentangle the traits and definitely opt for one Guna. These being broad divisions, a little change in the avocation will not disturb us much. We are to take the situation as our normal duty and do it as best as possible. The ideal of detached duty will release us from frustration and worry to a great extent. It will increase our capacity too by making us capable of adapting ourselves. A man has various inherent capacities all of which are not used at a time. Hence when one set of capacities finds it inconvenient, the other comes to the rescue. Moreover one's job is not a whole-day affair. To compensate, a consuming interest in a thing according to one's tendencies will give one the required satisfaction. Nowadays, hobbies are cultivated by people. This is good so far as it goes. It will be better still, if a 'hobby' is according to one's predominating quality and has some connection with the highest goal of life.

We are aware that this idea may be criticised by the revolutionists as a philosophy of a contented society. Their contention is, where fast growth is necessary, as it is in a backward economy, this idea of adjustment will retard progress by lessening the tempo. This is a wrong notion. Relaxed effort is more creative and productive. Moreover, this argument stresses the future goal of achievement too much, ignoring the joys and satisfactions of the present generation. This is the defect of all revolutionary theories. But anxiety and impatience may be good if they are limited to the people at the helm of affairs, and that only with regard to quick changes. But even then it is unnecessary to create the hysteria psychosis throughout the length and breadth of the country. It is done in the totalitarian countries and in some measure in other countries too by vigorous propaganda. The effect on the individual is not, however, good. The little joys that he could have are also marred by this psychosis. Everybody wants peace, they say. But peace does not mean only no-war, it means peace in a man's own environment as well as in his soul.

The principle of svadharma makes work easy and satisfying. The ideal of Karma Yoga elevates work to the status of a sacrament. Thus these two combined can stand guarantee for efficiency, satisfaction and purity. According to Vedanta, man's innate nature is perfection. So Svadharma may also mean one's duty according to his innate nature of perfection and holiness. It has a great social benefit, for the worker will be motivated by an ideal of purity and oneness and his methods also will pave the way for goodness and oneness. The solution of the problems of the world depends upon mutual understanding and purity of method. So this stressing on the perfect nature of man in everyday action will bring about the needed understanding among nations. Individually also each man will be benefited and have satisfaction as well as progress towards the ultimate goal of life.

THE GITA IMPERATIVES

THE Vaikuntha Ekadasi, the day on which Bhagavan Sri Krishna gave His Gita message, is a memorable day for all humanity, for it was really the people of all lands who were addressed by Sri Krishna through Arjuna. His message was valuable in the past, but it has acquired a greater value now, for it is a message of hope and strength. Life in the contemporary world is full of many threats. The problem modern man faces is global in character. Factors unpredictable and uncontrollable are often involved. As a result man is apt to be diffident. This outlook spreads to other departments of life too. A negative attitude towards the affairs of life becomes dominant. Hence is the imperative necessity of cultivating positive thinking. It may not be possible to control the external trends by an individual or a group. But there is no meaning in extending the negative attitude to other walks of life. This can at least be resisted by individuals. On its essential necessity Swami Vivekananda once said :

> No negative, all positive, I am, God is, everything is in me. Be conscious and bring it out.

Anxiety is mental; often its root is in our pessimistic thinking. Even when the social condition or world situation is not favourable, we must practise a constructive outlook to keep our life going, for it minimises much of the draining off of our vital energy. So Swamiji says :

> We should cultivate the optimistic temperament, and endeavour to see the good that dwells in everything.

If we sit down and lament over the imperfection of our bodies and minds, we profit nothing; it is the heroic endeavour to subdue adverse circumstances that carries our spirits upwards.

Cultivating a spiritual attitude towards life will help us much in achieving hope, calmness and poise. God is the anchor of our life. If we link our life to Him, it will be easier for us to defy the feeling of uncertainty and the resulting worry. Even physical extinction will not be able to scare us if we can convince ourselves of the immortal nature of our soul. The Vedantic realization is the realization of one's identity with the indestructible Atman. Even a glimpse of it will dispel all fear. Hence the Upanishads proclaimed:

> The knot of the heart is cut asunder, all doubts are dispelled and Karmas perish, when the higher and lower Brahman has been realised. (*Mundaka U.* 2.2.8.)

When we say this, we do not mean that there is no cause for fear. There is and it is real. People will have to try individually and collectively to remove it. But many improvements are not possible within the span of a man's life. Then what idea will sustain him and release him from tension? An attitude of detachment can only do it. The detachment idea is a special contribution of the Gita. In various ways it explains the philosophical attitude to be cultivated for the purpose.

A bold attitude towards life is the gift of our scriptures. As Swamiji says:

> It is only in our scriptures that this adjective is given to the Lord—*Abhih, Abhih*. We have to become *Abhih*, fearless, and our task will be done.

The Gita is a mine of strength. Sri Krishna exhorts man through Arjuna to shed all his nervousness and cowardice and fight the battle of life, boldly but calmly. So strength is what is necessary. Said Swami Vivekananda:

> Thinking all the time that we are diseased will not cure us; medicine is necesssary. Being reminded of weakness does not help much. Give strength, and strength does not come by thinking of weakness all the time. The remedy for weakness is not brooding over weakness but thinking of strength.

And again:

> Whatever you believe, that you will be. If you believe yourselves to be sages, sages you will be tomorrow. There is nothing to obstruct you.

Thoughts must be met by thoughts which have great influence on us. If we change our thoughts, we can radically change our life. To effect that change we must follow the imperatives of the scriptures and for that we must have faith. As the Gita says, 'Man consists of his faith; he verily is what his Sraddha is', '*yo yacchsraddhah sa eva sah*' (xvii. 3). Through faith we get clarity of vision, peace of mind and vitality of life. Our happiness and effectiveness depend upon the thoughts we think. Hence the urgency of changing our thought patterns. We must throw out unhelpful thoughts, thoughts that create unhappiness, fear, jealousy and the like. If our thought regarding others affect us, we must think only good thoughts, thoughts of goodwill, love and sympathy. Many of us might have developed the habit of complaining, grumbling or finding fault with others. We must recondition our thoughts to gain health, balance and happiness. It is the findings of modern psychology that a vast number of people become sick because of their thoughts, full of resentment and ill-will.

Holy words have wonderful power. There is no limit to

the creative force of an active idea. So it is better to commit
the slokas containing potent ideas to memory and repeat
them until they are indelibly printed on our subconscious
mind. By holding **thoughts full of faith, positive thoughts,** an
atmosphere propitious to success is generated. It will do us
good if we follow the meditational practice of burning all
sinful thoughts, or we may drop out one by one every destructive thought, every fear, every worry, then think of waves
of bliss permeating the body and mind and lastly fill the
mind with the thoughts of God.

As the Gita passages are charged with special power,
it will be very useful to soak our mind with a few ideas contained in some slokas which may be described as Sri Krishna's
commandments or the Gita imperatives. That can easily
be done by repeating the slokas now and then on appropriate
occasions. These are the words of the Bhagavan Himself.
For centuries they have been repeated by thousands of devotees and holy men. The latter fact itself is enough to charge a
passage with a special power. If repeated with devotion
our mind can feel this power more easily. Schooled for
centuries with the idea of the Gita's holiness, we can easily be
brought into the proper mood. So it is not a drawback
that we do not repeat the idea in our mother tongue. Of
course, it will be necessary to know the meaning of particular
couplets chosen for our purpose. There are scores of edi-
tions in different languages and we can get at their meaning
easily.

Among our scriptures the Gita is the most widely read
and repeated. The Parayana, the methodical reading itself is
capable of creating a spiritual mood of devotion and poise
in us. If it is done with understanding the result will be
better still. It is true that scriptures should be used as guide-
books, as something like a Railway Time Table, as a thinker

once said. But even reading without understanding but with devotion will create an atmosphere which can bring calmness to the mind. What spiritual realization devotion alone gives can be seen from an anecdote of Sri Chaitanya mentioned in the *Gospel of Sri Ramakrishna*. When Sri Chaitanya went on a pilgrimage to South India, he saw a devotee hearing the reading of the Gita and profusely shedding tears. He asked him afterwards what he liked therein. The devotee said that he did not understand the meaning, but whenever he listened to the reading of the Gita, he saw Sri Krishna standing on the chariot and giving His message to Arjuna.

Here we are advocating positive thinking by soaking the mind with scriptural passages. So an understanding of the meaning will be necessary. How many people have been comforted by the Gita passage like '*Kaunteya pratijanihi na me bhaktah pranasyati*', 'Arjuna, know it for certain, my devotee never perishes' (ix. 31). It works like a tonic to a despondent soul.

A few more such passages applicable to different situations of our life may be noted.

It is our common experience that often we feel unequal to our task. As a result, we become diffident. Arjuna had the same feeling on seeing his strong opponents as well as relatives on both sides ready to kill one another. And he said to Sri Krishna:

> Seeing, O Krishna, these my kinsmen gathered here eager for fight, my limbs fail me, and my mouth is parched up. I shiver all over, and my hair stands on end. The bow Gandiva slips from my hand, and my skin burns. (I. 28-29)

Then smiled the Lord and exhorted Arjuna with the famous words: '.... *Klaibyam masma gamah Partha, naitat tvayi upapadyate..*'

12

> In such a crisis, whence comes upon thee, O Arjuna,
> this dejection, un-Arya like, disgraceful and contrary to
> the attainment of heaven? Yield not to unmanliness,
> O son of Pritha! Ill doth it become thee. Cast off this
> mean faint-heartedness and arise, O scorcher of thy
> enemies! (II. 2-3)

These lines are charged with such power that they can raise
us too from our drooping spirit and infuse in us enthusiasm,
courage and hope.

The Lord then explained the world process and said that
Arjuna's opponents were already killed by their Karma.
Arjuna was only to be an instrument: 'Nimittamatram bhava
savyasacin'.

> Therefore do thou arise and acquire fame. Conquer
> the enemies, and enjoy the unrivalled dominion. Verily
> by Myself have they been already slain; be thou merely
> an apparent cause, O Arjuna. (XI. 33)

It is God's plan that sets forth everything, so one must work
unattached. So Krishna says:

> Renouncing all actions to Me, with mind centred on
> the Self, getting rid of hope and selfishness, fight,—free
> from (mental) fever. (III. 30)
> Therefore, cutting with the sword of knowledge this
> doubt about the Self, born of ignorance, residing in thy
> heart, take refuge in Yoga. Arise, O Bharata! (IV. 42)

In life too we often find that it works better if we are free from
the worry about the results. Then our mind remains clear;
the thinking faculty is at its best. So in all our undertakings,
specially when things seem unfavourable, let us follow Krishna's
advice, 'Yuddhyasva vigatajvarah', 'Fight being free from
mental fever' (VII. 30). While doing this we may fail, but
what does it matter? Striving is all that matters. The
main imperative of the Gita is detached action:

Therefore, do thou always perform actions which are obligatory, without attachment. By performing action without attachment, one attains to the highest. (III. 19)

But then we feel, if we are so indifferent to the result, can we work? Sri Krishna reminds us that we work impelled by our nature. Our senses will drag us to activity. If that is so, why not be willing workers and work to the best of our capacity? It may be argued that when we know of certain failure, is there any meaning in fruitless labour? Sri Krishna is quite definite about it. If all life is a Yajna, a sacrifice to the Divine, whatever work a man does becomes fruitful, for it is God who sees the effort and helps him. So He says: 'Svalpam api asya dharmasya trayate mahato bhayat'.

In this, there is no waste of the unfinished attempt, nor is there production of contrary results. Even very little of this Dharma protects from the great terror.
(II. 40)

Not only is a man spiritually benefited, God sends definite help too. As Sri Ramakrishna says, if we go one step towards the Mother, She comes forward a hundred steps towards the devotee.

Even in the so-called secular work, a man must remember Him and strive, 'Mam anusmara yudhya ca', 'Think of Me and fight' (VIII. 7). Not merely to think of Him but to work too. Every goal has some special way of Sadhana. If an enemy is to be conquered, fight is necessary. If an examination is to be passed, study is essential. But along with effort, there must be thought of God also. That will release us from tension, endow us with extra energy and some mysterious power may help us too.

No discipline is palatable in the beginning. 'That which is like poison in the beginning but like nectar at the end' is the best happiness, says the Gita (XVIII. 37). Sadhana requires practice, constant practice without flurry; '*Abhyasena tu kaunteya vairagyena ca grihyate*'. 'By practice, O Arjuna, and by calm detachment are things attained' (VI. 35).

Much of our energy is wasted because of our restlessness. So we lose all peace. The Gita points out:

> No knowledge has the unsteady. Nor has he meditation. To the unmeditative there is no peace. And how can one without peace have happiness? (II. 66)

Hence our mind must be made steady by regular practice, so that we can command the best of our innate power. So a poise, a calmness must be practised. And then with a joyous, optimistic mind we must face our problems and sorrows. As Sri Krishna says:

> In tranquillity, all sorrow is destroyed. For, the intellect of him who is tranquil-minded is soon established in firmness. (II. 65)

We waste much of our vitality by brooding over the past mistakes or worrying about the future gains or losses. It is futile. Sri Krishna says, '*Gatasun agatasun ca na anusocanti panditah*' (II. 11). The idea is that the wise grieve neither for the living nor the dead, they neither grieve over the past nor worry about the future.

The secret of work according to the Gita is Yoga, and Yoga is nothing but equanimity, balance, poise. It is also union with the Godhead. '*Yogah karmasu kausalam*' (II. 50) and '*Samatvam yoga ucyate*' (II. 48).

> Being steadfast in Yoga, O Dhananjaya, perform actions, abandoning attachment, remaining unconcerned as regards success and failure. This evenness of mind (in regard to success and failure) is known as Yoga.

This sloka gives three requirements for perfect work. First, perform work as Yoga; second, don't choose the nature of your work; and third, don't be anxious for the result. Whatever work is given by God is good. We must do it as Svadharma, as our duty. If we develop the habit of liking our work, the discontent will melt away. Thereby we will work better, feel less tired and our life, free from constant complaints, will be sweeter.

Jealousy is a great weakness of human character. It can be lessened if we realize, as Swamiji says, for one moment that whom God raises, rises; and whom He drops, falls. The Gita also says:

Whatever being there is great, prosperous or powerful, that know thou to be a product of a part of My splendour. (X. 41)

Having attained to the worlds of the righteous, and dwelling there for everlasting years, one fallen from Yoga reincarnates in the home of the pure and the prosperous. (VI. 41)

Much of our relationship breaks up because of our lack of patience and tolerance. A little more mutual understanding, a little more consideration can make things better. If necessary, even unilateral tolerance will be ultimately paying. It will change the other person or at least it will keep us in peace. Sri Krishna says, 'Titikshasva Bharata', 'Bear them patiently, O Arjuna' (II. 14).

In life it is impossible to avoid suffering, however much we might try. The period of life when diseases, one by one, overtake us is really a trying one. Then we can follow the behest of Sri Krishna, 'Duhkheshu anudvignamanah', 'In sorrow with mind unruffled' (II. 56). That is the only way. Or we may follow the man of realization:

Resting in Brahman, with intellect steady, and without delusion, the knower of Brahman neither rejoiceth on receiving what is pleasant, nor grieveth on receiving what is unpleasant. (V. 20)

Mortal as we are, often death takes its toll in our families. Near and dear ones sometimes leave us. The Gita reminds us *'Jatasya hi dhruvo mrityuh'*.

Of that which is born, death is certain, of that which is dead, birth is certain. Over the unavoidable, therefore, thou oughtest not to grieve. (II. 27)

It is not mere fatalism. The imperishable Atman is there always; only bodies are transitory.

As are childhood, youth and old age, in this body, to the embodied soul, so also is the attaining of another body. Calm souls are not deluded thereat. (II. 13)

Death may be terrible, but it is real, it is certain. So it is better to prepare for it too. How to do it? The Gita says:

And he who at the time of death, meditating on Me alone, goes forth, leaving the body, attains My Being: there is no doubt about this.

All the worlds, O Arjuna, including the realm of Brahma, are subject to return, but after attaining Me, O son of Kunti, there is no rebirth. (VIII. 5, 16)

Leading an ideal life is always difficult. The youthful natural enthusiasm often sags. Then there is an urgency of an incentive. Power, position or popularity no longer attracts a man. For him Sri Krishna supplies the incentive, 'Lokasangraha', 'setting an example to the people at large' (III. 20).

World brotherhood is our dream. Men of the whole world are our own. This feeling we can imbibe if we remember the Divinity in all creation. 'Sarvasya cahum hrdi sanni-vishtah', 'I am in the heart of all creation' (XV. 15). The wise know this. As the Gita describes:

> Relative existence has been conquered by them, even in this world, whose mind rests in evenness, since Brahman is even and without imperfection: therefore they indeed rest in Brahman. (V. 19)

Many of us are too dependent by nature. We may have many desires, but no energy to work for their fulfilment. And we think that by mere supplication to an unseen power we may get the result. But that is not the Gita way, for it says: 'Uddharet atmana atmanam', 'One must raise up oneself' (VI. 5); no short cut. As a Sanskrit saying goes, 'No animals enter as food into the mouth of a sleeping lion'. The lion must make efforts, then it can get its food.

But then, there is a stage in the evolution of a man when God Himself takes up his burden. That is possible when he lets go all his sense of doership and surrenders himself completely at the feet of the Lord. God then sends all his requirements, 'Yogakshemam vahamyaham', 'I bear the burden of finding and protecting his wherewithal' (IX. 22). That is the ultimate step a devotee can take, surrender all and wait for His mercy. Sri Krishna asks such devotees to sacrifice everything and take His refuge. 'Sarvadharman parityajya mamekam saranam vraja', 'Giving up all duties and efforts, take refuge in Me alone' (XVIII. 66). If we take refuge in Him and daily resurrender to Him to remind us of our pledge, there will be every time a surge of spiritual power which will drive off all fear, lethargy and despondency.

The Gita is a book of positive thinking. Let us absorb a few of its life-giving thoughts and make our life happy, peaceful and spiritually progressive.

THE HOLY SCRIPTURES

THE holy books have a great influence on society. They mould the life and thought, hope and aspiration, duty and conduct of the followers. Books in general also have much influence, but in comparison the scriptures have by far the greater influence. Among them again the basic scriptures are more authoritative. The later holy books base themselves on the former, and are generally the exposition of the truth in them with a special stress on one or two of its aspects. The sacred scriptures are deeply respected in every religion, for they are the revelations of eternal truth and embody the religious and cultural heritage of the people. Every religion has them. While the Semitic religions accept one book being a revelation at a particular point of time, Eastern religions which believe religion to be eternal, generally accept more than one.

The most authoritative book of the Hindu religion is of course the Vedas. In fact, they are so important that a faith or sect is considered *astika* or 'believer' if it accepts the authority of the Vedas. As a result, though Buddhism and Jainism are varieties of Hinduism and accepted as such, they are still considered to be *nastikas*, non-believers. The Vedas are the primary authority. Smritis, Puranas, etc., come next to them in importance. The Vedas are said to be the root of dharma—*Vedo dharmamulam*. Other scriptures get validity from them. The word 'Veda' means knowledge or wisdom. Naturally, the Vedas are accepted as impersonal and eternal (*apaurusheya* and *nitya*). They are truths revealed to the

Rishis or seers of old. They are called Sruti because they were directly heard from God or learnt through hearing them recited by the preceptor. Sri Sankaracharya defines Veda as 'a book which reveals the knowledge of supernatural methods (*alaukika upaya*) for the achievement of the desired object and avoidance of the undesirable.' Regarding the influence of the Vedas a writer says:

'No school of philosophy will be recognized as orthodox, if it is not supported by the authority of the Vedas. The whole life of a Hindu, from conception up to the last funeral rite, has to be sanctified by the recitation of Vedic mantras. From these facts it may easily be conceived how profound has been the influence of the Vedas upon this great and most ancient of the civilized nations of the world.'

(*Cultural Heritage of India,* Vol. I, p. 182.)

The Veda as a book has four parts—Rig-Veda, Sama-Veda, Yajur-Veda and Atharva-Veda. They were taught by Vyasa to Palita, Jaimini, Vaisampayana and Sumanta respectively. *Rigveda Samhita* is the earliest available book of the world. It is a collection of nearly 10,500 verses grouped into 1,017 hymns in 10 Mandalas addressed to different deities. The Atharva is the latest Veda, where worship of higher gods and popular worship have been blended. Originally only the first three were included as is signified by the name of the Vedas as trayi. Each Veda again is divided into four parts—Mantra or Samhita, Brahmana, Aranyaka and Upanishad, meant to be studied particularly in the four different Ashramas, viz. Brahmacharya, Garhastya, Vanaprastha and Sannyasa. Mantras are hymns to deities, the Brahmanas deal with sacrificial rites to please the gods, the Aranyakas raise the ritual to a philosophical level by reinterpretation and the Upanishads or Vedanta are the records of mystical utterances and philosophical thoughts of the ancients. Mantra and Brahmana are called the Karma-kanda, the Aranyaka and Upanishads are called Upasana and Jnana-kandas, dealing with these particular topics. The auxiliaries of the Vedas, called Vedanga, are meant for proper cultivation and understanding of the Vedic texts and their application in rituals. They are six in number: Phonetics, Ritual, Grammar, Etymology, prosody and Astronomy.

The Upanishads are the foundation of the philosophical Hinduism. Their influence is tremendous. There are at present about 250 Upanishads, both ancient and modern, but of them only some are very old. Most of them are however spurious, which fact proves the popularity of the Upanishads. 108 Upanishads were recorded in early days. The most important and authoritative are the ten Upanishads on which Acharya Sankara wrote the commentaries. They are Isa, Kena, Katha, Mundaka, Mandukya, Prasna, Taitti-riya, Aitareya, Chhandogya and Brihadaranyaka. Kaushi-taki, Svetasvatara, Kaivalya, Narayana, Jabala, Nrisimhata-pani etc. also are well known. The word 'Upanishad' primarily means knowledge or philosophy, and secondarily, books relating to it. The Upanishads are also called Vedanta, literally "the end "of the Vedas, either on account of their position at the end of certain books of the Vedas or on account of their representing the essence or conclusions of the Vedas. They are also called Rahasya, or secret, as only qualified initiates had access to them under the direct guidance of the teacher.

The principal topics of the Upanishads are the Soul, God and Nature. The identity of the indestructible Brahman and Atman, the unity of existence and the divine heritage of man, the theories of reincarnation and Karma, personal and impersonal God, final release and the disciplines for achieving it are the major teachings of the Vedanta.. The message of Vedanta is universal, giving us strength, fearlessness and hope and providing us a rationale of morality. It draws our attention to the inner life, and points out our goal to Infinity.

The Smritis are the secondary scriptures dealing with religious and other duties. The Dharma-sastras are the law-books to guide the members of society. They prescribe the do's and don'ts of conduct in tune with the Vedas, changing from time to time. The Samhitas or Smrtis of Manu, Yajnavalkya, Parasara and others are very well known.

Valmiki's Ramayana and Vyasa's Mahabharata are the two immortal epics. They are called the Itihasas. In a way these are the most widely read books of India. Many adaptations and translations of them in different languages have made the stories and the noble qualities represented by different characters familiar to every boy and girl of India, thereby moulding the society. They are so popular because they are the applications of the higher principles presented in the scriptures. Countless other stories, parables, dialogues,etc., have been arranged round the main ones. The Gita is thus taken as a part of the Mahabharata.

The Bhagavad Gita is a tremendously influential book. It contains the teachings of Sri Krishna, synthesizing the various spiritual approaches and disciplines. Its place is very high in Indian literature because in 700 slokas it gives the quintessence of the Hindu philosophical ideas.

The Puranas are meant for popularizing religious ideas among the people through stories, legends, etc. There are 18 main Puranas and 18 Upa-puranas. Different Puranas are popular among the followers of different sects. One of the most popular Puranas is the Bhagavata, narrating the different Incarnations of Vishnu. Sri Krishna's life and exploits are fully delineated in this book and it is regarded by the Vaishnavas.as the most authoritative text. The Devi Mahatmya, which is very popular among the Sakti worshippers, forms part of the Markandeya Purana.

The Agamas narrate the methods of worship according to Saivism, Saktism and Vaishnavism. The Tantras, which are nothing but Agamas, are specially applied to Saktism and Buddhism. While the Agamas are mostly theological, the six Darsanas are philosophical. They are Sankhya, Yoga, Nyaya, Vaiseshika, Purva Mimamsa and Uttara Mimamsa or Vedanta.

Among the philosophical books of Hinduism, the most authentic is the Brahma-sutra or Vedanta-sutra or Bhikshu-sutra. The main teachings of the Vedanta (or the Upanishads forming the end and aim of the Vedas) are systematized in it. As it was written in a very cryptic, terse form, it gave rise to various interpretations, the chief among them being by the Acharyas, Sankara, Ramanuja and Madhva. In four chapters the book points out Brahman as the Ultimate Reality as shown by the Vedas, meets the objections of opponents, speaks about the discipline and finally about the fruit of knowing Brahman.

In applied spirituality, the most outstanding book of influence is Patanjali's Yoga-sutra. It teaches about the technique of concentration. The eightfold path recommended by it has been accepted as part of spiritual discipline by almost all the religious schools.

The basic books widely studied by serious religious aspirants are the Upanishads, Brahma-sutra and the Gita, which together are called the Prasthanatraya. Based on the ideas of these fundamental books coupled with their own realizations, many saints and holy men have produced countless books in different languages. They are widely read and have great influence on the people.

We may now note also the most important scriptures of other religions. The Jains have as their scripture the Agamas. In their different sections like Angas, Upangas, etc., they deal with the world-view, doctrine of salvation, monastic rules and discipline, the moral code and the rules for ascetics. Astronomy, astrology, physiology, geography, etc., are also taught in them. .They were orally transmitted like the Sruti and written in the fifth century A.D.

Similarly the teachings of the Buddha were systematized and recorded later. They are together called the Tripitaka, the three baskets. The Sutra-pitaka includes in five divisions many hundreds of longer and shorter sermons and discourses on the doctrine of the Master and his disciples. The Vinaya-pitaka expounds and explains the monastic discipline. The Abhidharma-pitaka is mostly a later addition and is composed of discussions of doctrinal, philosophical and psychological themes. Among the Mahayana Buddhists, the Saddharma-pundarika, Prajna-paramita, etc., are very popular. The Dharmapada is a small book giving the essentials of the teachings of the Buddha and is widely read.

The sacred book of the Sikhs is the Adi-Granth. It is a collection of the teachings of the first five Gurus of Sikhism, beginning with Nanak, who was deeply influenced by Kabir. It includes hymns, prayers, theology and religious teaching. Though many hymns are addressed to different deities, this holy book is itself literally worshipped by the followers as the representative of the Gurus.

The Semitic religions are more or less book-centred. The whole religion revolves round a particular book given by the propounder in the form of his teachings. The Bible is the one authoritative book among the Christians, with more stress on the New Testament.

For Judaism the Old Testament and the Talmud are

important. The Talmud is an encyclopaedia of Jewish tradition supplementing the Old Testament. Law is its primary concern, but religion, ethics, etc., also are discussed in it.

The Koran is the holy book of Islam. In its 114 Suras containing 77,639 words are recorded the teachings of Prophet Mohammed received through the angel Gabriel. It urges submission to the one God, and the one faith of Islam which is the way to salvation. The day of judgement, rewards, punishments, laws, etc., have been discussed with fervour and with illustrations.

The sacred book of the Zoroastrians is the Zend Avesta. The Yasna are records relating to morality, theology and ceremony. The Gathas of Zarathustra belong to this section. There are other sections dealing with invocations, hymns of praise of the divine company surrounding Ahura Mazda, litanies and priestly duties.

Among the Chinese holy books the most famous are the *Analects* of Confucius and his disciples, being conversations on moral codes, and the *Tao Te Ching*, the classic of the Taoist school, which is a collection of aphorisms on the nature of the *Tao*, the cosmic ultimate and *Te* and its manifestation through human nature. The two chief books of the Japanese Shinto are the *Kojiki* and the *Nihongi* which are mainly chronicles of ancient times.

These are the main scriptures of the living religions of the world. They along with innumerable other books in tune with them inform the followers of the faith about the higher verities as well as their duties and codes of conduct and thus profoundly influence the life of the people and keep the religious ideas alive in society.

ADHYATMA RAMAYANA

'I constantly meditate upon that Ramachandra, the dust of whose lotus feet the Vedas search for, from whose navel-lotus arose Brahma, and whose name is relished as the essential treasure even by God Siva,'[1] so sang the *Adhyatma Ramayana*.

THE Ramayana is a book of great influence. The story of Sri Rama in the Valmiki Ramayana in olden days had such an impact on Indian consciousness that in every Indian language several translations and adaptations were brought out. As a result of all these Ramayanas, there is hardly a boy or girl in India who does not know about the detachment and dutifulness of Rama, love of Sita, service of Lakshmana and Bharata, devotion of Hanuman and examples of many other noble qualities. The Ramayanas in the local languages of course are naturally very popular, being accessible to the peasant as well as the learned. Down the centuries they have provided Indians with grand ethical and spiritual ideals. Most of the other Ramayanas have been greatly influenced by the *Adhyatma Ramayana* which was written in Sanskrit. It has been recognized by writers on Tulsidas

---

1. यत्पादपंकजरजः श्रुतिभिर्विमृग्यं
   यन्नाभिपंकजभवः कमलासनश्च ।
   यन्नामसाररसिको भगवान् पुरारिस्तं-
   रामचन्द्रमनिशं हृदि भावयामि ॥ (I. 5. 47)

that his *Ramacharitamanasa* has derived much from the Adhyatma Ramayana, specially whenever it deviates from the Valmiki Ramayana. In fact it has more similarity with the former in approach and narration of incidents than with the latter. The Adhyatma Ramayana is known throughout India but is specially popular in the North among the followers of the path of Jnana. It is widely read in the monastic circles too.

The Adhyatma Ramayana may be called a Bhagavata Ramayana. It deals with the character of Sri Rama more in tune with Srimad Bhagavata's dealing with the character of Sri Krishna. It is a remodelling of the Valmiki Ramayana, with the latter's beauty often retained but teachings made more explicit. The Valmiki Ramayana is like an ocean of literary beauty, ethical teachings and spiritual instructions but it requires deeper insight and good Samskaras to get at those truths. The human element, ethical quality and literary beauty are more predominant there. The Adhyatma Ramayana on the other hand gives the spiritual truth more explicitly. It is a lake with crystal clear water through which the gems below can be easily seen. Whereas in the Valmiki Ramayana the glory of Maya or Prakriti has been well presented, the Adhyatma Ramayana presents the glory of the Mayin or Paramatman.

In his Ramayana (Adi XV) Maharshi Valmiki says:

'Vishnu, who is the Paramatman and the whole, granted the aforesaid boon to the Devas and thought about Himself as a man and the place where He was to be born. And then the Bhagavan with lotus eyes willed to divide Himself into four parts and accept King Dasaratha as His father.'

So though Valmiki stresses the human aspect of Sri Rama, he also recognises that he is Vishnu Himself. But how the propriety of this dual character is maintained in the character of Rama has been clearly explained in the Adhyatma Ramayana. Lord Siva has given the secret of Sri Rama's real nature in this holy book. By reading this, the grand truth of the Avatara and his lila can be fully comprehended. It is a book laying stress like the Bhagavata on Jnana, Vijnana, Bhakti and Vairagya. It has earned a name as a book more given to Jnana because of its philosophical basis which is non-dualistic. But at the same time it retains all the grandeur of the Bhakti system.

The important idea in the Ramayana is the grand detachment of Sri Rama. It is also there in the Valmiki Ramayana. But in the Adhyatma Ramayana it has been the guiding idea. Hence at every step we are reminded that Rama was Paramatman incarnate.[2] His love and affection, sorrows and sufferings are only external. These pairs of opposites cannot really touch him.[3] He *as if* plays his part as is clear from Kausalya's prayer in this book.[4] Often an expression is seen which says, 'But if we analyse we find that he did not do anything; for he is changeless and measureless.'[5] Not only Sri Rama but even his relatives and companions and also his acquain-

---

2. रामं विद्धि परं ब्रह्म सच्चिदानन्दमद्वयम् ।
सर्वोपाधिविनिर्मुक्तं सत्तामात्रगोचरम् (I. 1. 32.)

3. विशुद्धविज्ञानघने रघूत्तमेऽविद्या कथं स्यात् परतः परात्मनि । (I. 1. 21.)

4. करोषीव न कर्त्ता त्वं गच्छसीव न गच्छसि ।
न शृणोषिश्रृणोषीव पश्यसीव न पश्यसि ॥ (I. 3. 26.)

5. अविकारी परिणामहीनो विचार्यमाणो न करोति किंचित् ॥
(I. 3. 71 to 66.)

13

tances and enemies are aware or made aware of their real
nature and they knowingly play the parts assigned to them.
It is true that this fact takes away a little of the literary excellence which depends upon real feeling of sympathy. But the
loss is made up by the spiritual gains of the realization of
the Avatarahood of Sri Rama. The idea is so predominant
that even the meaning of the word 'Rama' has been given
in this book in tune with this idea. It says:

> 'Rama is One in whom the Munis sport after the
> destruction of ignorance through knowledge or one
> who gives joy to the devotees by his beauty'.[6]

It is a general mistaken notion that the Adhyatma
Ramayana is an allegorical treatment of the original. But
the different characters are not presented in that way. It
is true that several characters have been pointed out as different metaphysical entities, e.g. Rama as Paramatman, Sita
as Prakriti or Yogamaya, Lakshmana as Jivatman. Basing himself on these philosophical ideas, the author reminds us and
the characters too at every step that they are mere tools in
the hand of God or Karma. Their part is only to become the
so called cause—Nimittamatram of the Gita. Like Arjuna
they know their real nature but still act according to Divine
Will. So we find that Ravana knows that he will be killed;
Sita knows that she will be abducted. Still they do their
functions as ordained.

The Adhyatma Ramayana again is very careful to
remove some of the objections raised against the Valmiki
Ramayana. As for example, the abduction of Sita. The

---

6. यस्मिन् रमन्ते मुनयो विद्यया ज्ञानविप्लवे ।
   तं गुरुः प्राह रामेति रमणाद्राम इत्यपि । (1. 3. 44 or 40)

Adhyatma Ramayana says that Rama informed Sita earlier
that Ravana was coming and asked her to stay with Agni
for one year leaving behind the Maya-Sita.[7] And even then
when Ravana came, he took the entire block of earth on
which she stood[8] and kept her in Asokavana 'like a mother'.[9]
Tulsidas, Kamban and other writers of the Ramayana have
followed the author in one or the other part. This shows the
influence exerted by the Adhyatma Ramayana on the later
writers. The Adhyatma Ramayana (with 7 Kandas and 66
chapters including the Anukramanika and over 4.300 Slokas)
is said to belong to the Brahmanda Purana, Uttara Khanda
and written by Veda Vyasa who is the traditional author of
all the Puranas. About the origin of the book, the *Anukramanika* says that Mother Parvati wanted to know of the
nature of Sri Rama and the answer given by Bhagavan Siva
has become famous as the Adhyatma Ramayana (Anu.
19-20). It is called 'Adhyatma' or spiritualized Ramayana
because it is full of instructions on Bhakti, Jnana, worship,
right conduct, etc., remembering always the metaphysical
background. The Adhyatma Ramayana is also known as
Rama Gita (Anu. 48). It has been described as the nectar
churned out of the ocean of the Upanishads.[10] This statement reminds us of the similar one regarding the Gita.   Like

---

7. रावणो भिक्षुकरूपेण आगमिष्यतिकम् ।
   त्वन्तु छायां त्वदाकारं स्थापयित्वोटजे विश ॥   (III. 7. 2)

8. ततो विदार्य धरणीं नखैरुद्धृत्य बाहुभिः ।
   तोलयित्वा रथे क्षिप्त्वा ययौ क्षिप्रं विहायसा ॥ (III. 7. 51.)

9. मातृबुद्ध्यानुपालयत् ।   (III. 7. 65.)

10. रामेणोपनिषत्सिन्धुमुन्मथ्योत्पादितां पुरा ।   (Anu. 49.)

Sri Krishna in the Bhagavad Gita, Sri Rama too gives his
message while instructing Lakshmana and others. The
purpose of the book is purification of the minds of the
people. As it has been said:

'This Ganga of Adhyatma Ramayana arises from the
mountain of Siva, meets the ccean of Rama and purifies
the three worlds on the way.'[11]

As told before, Jnana, Vijnana, Bhakti and Vairagya are
forcefully presented here (I. i.9). The discussion started
with the question whether Sri Rama forgot his real nature;
for otherwise why should he weep for Sita? (I. 1.13). As
answer the basic philosophy which is non-dualistic but rein-
forced by devotion has been presented. Sita gives the gist
of this in the Samkshepa Ramayana saying that Rama is
Purusha, she is Prakriti and the Jiva is free from ignorance
when he understands the meaning of *Tat-twam-asi*, that he is
of the nature of Brahman and the Jiva has been described by
Siva as Rama-Hridaya, the heart of Rama (I. 1.56). By
reading and understanding this a devotee can realize the
Highest. Devotion to the Lord also gives the same result.[12]

This book has a good number of stotras or hymns
expressing the noblest sentiments of devotion and subtlest
reaches of knowledge. Some of them casually deal with the
philosophy of religion, of the nature of Brahman, Atman,
God, Jiva, Prakriti, creative processes, etc. The Avatarahood

---

11. पुरारिगिरिसम्भूता श्रीरामार्णवसंगता ।
    अध्यात्मरामगंगेयं पुनाति भुवनत्रयम् ॥   (I. 1. 5.)
12. अतो मद्भक्तियुक्तस्य ज्ञानं विज्ञानमेव च ।
    वैराग्यं च भवेच्छीघ्रं ततो मुक्तिमवाप्नुयात् ॥   (III. 4. 51.)

of Sri Rama is also mentioned in all of them. Even
Vasishtha and Kausalya utter prayers addressed to him.
Valmiki sometimes refers to Rama as Vishnutulya, like
Vishnu, but in the Adhyatma Ramayana, he is always in his
original glory. Among the hymns, however, the most
appealing are those that speak of motiveless devotion and
self-surrender. As for example, Ahalya prays to Rama:

'In whatever place I be, O Lord, may I always have
deep devotion to you.'[13]

Or Parasurama prays:

'May I have undeflected devotion to you and may I
have the company of your devotees.'[14]

Another thing often prayed for is to remain free from Maya.
Kabandha prays:

'Save me O Lord of the universe. Let not your Maya
cover my consciousness.'[15]

To Sabari, Rama assures that Bhakti is the one thing necessary
and there is no other consideration of birth or lineage.[16]
Following the Gita-idea Sri Rama too says, 'Like a wish-
fulfilling tree I do as the devotees wish me to.'   (II. 9.66.)

---

13. देव मे यत्र कुत्रापि स्थितायाा अपि सर्वंदा ।
   त्वत्पादकमले सक्ता भक्तिरेव सदास्तु मे ।   (I. 5. 58)
14. त्वद्भक्तवसंगस्त्वत्पादे दृढा भक्तिः सदास्तु मे ॥
                                        (I. 7. 44 or 58)
15. त्राहि त्राहि जगन्नाथ मां माया नावृणोतु ते ।   (III. 9. 54)
16. मद्भजने भक्तिरेव हि कारणम् ।   (III. 10. 20.)

The above quotations will amply show that the Adhyatma Ramayana stresses Bhakti as much as Jnana. By following these paths a man can realize the goal of life. Jnana-misra Bhakti is the path specially recommended by this holy book.

Lilasmarana, thinking of the life and exploits of the Lord is itself accepted in the Bhakti system as a Sadhana. The Adhyatma Ramayana says that whoever reads and thinks of Rama will be spiritually benefited (Anu. 38), nay, he will attain Jivanmukti.[17]

---

17. यस्तु प्रत्यहमध्यात्म-रामायणमनन्यधीः ।
　　यथाशक्तिपठेद्भक्त्या स जीवन्मुच्यते नरः ॥ (Anu. 30.)

IN SEARCH OF SECURITY

SEARCH for security has been the concern of man from the beginning of history. For physical safety he, as a primitive man, had to fight against the natural forces and other creatures. With the growth of civilization, the uncertainty and anxiety lessened a little but still it remained the dominant note in the life of man. The different movements inspired by ethics, philosophy and politics are all busy in finding out material security for him. Science and technology are primarily aimed at that. For physical security, food is the first thing necessary. Man has given up his nomadic life in search of a peaceful, secure life of agriculture. Every improvement of the means of production has helped him to meet this requirement. With the growth of industrialization, the economic forces have gone out of control of the common man. In earlier days there might not have been much of the modern conveniences, but man was the master of his situation. The village community was more or less self-contained and self-supporting regarding the basic necessities of life. To fight other creatures man had to live in groups. Individuals, however, joined in a natural family. The undivided family was the order of the day. It had many advantages too, for it provided security to weaker members.

With the change of the rural structure of society the individual hold over land, the direct means of getting food, went out of the hands of the individual. New methods had to be found for providing security to man in old age and illness, which was provided earlier by the joint family. Various social security measures thus evolved with the passage of time. Several countries in the West have developed so much in this direction, that their citizens are insured against all eventualities. The Chinese experiment with communes is yet another search for finding complete security for all people in the shortest possible time. It is claimed that all possible securities are assured in this system, for everyone is equally a member of the society. But this requires total regimentation, which is very much resented by educated people. The Sarvodaya movement wanted to provide almost the same security but through democratic means and voluntary efforts. This is the goal of human endeavour, the Utopia of social workers, to provide complete material security to man, without losing freedom if possible.

Security of the basic necessities of life is essential. Without some measure of this security no higher thinking is possible. As Sri Ramakrishna has said, 'Religious life is not possible for empty stomachs'. But it has been reported recently from Sweden, the most progreessive country in the West in providing social security, that too much security is also not good for man. A large number of cases of mental disturbance and neurosis proves that there must be something in the environment of man to fight against so that he finds a purpose in life. And the need to fight keeps him alert. Moreover, 'man does not live by bread alone'.

The instinct of self-preservation is predominantly evident in primitive man as well as in children. It is present in every other being too. But then there are other securities, the necessity of which is felt by man. Emotional security is a great need for the proper growth of children. The troubles and agony through which the adolescents and young people pass are due to unknown fields of experience and uncertainities of life. If they have suitable emotional security through the love of relatives and friends, the adjustment becomes easy. Much of delinquency and anti-social attitudes are often traceable to emotional insecurity in childhood and not so much to physical insecurity.

Then there is the question of spiritual security. Dr. Jung says that for a vast majority of people after 35, the urgent need is to discover the purpose of life. Often psychological troubles have been traced to the lack of a goal of life.

We can enumerate other securities, viz., economic, military, intellectual and the like. But they may be included more or less in the broader classification of physical, mental and spiritual. When a man is possessed with a purpose, he can ignore other securities and take risks. This can be seen in the austerity and hardship courted by religious men, patriots, soldiers, scholars, adventurers and many others. Insecurity as such, as we said, is not always bad. It makes a man of better mettle.

Spiritual security must be discovered by every man in his own heart. Now-a-days doctors and psychologists advise people to engage in purposeful, creative activity. This of course must be supplemented by an intellectual understanding of the scheme of the universe and one's own place in it. The spiritual understanding that there is One who is the root of all, can give permanence to this sense of security. Religions down the ages have preached surrender to God, which automatically gives security even to the despondent soul.

As an antidote to the feeling of insecurity and fear, cultivation of the positive attitudes of courage and strength is also necessary. Danger is not so much in objective situations as in our thinking. If the attitude of fight and not submission is cultivated, many of the worries regarding the future will melt away. Even when there is real difficulty, an attitude of fearlessness and strength will make man more capable to face the situation better. Fearlessness hence has been described as a cardinal virtue. Swami Vivekananda exhorted his countrymen in these energizing words:

> What makes you weep, my friend? In you is all power. Summon up your all-powerful nature, oh mighty one, and this whole universe will lie at your feet. It is the Self alone that predominates, and not matter. It is those foolish people who identify themselves with their bodies that piteously cry, 'Weak, weak, we are weak'. What the nation wants is pluck and scientific genius. We want great spirit, tremendous energy and boundless enthusiasm, no womanishness will do. It is the man of action, the lion-heart, that the goddess of wealth resorts to. No need of looking behind. Forward! We want infinite energy, infinite zeal, infinite courage, and infinite patience, then only will great things be achieved.

In our scriptures God has been identified with Abhayam, fearlessness. The *Gita* considers Abhayam as a Sattvic quality. Its great usefulness has been forcefully presented by a noted writer thus:

> Who is there who today is not enveloped by mundane fears—fear of starvation, of nakedness, of poverty; fear of myriad possessions, of plenty, of prosperity which may be lost; everyone's life is permeated with insecurity and security is sought through armies and aircraft, and in other dubious ways. Courage alone feels secure, for through it a man gains his own Soul by losing the whole world. This courage alone is the help of the helpless, and in dire calamity it stands its possessor in good stead. Did it not enable Gandhiji to die with understanding in his heart, love in his mind, forgiveness on his lips?

(B. P. Wadia: *Thus have I heard,* p. 378.)

Shakespeare's advice in such a situation is worth noting:

> 'Tis true that we are in great danger;
> The greater therefore should our courage be.

Strength is the greatest security against all weakness. Weakness of body, mind, and soul can each be counteracted by the corresponding strength. The mind being stronger than the body, the mental strength can engender even physical strength to a large extent. Spiritual strength, however, is the best.

In the scriptures mention has been made of various methods of cultivating spiritual strength. Surrender to the Divine Being is the easiest method, suitable for most people. In the Vaishnavite books, different factors of surrender have been noted. Of these, there is one which asks us to have 'faith that He will protect'—*Rakshishyati iti visvasah.* Faith in the existence of God and in His mercy has a great sustaining power.

Great souls also can infuse faith and courage in us by their bold assertion born of realization. Sri Sankara in his *Vivekachudamani* rises to this height when he declares:

> Fear not, O learned one, there is no death for thee; there is a means of crossing this sea of Samsara; that very way by which sages have gone beyond it, I shall teach thee. (43)

God is the only ultimate refuge of man. Property, friends and society are only relative ones. As Acharya Nimbarka says, 'There is no refuge other than the lotus feet of Krishna'—*Nanya gatih Krsnapadaravindat.* The *Gita,* that mine of advice regarding all human situations, says:

> And having obtained which, a man regards no other acquisition superior to that, and where established,

he is not moved even by heavy sorrow —let that be known as the state called by the name of Yoga—a state of severance from the contact of pain. (VI. 22-23)

Sri Krishna Himself proclaims about His devotee:

Soon does he become righteous and attain eternal Peace, O son of Kunti; boldly can you proclaim, that My devotee is never destroyed. (IX. 31)

When we read this we know we are safe in His care as soon as we take refuge in Him. The burden of sin and misdeeds often hangs heavy on us. Sri Krishna assures:

Relinquishing all Dharmas take refuge in Me alone; I will liberate you from all sins; grieve not. (XVIII. 66)

Although surrender or the path of devotion is most suited to many people, there are people of other natures who require other methods. The Stoic philosophers practised determinedly endurance of all hardships. Their motto was, as said by Marcus Aurelius, 'A man's life is what his thoughts make of it.' And they applied this principle in their life. The spiritual aspirants following the path of Knowledge go to the roots and build up their strength. According to the *Brihadaranyaka Upanishad*, 'fear comes from the existence of a second one'. But the Vedanta asserts that there is only one existence, one reality, and hence there is no cause of fear. So the Jnanis doggedly practise the art of avoiding reactions to all pairs of opposites like happiness and sorrow. As the *Gita* puts it:

Having made pain and pleasure, gain and loss, conquest and defeat, the same, engage then in battle. So shall you incur no sin. (II. 38)

For regular practice it advises further:

> He whose mind is not shaken by adversity, who does
> not hanker after happiness, who has become free from
> affection, fear and wrath, is indeed the Muni of steady
> wisdom.   (II. 56.)

The Yogis, however, have perfected the method of mind
control. It is in the mind of man that all feelings of fear,
worry, anxiety and insecurity are born. If a man gets control
over his mind, he becomes the master of the situation. So
Rajayoga advises the method of meditation through gathering, fixing and concentrating the mind. As a result, mastery
of the mind is achieved, which frees a Yogi from all unpleasant feelings.

The followers of the path of Karma, however, consciously
practise detachment and action. Action has been accepted
as an antidote to all paralyzing emotions like fear and insecurity. The practice of detachment gives a strong mental fibre
to the man of action.

Thus through these various disciplines the scriptures
try to take us to a haven of peace and security. The spiritual
method is not a palliative or a tranquilliser, meant for temporary relief. It goes to the root of the problem and has no
adverse effects. As this leads to the highest goal of life, there
will be no necessity to discard it on the way.

Above are the broad divisions of spiritual discipline to
attain peace, happiness and security. Even if they are practised
partially, they are capable of giving man a great measure of
the sense of security. As the *Gita* puts it:

> In this, there is no waste of the unfinished attempt,
> nor is there production of contrary results. Even very
> little of this Dharma protects from the great terror.
> (II. 40.)

The disciplines need not be thought of as difficult. The
approach to God is very simple. Believe now and make it
a reality. Practise it right now and you get the benefit.
God has been described in the theistic systems as Father or
Mother. A child feels most secure in the arms of its parents.
As God becomes real in our life, the feeling of all insecurity
vanishes. The growth of terribly destructive weapons have
brought in now-a-days new insecurities, for inner life has not
been elevated. Modern economics and politics have made
individuals helpless regarding external situations. It is only
in the inner life he is still the master. So if the feeling of
insecurity, physical, mental or spiritual, troubles him, he
can dive deep into his soul and forget the environment for the
time being and come back with renewed strength, hope and
faith to face the situation better. If genuine love for God
develops, He Himself will take the reins of his life. And
there will be no more fear. Such a man will rest in the arms
of God forever.

THE IDEAL OF SAINT-MAKING

THE lives of saints have always been an ennobling study. The study is pleasant too. It is pleasant to those who hunger for a higher life. In their search for a meaning of life men find from the lives of saints a purpose, a goal. Often it is seen a man begins his life in an ordinary way, keeping himself occupied with daily pleasures and joys, sufferings and sorrows. After the enjoyment is partially satisfied and the man grows in experience in life, he pines for something that he does not even know. Then gradually, if the samskara is good or earlier upbringing gave him some contact, he becomes aware of a new realm and a fresh field of study and contemplation. Then he becomes acquainted with the spiritual verities. And in this field, the lives and exploits of saints attract him much. He discovers that here are some souls who completely ignored the demands of the flesh and were fully occupied with something higher, nobler and subtler. With study, faith grows. And he comes to believe in the realization of the saints. It becomes a source of great solace to him. That is why we find hundreds of people devote their well-earned rest after retirement from active life to this study. People who do not have such Samskaras go in search of various excitements for which, alas, they often have little capacity.

From this probably an idea has grown among common people that religious life is for old people only. With this idea they praise the old Indian scheme of four divisions of life where total pursuit of the way of Liberation has been put off to the fag end of life. Of course, this is not a correct view, for without earlier preparation nobody can follow the lead of the saints to the dizzy heights of metaphysical truths or in the exacting discipline necessary for spiritual progress. Hence the same old Indian scheme of life put the stage of Brahmacharya first— a life full of austerity, deep study and contemplation. The seeds of the yearning for the ideal of Liberation were put at that time itself, which grew steadly through the life of Garhasthya and culminated in Vanaprastha and Sannyasa. In Vanaprastha slowly the householder was advised to separate himself from the family and repair to the forest with his wife to contemplate on God. And he was to be completely free during Sannyasa. This scheme of life was to guide man gradually into the mysteries of spiritual life. It was smooth too. The entire life, it will be noticed, was oriented to that one great goal, Moksha or Liberation.

It is because of this scheme of life it is said that India opted for the ideal of saint-making as against the West trying for the material improvement of society. We may, however, ignore such contradictories where one is put against the other to bring out a quality in bold relief, for religious souls were there in every country, and before the materialistic philosophy gained ground in recent centuries, the ideal of every society was the same, i.e., the realization of God and Salvation. This ideal was an axiom with the ancient people, though of course human limitations and difference of temperaments were recognized. For this difference several explanations have been given. The theory of Karma appeals to many as more rational, for it explains why one man has more spiritual development and the other less. This theory states that the ultimate goal of life is Liberation, through the experience of joys and sorrows. Every soul must have it today or tomorrow. Some begin their conscious march in this life itself, but many require a few more to work out the results of accumulated action to be fully ready for ultimate Liberation. Some others may be quite unconcerned about spiritual life; they may be impervious to spiritual ideas, or may be agnostic or materialistic. But a time will come after prolonged experience through a succession of births when they also will be ready for Liberation. The theories of Karma and reincarnation are thus bound together to give a cogent explanation of this world process.

All the religious schools of India agree that when a soul is ready for illumination it becomes interested in spiritual things and not before. Then the question may naturally arise why should there be preaching of spiritual ideas at all. It is pointed out that by propagation, souls who are ready for the ideas but have not yet found the way will have a sort of an awakening. The thin veil of delusion shutting them out from the discovery of the existence of spiritual truth will be torn off and the latter will shine in all its glory. Then the individual will make a determined effort and gradually come to understand the Ultimate Reality.

It has been held in different systems that knowledge of truth is instantaneous. The Advaita system believes that as soon as a fit aspirant hears the Mahavakya from his Guru, the knowledge comes immediately, *acirena,* as the ancient scriptures say. In a different context it has been argued that when the mind is fully purified Jnana dawns automatically and immediately. 'The dark room of a thousand years is illumined in a flash', as Sri Ramakrishna said. The Bhakti schools also believe that love of God comes as soon as a devotee repeats the name of God becoming free from all sins. Of course, all the religious systems recognize the prior struggles of a spiritual aspirant before final illumination. In the analysis

14

of the lives of mystics, it has been pointed out that they had to pass through different stages.

Saints may be both mystical as well as of the Jnani type. Prof. P. N. Srinivasachari has written a fine, exhaustive book, *Mystics and Mysticism*. In it he has described the life and views of only the mystics, that is, of those who had the experience of at-one-ment with the Godhead. The non-inclusion of the saints of the Jnani type shows that he makes a distinction between the mystic and the Knower. In the course of discussion, he says:

> Pure Advaita thus established by *adhyasavada* and *aikya-jnana* is different from mysticism which stresses the unitary consciousness and not identity. The self and God are distinct but they are not separate and to the mystic, *mukti* is both the apprehension of unity and the attainment of union. But it may glide into Advaita-mukti or non-duality. (p. 41)

The saint, however, includes all the types—those who worship the Deity and realize unity with Him as well as those who intuit their identity with God. R. D. Ranade observes in his *Mysticism in Maharashtra*:

> All these mystics constitute the musical band of God, and each contributes his note in such a way that the whole becomes a harmony, and a symphony wonderful. (p. 482)

The different realizations, as pointed out by Swami Vivekananda, can be broadly classified under the three well-known heads, viz., Dvaita, Vishishtadvaita and Advaita. Though other systems will not a hundred percent tally with Dualism, Qualified Non-dualism and Non-dualism, broadly speaking, in their realizations the saints come to realize their proximity, unity or identity in accordance with their attitude. The term 'Saint' being a broad one, encompasses all the noble souls having various types of realization.

Another distinction is also made among saints. It is often noticed that those who became great saints afterwards led not a very extraordinary life earlier. But then, all on a sudden as if in a flash they intuit some higher thing, and as a result a total change comes over them. In such cases there is no premeditation or gradual preparation. But the vast majority of saints grew out of definite preparation and practice of spiritual discipline. This process is known as yoga in the scriptures. In the former there is a chance of developing eccentricity, queer habits and ideas, so it is enjoined in the scriptures that definite religious discipline must be practised. They insist on a determined attempt at living a life of ethical perfection and generally discourage all miraculous powers. The commom man, however, gives more value to these powers and think these as the proof of one's sainthood. Often such saints are not bound by rules and regulations, manners and customs. Sects have arisen following them,which do not believe in any restriction. This along with intense feeling for God may be all right, but often such aspirants fall by the way side due to sheer exhaustion, irregularity or demand of the flesh. Hence we find many saintly persons appearing among such groups, and at the same time many acts of debauchery are also committed. So the scriptures stress a methodical, ordered life rather than an unfettered life of intense feeling. Achara, habits of religious purity, has been an important thing in all spiritual traditions, specially so in India.

While giving a rational explanation regarding experience, Swami Vivekananda explains in *Rajayoga*. that such saints 'stumbled into realization', as it were. Hence it is often found that many queer ideas and hatred for other groups remain in them in spite of their realization. The ethical perfection, the acquisition of many virtues that we associate with a man of realization were not always manifest in them.

Then there is the danger of spurious claims too. Charlatans are not wanting who quote scriptures to support their depraved ways of life. Hence among the ancient monastic orders there is the custom of selecting as the head, a monk who is austere, learned and who has good habits and has led the life of purity and holiness for a number of years and not those who claim to have some visions merely. This should be the method if sainthood is to be developed consciously and not left to chance.

Thus religious life has two aspects. One stands for realization through ethical perfection and purification of mind and habits and the other for a direct mystic communion with the Godhead sheerly through intense feeling. The latter has a greater appeal, the former has a greater social value. The latter is unpredictable, the former is gradual and definite. The latter has many pitfalls, the former is free from them. The latter being accidental, has no particular training, the former has definite methods to follow. The latter gives no hope to others about success, the former does so. But the latter, if genuine, is more fruitful and quick.

How do the spiritual disciplines originate? First comes the saint. He has access to the realm of spiritual values. In the progressive moral life of man the ideal values of truth, goodness and beauty are revealed. Saints discover the underlying spiritual principle whose manifestations things of the world are. As Carlyle assures us in his *Sartor Resartus,* the material world is but a vesture or symbol through which the spirit reveals itself. While this is a matter of intellectual consciousness with the philosopher, it is a matter of personal experience with the mystic. The mystic travels through the stages of purification and illumination and reaches the ecstatic state where he realizes the Divine Oneness. The Upanishads describe this realization of unity arrived at through intuition and not reasoning. The variegated realization gave the idea of unity in variety. While giving expression to their mystic realization, saints often burst into lyrical composition. While contemplating on this, many of their followers do the same. That is why we find most of the saintly followers are remembered probably more than their teachers because of their lyrics and poems. In fact, the melodious mystics are the most popular among the people. With the passage of time the mystic realization and the lyrical compositions give rise to methodical, serious thinking. Systematic thought by its very nature gives rise to objectivity. Through thorough analysis the essentials are sifted and a consistent technique to get at that realization is evolved. The later aspirants follow that discipline and are blessed in their turn. Thus a succession of saints is maintained, though many of them are not well-known. Systematic thought is given by many saints themselves, who are propounders of new faiths. Many of them are thus great philosophers also. There is an advantage in this, for if men of direct realization write their views about their realization and ways to have it, the system remains purer. People lacking direct access to them cannot spoil their views with speculative thinking. Great harm has been done by later interpreters by mixing their own ideas. The teachers, who had access to this realization and had a clear grasp of the views of the Master, corrected the people and thereby the religious system. Sankara and others propounded the path of Knowledge. Among the teachers of Bhakti in India, Ramanuja, Madhva, Chaitanya, Vallabha, Nimbarka, Ramananda—each is a propounder of a particular school of devotional philosophy. Kabir, Dadu and others have also particular sects following them. Though no particular large sects follow them, many other saints, like those of Maharashtra, have a large body of people devoted to them. In fact, some scholars are of opinion from a study of the religious life in Maharashtra, that individual, unorganized religious life is the normal one in that area. This may be said to be true in a way for the whole of India, for even the followers of a particular sect gather round a teacher belonging nominally to a major sect. Hence there are differences in spiritual practices and disciplines.

About the pragmatic value of the realizations and existence of saints much has been said by William James, Evelyn Underhill, Dean Inge and other noted writers on mysticism. The saints bring to the people the message of goodwill, harmony, hope and illumination. Evelyn Underhill says:

> Through the vital personalities of the mystics and the saints the radiance of the spiritual streams out upon the race. God speaks to man through man. Such personalities act as receivers and transmitters. They distribute the flashes of the Uncreated Light.

Spiritual training develops good qualities but mere virtues do not make a saint. He has something emergent in him He must have a communion with God, maybe through self-effort, environmental influence or grace. As a result of his communion a special outlook, a particular conviction, a definite idea of sharing develops in him. Through it, his personality becomes ennobling and irresistible. If a character developed through definite ethical preparation is' blessed thus with realization, it becomes more beneficial to other aspirants. Such saints become models for later generations to follow. In the case of other mystics, their yearning being exceptionally intense and realization sudden, people find their lives more difficult to imitate. They, however, inspire others by bearing testimony to the reality of the spiritual verities. Our ideal is to accept all the saints and their methods. 'As many faiths, so many paths', as Sri Ramakrishna said. Hence it will be proper for us to recognize and follow according to our temperaments the disciplines evolved by founders of different systems and at the same time derive enthusiasm and inspiration from other mystics. This will be the proper technique for saint-making, producing the best results. The ideal of saints is an eternal ideal. Our vision may be clouded occasionally but with further development of human society, we hope, this ideal will reassert itself. As Aldous Huxley points out in his *Perennial Philosophy,* 'Except by saints, the problem of power is finally insoluble' To have such saints the ideal of saints must be held aloft and the technique of saint-making must be put into practice more enthusiastically.

SWAMI RAMAKRISHNANANDA

THE IMPLICATIONS OF HIS LIFE

The Unique Worshipper

ON a sultry day of June in Madras a devotee lay down for rest. He, however, felt very uneasy because of excessive heat. He became quite restless, and then all of a sudden he got up and entered the shrine quietly, thinking that the heat was unbearable also to his Lord. So he began to fan the portrait of his Master. And then flowed a stream of soft, loving words from his lips: 'My Master! O the beloved of my heart! O my Master, O the beloved of my heart!' Thus he went on for two hours. As he fanned and hummed these endearing words he forgot all about his surroundings, all about his existence and all about the burning heat; only the living presence of the Master was real to him.

One evening a group of devotees came to the Math to meet him. They understood that he was in the shrine and waited for him. Presently they heard him calling out in loud and angry tones:

'You have brought me here, Old Man, and left me helpless! Are you testing my powers of patience and endurance? I will not go and beg hereafter for my sake or even for yours. If anything comes unasked, I will offer it to you and share the Prasada. Or I will bring sea-sand for offering to you and I shall live upon that.'

The devotees, who were waiting outside the shrine, did not quite follow his words. They guessed that he was quarrelling with somebody. But, in fact, he was in a distressed mood unburdening himself to his Master.

Once he took hot milk into the shrine for offering. While testing the warmth of the milk by dipping his finger into it he happened to burn and blister the finger. He then placed the milk before the portrait and said in a complaining tone, 'You want to drink warm milk and my finger is burnt!'

Such was Swami Ramakrishnananda, a direct disciple of Sri Ramakrishna. The few incidents cited above will amply show how surcharged he was with the feeling of the living presence of the Master. Whoever had seen the Swami performing worship in the shrine was deeply impressed by his ecstatic devotion. The love for ceremonial worship was in his blood. His father was an expert in this art. His Guru had his realizations through it. In fact, he believed that deities actually dwell in the temples and they talk to the devotees too. Once when a devotee was going to take leave after a long conversation, the Swami said, 'Wait, Guru Maharaj is taking tiffin. I shall give you a little Prasada'. Though the gentleman did not quite comprehend this attitude, he was sure that the Swami was perfectly sincere. The Swami himself once observed that the eyes and mind of the real devotee got peculiarly transformed, and if others had not such eyes and mind, it was not the fault of the devotee.

In The Mould

Swami Ramakrishnananda was born in an obscure village in Bengal in 1863 of very pious parents, his father being a great worshipper of the Divine Mother. As a boy Sasibhushan—such was his pre-monastic name—showed great promise. He was uniformly developed in hand, head and heart, often spoken of by Swami Vivekananda as the constituents of an ideal character. He was very strong in physique, exceptionally brilliant in his studies and intensely susceptible to spiritual ideas. As he grew up to be a young

man his hunger for spiritual knowledge increased.   Though
a son of an orthodox father, he joined the Brahmo Samaj
which at that time was attracting educated and sincere seekers.
But he was anxious to see spirituality translated in one's
life; he was thirsting for realization.   If there is truth, it
must be found out; if there is God, He must be seen.   At
this juncture of his life he came in contàct with the Saint of
Dakshineswar, and all his doubts were set at rest.   Here
was a man 'who took his stand on the adamantine rock of
realization, and not on the quick-sands of reasoning or
learning'.   He was not merely a man but a movement, the
harbinger of a spiritual renaissance unprecedented in the
history of India.   On hearing of the saint from Kesav Chandra
Sen, he went to see him.   He 'talked a great deal that day;
but never again.'

The first meeting made a tremendous impression on his
mind and his life took a new turn.   He began to practise
spiritual disciplines with great earnestness.   When Sri Ramakrishna fell seriousɟy ill, he gave up his career to serve him
heart and soul.   Imperceptibly he was being trained also
by the Master,who was fully aware of the spiritual potentiality
of this young man.

A saint-maker that Sri Ramakrishna was, he cast souls
of his choice in a supreme mould of perfection in a way which
escaped detection and imitation.   And when he passed away,
he left behind him a band of disciples whom the world afterwards recognized as rare spiritual luminaries.

One day when the young Sasi was going out of his room
on some urgent business, the Master interrupted him and
said pointing his finger to himself, 'You see, He whom you
seek is this, He is this.'   That gave him the clue to his life's
ideal and with this he solved all his problems and the problems of others.   'The Guru's work is to give the right

direction,' said he in later life. His Guru also gave him by that one sentence the key to all understanding. The purpose of his life was found, the goal fixed, and what remained was only practical testing and demonstration of this truth in life.

A Saga of Service

After the passing away of Sri Ramakrishna, Sasi Maharaj kept a vigil over his relics. He did it with great attention and one-pointed love, observing meticulously all the minute details of service which he was rendering even when the Master was in flesh and blood. When all his brother-disciples were intensely engaged in practising rigorous spiritual disciplines and were now and then going out of the monastery for visiting places of pilgrimage, it was Sasi Maharaj who stuck to the service of the Master. And that was the beginning of the Order of Ramakrishna. Swami Vivekananda who actually gave shape to the Order and founded the Ramakrishna Mission recognized his great contribution. He said:

'He was the main pillar of the Math. Without him life in the monastery would have been impossible. Often the monks would be lost in prayer and meditation with no thought of food, and Sasi would wait with their meals ready, and even drag them out of their meditation.'

Thus he continued for twelve long years serving the Master in the shrine and looking after the needs of the residents of the Baranagar and Alambazar Maths. Love of service was ingrained in him. As a boy he was very dutiful and serviceable to his parents. And even in later life he felt that he could not render enough service to them, for a higher call had come. Though he was very scrupulous regarding the rules of monastic life, he did not hesitate to take to teaching in a school at Baranagar to maintain the Math and thus serve the Master and brother-monks. This spirit of service was manifest even in his dealings with the people who came to visit the Math. He was so much imbued with the spirit of service, that he preferred to do all the work of the Master with his own hands, though his assistants were always eager to help him. He laid down his life working rather too hard for the cause of the Master. He spent the major part of his stay in Madras in an annexe undergoing many physical inconveniences as well as financial uncertainty. He used to take a good number of classes every week in different parts of the city, over and above private interviews and conversations. He went out for preaching the message of the Master to many distant places including Bombay, Ceylon and Burma. He had to go to almost all parts of South India. Through his inspiration and supervision the activities in the states of Mysore and Kerala were started. He invited Swami Brahmananda and the Holy Mother to Madras and spared no pains to make their stay comfortable. With them he went down to Rameshwaram and other holy places to look to their needs. He never went out for any other pilgrimage. Thus he worked for fourteen long years in Madras. As a result, his robust health broke down. This is the price a pioneer pays for his uphill task. His work was unostentatious and potent, and it is flowering now. The seed that he sowed has grown into a mighty tree. The present success is really due to his self-immolation. Even as the blood of the martyrs is the seed of the Church, so is the self-immolation of Swami Ramakrishnananda for the growth of the Order. Rightly has his life been described as a saga of service.

Personal and Impersonal

As a result of his wonderful constancy of devotion, the ritualistic worship of the Master became established in the

Order. He was thus the originator of the ritualistic aspect which is the concrete form of the spirit for which the Ramakrishna Brotherhood stands. Swami Premananda, who himself especially represented the devotional and ritualistic aspect of this Movement, said appreciatively of the Swami, 'In fact, he and none of us is the founder of the Math and its shrine. I can proclaim emphatically that he is the creator of all this.' He evolved a detailed system of worship of the Master culling appropriate mantras from the ancient scriptures. It was he who gave a shape to the vows of Brahmacharya initiation that the young novitiates take.

Every great spiritual movement has two sets of interdependent teachings. One represents the aspect of ritual, which is centred on a personality, and the other represents the aspect of philosophy, centred on principles. The gospel of detached action and love and worship of Sri Krishna, the Four Noble Truths and the Godhood of Gautama Buddha, the Sermon on the Mount and the sonship of Jesus Christ and the teachings about the Unity of God and the Prophethood of Mohammad represent these two aspects. There is an organic relation between the two. Mere worship of a personality without the idea of the impersonal at the background makes the devotee sentimental or fanatical; mere philosophical principles without a scope for concrete expression degenerate into feeble intellectualism and vapid cosmopolitanism.

Swami Ramakrishnanada represents both the aspects. But his especial contribution consists in holding a concrete ideal before the members and devotees of the Order who require a way of life, a programme for practical spirituality, that will help them to imbibe the impersonal ideas the Master embodied in his life. By trying to relate all their activities to the Master, they will gradually be able to forget their selfish

ends and remember constantly the Master for whom they
work. 'As the devotee empties himself of himself he is
infilled with God,' said the Swami. Thus there will be 'a
complete shifting of the centre of gravity of their life,' as
Sister Nivedita puts it, from their little self to the Higher
Self. That is the goal of all religions, of all spiritual disciplines. When a **devotee** engages himself in the work and
worship of the Master throughout the day, he will slowly be
full of him, and gradually it will dawn on him that the Master
in human form is the manifestaton of the Divine, an incarnation of God. The worship and contemplation of Sri Ramakrishna the person, will lead them to understand and appreciate Sri Ramakrishna the Principle.

Commissioned

Swami Ramakrishnananda had a mission in life. When
we study his life and his contributions to the Order, it seems
to us that his special mission consisted in his holding Sri
Ramakrishna before others as an Incarnation of God who
was a living presence and whose life and personality have
opened a new way of salvation.

Swami Vivekananda viewed the Ramakrishna Ideal
as the integration of the various methods of God-realization.
The modern age being a complex one, the human character
should be the perfect efflorescence of the total man which
can face the terrific challenges of the times. Differences
in various walks of life arise because of various approaches
to problems. Hence to be able to live in peace and harmony
in this contracted world of today, modern man must develop
a wider outlook and a richer personality. Likewise man's
approach to the ultimate problems of life—his approach to
God or the Absolute—has also to undergo a necessary orientation. In the traditional way, a particular method was

followed. The intellectual would realize through discrimination, the emotional through devotion, the mystic through meditation and the active through work. Though the practice of all the four is the ideal, a spiritual aspirant can realize the ultimate goal through any of these methods. Moreover, he showed that they were inter-related, as the very nature of man is the combination of these psychological aptitudes. But his most predominant contribution in this field is the gospel of service, of viewing man as God, which is rooted in his and in the Master's Advaitic realization of the Divine in all creatures.

The combination of the traditional method of worship emphasized by Swami Ramakrishnananda and the dynamic way of viewing God in man promulgated by Swami Vivekananda is very significant. By this, work and worship, traditionalism and dynamism, personal and impersonal, finite and infinite, human and divine, cult and culture are all perfectly harmonized and blended into a complete ideal that can be emulated with profit by men of different temperaments and endowments.

Swami Ramakrishnananda went out to various places for spreading the message of the Master and it was he who actually founded, organized and infused life and blood into the Ramakrishna Movement in South India. At once an ideal monk, an ecstatic devotee and an astute scholar, the Swami left profound and abiding impressions wherever he went to preach the gospel of the Master. Calm and quiet, austere in habits and grave in appearance, Swami Ramakrishnananda presented in himself a beautiful contrast to the Cyclonic Monk, Swami Vivekananda.

While Swamiji commanded, Sasi Maharaj appealed to reason and heart. Swamiji was a great leader who created a vast upheaval in the whole society; Sasi Maharaj had comparatively a limited field. This was, as it were, a division of labour. Both upheaval and settling down, stirring of emotion and the judicial canalizing of it, generating enthusiasm and the sustaining of it, organizing of a movement and the consolidation of it, were essential. And Swami Vivekananda had attempted both, but he did not live long. So while it was the work of the short-lived leader to inspire and organize the enthusiasm of the whole society, it fell to the share of Sasi Maharaj to maintain, increase and direct that enthusiasm to the cherished goal.

The formative influence that he exerted on a few individuals speaks volumes about the quality of the work Sasi Maharaj did. And this he did in the most natural way. He was ever full of Sri Ramakrishna and would always talk about him. To him the Master was an Incarnation of the age who came into this sophisticated world as an unlettered man yet possessing the highest wisdom by which he changed the lives of many. 'In an age in which money is the measure of greatness, he stood for non-possession. When individualism and egotism are the law, he had no egotism at all. He could seldom utter the two words "I" and "mine". As his own ego was totally obliterated, the cosmic "I" of God took hold of him and manifested itself through him.' Thus he would speak of Sri Ramakrishna in such inspiring terms and with so much devotion that people came to know of the Master. People were enamoured of, nay dazzled by, Swami Vivekananda for his dynamism, his great intellectual brilliance, his regal bearing, his leonine form, his patriotism and his love for the masses. But they had no chance to know Sri Ramakrishna, the power behind this great personality. But Swami Ramakrishnananda was essentially a devotee. His voice would be choked when speaking of the Master. Through him the people of the South came to know of Sri Ramakrishna and a few chosen people took him as their life's ideal. He entered the lives of these devotees and changed them. It was they who were his active assistants in working out the programme of work given by Swamiji.

Vivekananda's Plan Materialized

Swami Vivekananda had an idea of bringing together both the lay and monastic devotees of Sri Ramakrishna in the service of the Master, and so we find that one of the objects of the Ramakrishna Mission is 'to carry on, in conjunction with lay workers, religious, philanthropic and charitable activities, looking upon all men, women and children irrespective of caste, creed, nationality and colour, as veritable manifestations of the Divine'. While organizing the activities of the Mission Sasi Maharaj worked out this plan of the leader. He inspired the householder devotees to work for the cause of the Master, howsoever modest the work might be. And he took active part in starting and guiding the various activities of the Mission. Because of his inspiration and guidance, a good number of institutions came up in South India and continue to thrive today. The combination of the lay and monastic workers was due to his conscious absorption of the idea of Swami Vivekananda on this point.

To make religion vital in the life of the nation it will not do to keep it reserved only for a few all-renouncing monks. He repeatedly declared that Sri Ramakrishna came to reinstate Dharma in all its aspects. He came to fulfil and not to destroy. So he wanted pious and selfless householders to come forward to serve the Master and thus be blessed.

His Orthodoxy and Catholicity

Sri Ramakrishna had the realization of the ultimate Reality through different paths extant in the world. He

15

underwent the disciplines recommended by Vaishnavism and Saktaism, Advaita and Dvaita systems, as well as Christianity and Islam. This harmony of faiths is a great contribution of Sri Ramakrishna. Swami Ramakrishnananda imbibed this spirit of harmony from his Master and so there was a wonderful blending of orthodoxy and catholicity in him. The orthodoxy of observing ritualistic details in worship and of following rules about food and dress was in his very nature. So Swami Vivekananda, while selecting a suitable monk for the South, which is famous for its orthodoxy and for its love of the ancient culture, chose Swami Ramakrishnananda and sent him to Madras with the remark, 'I shall send you one who is more orthodox than your most orthodox men of the South and who is at the same time unique and unsurpassed in his worship and meditation on God.'

Swami Ramakrishnananda of course satisfied the orthodox people by observing all the accepted codes of orthodoxy. But his was not the usual type of orthodoxy. He was orthodox in a deeper sense. His Master was a veritable Incarnation of catholicity, and Swami Ramakrishnananda was orthodox in pursuance of this catholicity of the Master. Orthodoxy is often synonymous with bigotry, which denies unfamiliar aspects of the manifestation of the Divine. But Swami Ramakrishnananda was always devoted, in acknowledging the totality of the manifestation of the Divinity and carried through the implications in the realities of life. He was equally respectful towards all faiths and all incarnations. His book *Sri Krishna the Pastoral and King-maker* shows his deep reverence to this great Avatar. His reflections on the Koran show how deeply he entered into the spirit of this holy book: He wrote a classical life of Sri Ramanuja which records his great esteem for the Acharya. His love for Jesus was unique. He was so catholic, that he would be seen now and then to kneel down before the altar in the Santhome Church in Madras. Incarnations to him were the embodiments of Eternal Religion 'which never deteriorates; it is man that deteriorates. And the incarnations 'come to redeem humanity.' So we must show our veneration to all of them, and that was his catholicity. That is why, when a speaker spoke against Sri Sankara in course of his talk, Swami Ramakrishnananda protested immediately.

Though he was very catholic in his attitude towards all faiths, he was no eclectic. An eclectic culls truths from various sources and makes of them a bouquet. But as it is not rooted in the genius of a particular group, community or culture and as its new anthological scripture has no experiential validity, it cannot produce the desired result. It is good as a comparative study but it fails as a faith with enduring vitality. The orthodoxy on the other hand has depth and intensity but it lacks width of vision and charity. Swami Ramakrishnananda's catholicity was rooted in the synthesizing and harmonizing realizations of his Master. This synthetic attitude combines the ardour and intensity of the orthodox with the breadth and generosity of the eclectic. It affirms that all faiths are true and all teachers are great. It sees the unity running through the diverse manifestations. It does not believe in uniformity through standardization. His catholicity was not rootless, it resulted from his realization of the unity of existence. As it takes its stand on the realization of the ultimate principle, it is not afraid of truth from whichever quarter it might come. And this spirit he imbibed because of his deep faith in his Guru whom he viewed as the fulfilment of all incarnations.

As Sri Ramakrishna was unique as an Incarnation, Swami Ramakrishnananda also was unique as a disciple of such an Incarnation.

'I AM THE WAY'

WHILE we discuss the equal validity of all religions as propounded by Sri Ramakrishna and Vedanta, often a question is asked, 'But Christ himself said, "I am the way.".' This appears to be a genuine problem of sincere followers of any particular religion. The early Church flourished on the slogan 'The only way to God'. Even now some evangelists speak about 'the one way'. The reference is to Christ's reply to Thomas, who asked, 'Lord, we know not whither thou goest, and how can we know the way?' And Jesus replied, 'I am the way, the truth and the life; no man cometh unto the Father, but by me.' In another context he said, 'I am the door,' and also 'I am come as a light unto the world, that whosoever believeth in me should not abide in darkness.' (John 14.5-6, 10.9, 11.46)

Comparative religion now makes us aware of similar statements of great teachers in almost all religions. Sri Krishna says, 'Relinquishing all Dharmas take refuge in Me alone, I will liberate thee from all sins, grieve not.' (Gita 18.66) The Koran declared, 'There is only one God and Mohammed is His messenger.' How to reconcile these seemingly exclusive claims by different world teachers? If we cannot do it, all of them become suspect.

To reconcile these statements a passage from the commentary of Acharya Sankara will be useful. Sankara, while commenting on a passage in the Brihadaranyaka Upanishad (1.4.10), quotes the sage Vamadeva, saying 'I was Manu, and the sun (Rig Veda 4.26.1) and explains that Vamadeva realized his own Self as identical with Brahman and "in that state of realization of the Self and Brahman, visualized these Mantras' (p. 61, Swami Madhavananda's translation of the commentary). Herein we find the harmonizing principle of the philosophy of Vedanta operating. This enables us to understand that all the great teachers who declared themselves to be the main avenue to God or as the ultimate refuge, really told this not as human beings, but because they realized their identity or intimate relationship with the Godhead. The speciality is their realization but, of course, it is not exclusive. This is how we can accept all the great teachers claiming the uniqueness to be true and need not throw out others for the sake of one, creating a cleavage among the followers of different religions. It will free us from the doubt about our exclusvive position when we face a good votary of another religion. In these days of open knowledge, this is the only way.

In another way we can look at it which amounts to the same thing. The great teachers have been recognized in some of the religions as Incarnations of God. God comes down to earth when virtue declines or vice prevails. Or He sends His messengers with special powers. So it is natural for them to declare their uniqueness. No one will hear a teacher, says Sri Ramakrishna, unless he has a command from God. In such a case he is particularly conscious of his mandate. An Avatar naturally has a feeling of mission in his life, even from his early days.

Moreover, in Hinduism there is an idea of an Incarnation of the age. Such teachers stress particular teachings according to the needs of the times. The faith of the people quickens by a direct declaration of a great teacher about the uniqueness of the teaching or his mandate and the mission. Humanity down the ages has followed such great teachers. In these days of easy travel and communication, it is impossible to be exclusive. Such a method of reconciling sustains our reverence for all the teachers and so will pave the way for better understanding among religious groups of the world.

THE STRUGGLE FOR THE IDEAL

MAN needs an ideal. It is necessary for making his life purposeful. It helps him to direct his energies to a desired goal. But how difficult it is to choose an ideal! The very first problem for him is whether to opt for a life of idealism. Will it be practicable? Is he fit for it? The vast majority of people throughout the world are running after the ordinary joys of life. They feel, having any ideal is detrimental to the proper enjoyment of the pleasures of life. Ideals create conflict, because life consists, they say, of compromises. So they think it is better to do away with all idealism and thus free the mind from all compunctions, and this alone can ensure undisturbed enjoyment of the things of the world. Hence, often they are against all idealism and ridicule those who try to follow an ideal.

Again a vast number of people in the world recognize the existence of higher ideals and their beauty but they think these are reserved for a chosen few. Weak people as they are, how can they think of practising these high ideals? So drifting, falling in inertia, is the only way out. The amount of awareness and the preparedness to look for defects in their life and thinking that is necessary for following an ideal is too much for them.

Then there are people who have opted for a life of idealism. But how difficult they find it on the way! When they made the choice they thought all struggles would be over. But alas! the ideal has a tendency of receding farther and farther. Finer and subtler ramifications of the same ideal present themselves and at times they feel it is too much for them.

True, they are not as grossly non-idealistic as many are, but still with regard to the high ideal they feel their incompetence. Feeling one's insignificance is not pleasant. Moreover, doubt comes, if the ideal becomes more and more subtle and difficult, is it possible to realize it at all? Is it worth partially doing so? If the goal is too distant, is it not proper and more sensible to accept only a suitable ideal, realizable in one's duration of life and in the foreseeable future? The belief nowadays in future births is not strong. The prospect of a continuous struggle for a succession of lives is too discouraging. Hence many people prefer to pitch their aspiration on a lower ideal, on a par with their capacity.

The higher the prize the harder is the exertion. The nobler the goal the greater is the sacrifice. It is of course human to be staggered at the immensity of the task ahead. But proportionate effort is the rule of all successful undertakings in the world. Great men will all testify to this. Edison failed 20,000 times; still he was indomitable. Was his effort a total failure? No. 'I have learnt 20,000 ways in which the thing cannot be done,' he said. Such are the courage and patience, energy and perseverance that are wanted from a man with an ambitious ideal. This is true in the spiritual realm also. Unless we are prepared to forgo the little gratifications, we cannot aspire after the higher ideal. Of course, when a man is honest and feels that he is not equal to the task, a lower ideal is a necessity for him. Hypocrisy is more objectionable than proper appraisal of one's capacity and weakness. But denouncing a higher ideal simply because one thinks it is impracticable is moral cowardice.

Failure in a life of idealism is inevitable. But it does not mean that idealists should view failures with too much concern. The founders of great idealistic movements advise us not to be cowed down by failures, for effort is what is necessary; and according to spiritual teachers no effort is in vain; each contributes to the final emancipation. About failures and efforts, Swami Vivekananda says:

> Never mind failures; they are quite natural, they are the beauty of life, these failures. What would life be without them? It would not be worth having if it were not for struggles. Where would be the poetry of life? Never mind the struggles, the mistakes. I never heard a cow tell a lie, but it is only a cow—never a man. So never mind these failures, these little backslidings; hold the ideal a thousand times, and if you fail a thousand times, make the attempt once more. (*Complete Works*, Vol. II, p. 152.)

> He who struggles is better than he who never attempts. Even to look on one who has given up has a purifying effect. Stand up for God; let the world go. Make no compromise. (VII. 99)

It is open to anyone to say that human nature has not been known to rise to such heights. But if we have made unexpected progress in physical sciences, why should we do less in the science of the soul? (114)

> For a fighter, the fight itself is victory, for he takes delight in it alone. (581)
> The goal ever recedes from us. The greater the progress, the greater the recognition of our unworthiness. Satisfaction lies in the effort, not in the attainment. Full effort is full victory. (63.)
> Joy lies in the fight, in the attempt, in the suffering involved, not in the victory itself. For, victory is implied in such an attempt. (583)

The problem of choosing an ideal becomes more difficult for young people. But adolescence is the time for opting for an ideal. Often it is done unconsciously, probably on coming in contact with a man of idealism. But soon the youth wants to find out the support for it. That support must be both intellectual and social. With the growth of his intellect, the educated youth wants to test everything in the fire of reason. As his experience is less, imagination plays a great part. Then he requires social acceptance of the ideal chosen. If the society is indifferent, he is very much disheartened. Often he is depressed and becomes critical. Sometimes he becomes a revolutionary and wants to bring the entire society by force to his way of thinking. But alas! society is by nature given to inertia, sloth. Members are often self-seeking. It is a terrible struggle for all adolescents to adjust to such a society. It becomes more so for those who opt for an ideal. Psychologists may tell us that from imagination the adolescent comes down to the level of reality. But does that satisfy an idealistic mind? His anxious query, why things are what they are, rings through the atmosphere. Worldly-wise people may try to make him acquainted with the 'real' life. But is that beneficial? What about the progress of society? How did it march forward? Is it not because of the efforts of idealistic men and women? So is it not unnecessary then to make all people 'realistic'? The world needs the idealists. They are the salt of the earth. Moreover, without any ideal, life loses all its value, at least for the sensitive minds. Swamiji echoes the sentiment when he says:

> It is a great thing to take up a grand ideal in life and then give up one's whole life to it. For what otherwise is the value of life, this vegetating, little, low life of man? Subordinating it to one high ideal is the only value that life has. (III. 168.)

But alas! how difficult, how agonizing is the path to idealism! Difficult is the realization of the ideal, even after choosing it, for it is often seen that we compromise on the way. Not that we give up the ideal wholesale. We still swear by it.

But the tendency is to compromise. Practical difficulties are there, and must be reckoned with. But ultimately what do we see? In a short time the standard goes so much down that the ideal is practically lost. But protagonists of a life of idealism have warned us: Do not compromise, do not lower the ideal. Even if it is impossible to realize it, it must remain in its pristine purity. Probably better men will come forward in the future who will put it into practice. As Swami Vivekananda said:

> There are two tendencies in human nature, one to harmonise the ideal with the life, and the other to elevate the life to the ideal. (II. 291)

> You must struggle towards the ideal, and if a man comes who wants to bring that ideal down to your level, and teach a religion that does not carry that highest ideal, do not listen to him. (II. 296)

> Mark you, let us all be honest. If we cannot follow the ideal, let us confess our weakness, but not degrade it; let not any try to pull it down. (IV. 141)

> If a hundred fall in the fight, seize the flag and carry it on. God is true for all that, no matter who fails. Let him who falls hand on the flag to another to carry on; it can never fall. (VII. 98)

Though the flag must be held aloft, we sometimes wonder, is it not better for weak individuals to have an intermediate ideal which is easier, more tangible and more realizable? In real life we actually do that. But if we know the connection between the highest ideal and the intermediate one, and if the lower is so designed that it leads to the higher, much of despair, anxiety and sense of failure might vanish, and at the same time progress towards the ultimate goal also will be achieved. It was for this that the ancient Rishis fixed the goal of life as Liberation but at the same time accorded an honoured place to all the legitimate pursuits of life. This accommodation was done with an integrated philosophy. The idea of the fourfold goal of life with the ultimate ideal of Liberation shows that this scheme took into consideration the various factors of human life and made suitable and necessary concessions to the human temperaments and requirements. But in so doing, it never gave up the goal. A man following this scheme is apt to get at the ideal by stages. If they did not so accommodate, men, weak as they are, were apt to go out of the purview of the ideal, with painful struggle on the way and with disastrous results at the end for both themselves and the society at large.

For most of us the immediate moments of life are quite important. So we are advised that **we should pay as much attention to** the means as to the end. The advantage is, that thereby we become thorough regarding immediate duty, it being limited, and moreover we do not meet with failure and disappointment. Little efforts for little successes prepare the mind for bigger exertions and nobler objectives. And ultimately perfection, the highest goal, also may be achieved.

The great thought-leaders of the world admitted the necessity of this. Swami Vivekananda says:

Every man should take up his own ideal and endeavour to accomplish it. That is a surer way of progress than taking up other men's ideals, which he can never hope to accomplish. For instance, we take a child and at once set him the task of walking twenty miles. Either the little one dies, or one in a thousand crawls the twenty miles to reach the end exhausted and half-dead. That is like what we generally try to do with the world. All the men and women in any society, are not of the same mind, capacity, or of the same power to do things; they must have different ideals, and we have no right to sneer at any ideal. Let everyone do the best he can for realising his own ideal. Nor is it right that I should be judged by your standard or you by mine. The apple tree should not be judged by the standard of the oak, nor the oak by that of the apple. To judge the apple tree you must take the apple standard, and for the oak, its own standard. (I. 39)

Our duty is to encourage everyone in his struggle to live up to his own highest ideal, and strive at the same time to make the ideal as near as possible to the truth. (I. 39)

The ideal of man is to see God in everything. But if you cannot, see Him in one thing, in that thing which you like best, and then see Him in another. So on you can go. There is infinite life before the soul. Take your time and you will achieve your end. (II. 153)

So we see Swami Vivekananda repeatedly reminding us that every man must be judged by his own ideals. If he strives for his own ideal well, he has done his part.

In judging others we always judge them by our own ideals. That is not as it should be. Everyone must be judged according to his own ideal, and not by that of anyone else. (II. 105)

The great lesson to learn is that I am not the standard by which the whole universe is to be judged; each man is to be judged by his own ideal. (V. 168)

What exactly does this intermediate ideal or the middle way mean? It will be found that the passage to the goal constitutes that intermediate ideal. So when Moksha is the goal, Dharma, Artha and Kama are the intermediate goals. If equality is the goal, then whatever enhances equality is the intermediate one. If brotherhood is the goal, then whatever helps the growth of it is the middle one. If love, oneness, unity, are the goal, then whatever tends to increase these is the intermediate goal which is in a sense the means or step to the ultimate goal. And this is the only way of realizing an ideal, from a smaller to the bigger, from a lower to the higher, from a grosser to the subtler. That is the method. The advantage of this is that our enthusiasm is not dampened before an ideal that is too high. If the highest peak to scale is not within our present capacities, the smaller ones can be conquered. These victories in their turn will supply the necessary strength and courage for higher and more difficult objectives. This will show that as much attention will have to be paid to this realizable ideal as is demanded by the ultimate ideal. And this is a cardinal idea of Karma Yoga: Give as much attention to the means as to the goal.

Moreover, while struggling for this intermediate ideal, i.e., for the means, we may, without harm, even forget the ultimate ideal. It is not necessary to think of the goal at every step. Of course, it will be good to remember the goal now and then. That will make us aware whether we are on the right track. And as we cross each obstacle, our spirit will be stronger, determination firmer, confidence greater and we will be prepared for the next stage. It is for this that the well-known saying appeals to us so much: 'One step enough for me'. In this way if we can lead the civilization to higher and higher steps, it is quite probable that the highest ideal will one day become real. Even otherwise, as individuals we will be satisfied that we have done our part and met with some success, however meagre it may be. The full detachment, the entire unconcern, the complete abandon may be reserved for the few, but for the vast majority of us who are not so stout-hearted, nor very faint-hearted, this idea of an intermediate goal will be quite sufficient and beneficial. As it will be in tune with the highest, it will gradually lead us to the ultimate goal, the *summum bonum* of life, the acme of all human endeavour.

THE GOSPEL OF SERVICE AND SAINT TUKARAM

SAINTS have great influence on society. In fact, it is
because of these men of God that all higher values persist in
it. Otherwise the gravitational pull of life would have
dragged man down to the lowest rung of culture. Among
them, the Avataras or Divine incarnations have great
enduring influence. Sister Nivedita once described this phenomenon, saying that the society tends to lie low, horizontal;
it is these great souls who are, as it were, perpendicular.
uncompromising to the society's tendency of lying low.
Their teachings try to pull society up in the direction of
culture and nobler virtues. But with the passage of time,
the strength and society goes down to its original position.
Then arises another Avatara. So it can safely be said, saints
are the leaders of society, especially in the field of thought.
Through their exhortations people derive spiritual, moral
and often social sustenance. The history of different
regions substantiates this point. Competent scholars on
Maharashtra have pointed out that a potent factor in the
development of the idea of nationhood was the teachings of
the medieval saints, Tukaram, Ramdas and others. Prof.
Limaye says that the Maratha nobles contributed material
power and 'the moral force of the movement was derived from
the preaching of the great saints'. Justice Ranade too said
that, as a result of the work done by the saints and prophets
of Maharashtra, 'there came into existence the beginnings
of a national mind.' Prof. Patwardhan states in the following
strain regarding the democratizing influence of saints:

'For five successive centuries Maharashtra was the abode of that noblest and truest of all democracies, the democracy of the *Bhakti* school. . . . (The saints) not only made the literature but also made the people a nation'. (Cf. *Life and Teachings of Tukaram* by Fraser & Edwards, p. 19-21).

The ideal of a nation is thus the cumulative effect of the teachings of saints and thought-leaders. In encouraging man to strive for God, they stress some of the social virtues. The national ideal may be taken as the teachings common more or less to all these thought-leaders. Renunciation and service, according to Swami Vivekananda, are such ideals. They are the two broad terms which can cover the different facets of spiritual and social striving. The gospel of service to fellowmen is a grand one. The importance of love of others and serving them is well recognized in the religious tradition. As a scholar on the Bhakti school remarks:

This definition of Truth as *Love of others as thy own self* is given in the *Bhagavata Purana* which is universally regarded as the standard authority of the devotional school second only to the Bhagavad Gita or the Celestial Song, worshipped as India's New Testament. In several places it expressedly declares that he is the highest Yogi (man of contemplation and action) who looks upon and treats others as his own self. Taking up that teaching, Jnaneshwar, the premier saint of Maharashtra, to 'whom all succeeding saints including Tukaram, owed a good deal of their religion, and who is regarded as the progenitor of Maratha nationality, which culminated in the great Sivaji's Maratha Empire, declared that there is no acquisition equal to that of *samya*, i.e., the power of regarding others and treating them as your own self. If we interpret that by the light of the texts in the Upanishads and the books of our Saints, which say that there is nothing higher than or even equal to Truth, we come to the same idea of Truth as that defined in the *Bhagavata*

Purana. That is made clear beyond doubt by Sivaji's spiritual adviser, Saint Ramadas, who defined Truth in the Marathi language of Western India as *Ananyapana,* i.e., 'the condition of loving others as thy own self.'

(N. G. Chandavarakar)

It will be found that though Swami Vivekananda was the first in modern days to give much stress on this idea of service, it had never been lacking in the older tradition. The sayings of Saint Tukaram of Maharashtra may be taken as an illustration. He says in one of the Abhangas that a devotee of God has many qualities, but compassion to all beings is the most striking one.

> Much and weighty though a man's merit be, if he is merciful towards all creatures, then alone is he a devotee of Hari. He styles himself their messenger; the slave of his own slaves, if they follow Hari in body, speech and mind. If a man is merciful to all creatures, if he sees everywhere the Lord of the Senses, such a man he never forgets, he follows him everywhere. Tuka says: To his suppliants he is a retreat of adamant, immovable. Such as wait on him come back to rebirth no more.

(2251—Fraser & Marathe)

As a religious leader, Tukaram naturally gives his views about the conduct of a saint. He dwells with special earnestness on the services of the saints to mankind. Often he bursts out into statements like the following, showing the importance of service in a God-guided life.

> 'It is the glory of the saints that they came to bless the world; they wear out their bodies in serving others; forbearing love is their stock in trade; there is no self-love within them. Tuka says: Their happiness is in the happiness of others.'   (2375)

Tukaram again exhorts man to keep the company of saints and holy men 'who help to save mankind by serving their fellows'.

16

A developed soul sees God not only in man but in the lower creations too. So Tukaram speaks of service even of animals:

> 'Despise dogs and pigs for their bodies, but show them respect for their souls—embrace spiritually beasts and trees.'   (876)

In one of his songs Tukaram speaks about the friend of the oppressed whom he considers 'as the very image of the divine'.

> 'Whoever makes himself the friend of the oppressed should be recognized as a true saint.
>
> Know that God dwells in him.
>
> Mild as butter both within and without, such is the nature of a good man.
>
> He who takes the unprotected to his heart, who shows to his servants and to his own son the same compassion.
>
> Tuka says: How often shall I tell you that he is the very image of the Divine?'   (266—Deming)

Saint Tukaram was a devotee through and through. He is all for direct contact with God. Mere rituals have no meaning for him. Service to others, according to him, is the sure way of the manifestation of God in a devotee.

> 'He who renounces all is ever pure, even as the flame that clings not to any impurity.
>
> He who is truthful in speech throughout this worldly course is like the lotus to which the water never clings.
>
> He who serves other creatures and shows them compassion, in him the supreme Spirit dwells.
>
> He who utters not nor listens to criticism of others, is indeed Janardan dwelling in the world.

Tuka says: He who knows not the secret, is exhausted by ritual observances.'   (267—D)

The problem of good and evil, of merit and sin, is an eternal one. The great sage Vyasa said that helping others is Punya, virtue; and tyrannizing over others is Papa, sin: Saint Tukaram in the same strain says:

'Merit consists in service to others; sin is injury done to them; there is no other way of gaining anything.'
(268-D)

Then he adds:

'Tuka says: Our own gain or destruction lies clear before us; let each do as he chooses.'

When the good and the bad are known through discrimination, guided by the directions of saints, it remains for us to practise the good and shun the evil.

Service of man in the case of a devotee is the overflowing of his love for God. He sees his chosen Lord in all creatures and goes to love them. As the saint says:

'God is our friend; through Him all are our friends.'
(224-D)

But even in the act of loving he is ever conscious of the Lord through whom he is related to all created beings. So in another hymn he says:

'Do but this; let the wives and wealth of others be nothing to you.

Be not covetous, but follow your occupation comfortably.

Live peacefully without any covert struggle.

Enjoy the sweet and fragrant name; be not slothful in uttering the name of Rama.

Be the friend of everyone; speak no word of evil import.

> Avoid the wicked; exert yourself for the saints.
>
> If you form any hopes apart from God, they will end in the loss of all hopes.
>
> If you foster the thirst for things, you will never find happiness.
>
> Trust and be patient; let God be your stay.
>
> God will always take care of such; no one will be an exception, says Tuka.'   (269-D)

Service takes various forms.   It can be physical help to a needy person, or enlightenment to an intellectually deficient man, or moral and spiritual help to an exasperated soul.   As a leader of eternal values Saint Tukaram naturally lays more stress on spiritual service.

> 'The good one will make it his aim to proclaim his true blessings, and will make known such moral rules as he perceives.
>
> Yet we are in the hands of One who sets us dancing as he sees fit.
>
> Infinite is the merit of him who points the way to others; countless the obligations he lays upon us.
>
> Tuka says, You have been merciful, O saints; you have done your duty.'   (270-D)

The idea of Karma is paramount in Indian consciousness. Our religion and philsophy have been deeply influenced by this idea of effect being produced commensurate with the cause.   So the saint warns us that unsympathetic people and tyrants will lose all their accumulated   merits.

> 'If a man rejoices over the misfortunes of others; his own feelings and their pain will recoil upon himself.
>
> Harbour not such thoughts in your mind; do not store up for yourself a capital of sin.
>
> This will linger in your mind as torment and affliction; it will be consumed by fire and its place of rest burned up.

> Tuka says: Thus all your merits will be destroyed; whatever is destined for us will be brought to pass by the operation of our past.' (271-D)

The philosophy of work for a religious man has two sources. A theist looks upon God as the Supreme. All created beings are His creatures. So love of the Jiva is also essential for a theist. The Advaitin believes in the unity of existence. Brahman is all pervading; in fact He is all that exists. So a follower of Advaita sees God in everything. The devotee Tukaram also gets this mood of one existence and says that a man with this realization sees God everywhere.

> 'A man who has truly become God himself will look on all mankind as gods. Others do but tell idle tales to amuse their hearers. A man who has dined cannot understand that others are hungry and thirsty; he thinks they are comfortable like himself. Tuka says: What we want is experience; tall talk is idle.' (2208)

Thus we see that the idea of dedicated service takes various forms and has its inspiration from different sources. But one thing is common, that all people must serve humanity whatever their philosophical persuasion. Saints like Tukaram have raised our social conscience down the centuries, and when we find these holy men stressing service as an ideal, we can easily understand why Swami Vivekananda spoke of it as one of the national ideals of India. Service is in fact becoming a world ideal. The importance of our acquaintance with their writings is that it will free service from the materialistic idea of self-interest and make it spiritually motivated. It is precisely because of this that Swami Vivekananda spoke about the twin ideals of renunciation and service, 'for one's own liberation and for the good of the world.'

SUDDEN CONVERSION

Sri Ramakrishna said:

'There are two kinds of Siddhas (perfect men), Sadhana-siddhas and Kripasiddhas (those who have gained perfection through religious discipline and those who have gained perfection through grace). To get a good crop, some have to irrigate their fields with great labour by cutting canals, or by drawing water. But some others are lucky enough to be saved all this trouble of getting water; for there comes the rain and floods the whole field. Almost all have to perform devotional practices assiduously in order to get freedom from the shackles of Maya. But Kripa-siddhas are saved from all this trouble; they attain perfection through the grace of God. Their number, however, is extremely small.'

In spiritual communion there is a peculiar fraternity of saints. When we study the lives of holy men and women of different countries we find the two types of them, those who realize God through a definite spiritual discipline passing through gradual development, and also those who realize suddenly only through His grace. The latter idea covers a substantial portion of the literature of saints and mystics in the form of confession, autobiography or songs. It is known as sudden conversion, when there is no apparent cause or previous preparation.

The word conversion is from the Latin *conversio* (from *convertere:* to turn or change). Hence conversion means 'a turning about' or changing, transporting or converting. It is used principally in four senses: logical, religious, legal and economic. Of these, we are at present concerned with the religious conversion, not the one of changing religion for a genuine spiritual reason or the debased expression of it in the mass conversion prevalent in some groups. It has been pointed out that 'true moral conversion is an actual overturning of values and involves a species of new creation'. It has been defined as 'a mutation of life occurring under the impulse of an ultraterrestrial ideal' (Sante de Sanctis). Or again: 'a reaction taking the form of a psychological surrender to an ideal and issuing in moral development' (Underwood). It has been further subdivided into gradual and sudden, or, as De Sanctis calls it, fulminative and progressive, and E.D. Starbuck, 'impulsive and volitional.' (*Encyclopaedia Britannica,* p. 357.)

Conversion in its real sense involves 'a change from an unorganized life to a life organized around a central idea'. When this central idea is God, it may strictly be called a religious conversion. 'It is the most momentous event in the life of every individual and is indispensable to the task of making the best use of that life.' It is thus a psychological phenomenon of profound significance and is perfectly normal. It is the most fundamental change in human character, making it God-centred. The selfish or 'this worldly' outlook is changed completely to an unselfish or 'other worldly' outlook. The material values give place to spiritual values. Its essential feature is the unification of character centred on God, involving both a new and intense conviction of the existence of God and a strong sense of obligation to obey His will. In this unification all the faculties and emotions, including man's natural instincts and appetites, are drawn to a new harmony.

There are various grades of this conversion. But the ideal type is seen in the lives of saints who never turn back from God afterwards. They lose all attraction for the things of the world. This distaste for things worldly is a counterpart of their positive conviction about God. Often it passes through a conviction of one's sin and utter worthlessness. There are of course conversions which, though genuine, are of a less stable nature. Even they produce great and some lasting effect on the lives of the converts. Conversion gives rise to the formation of new dispositions or 'sentiments' and has often been compared to falling in love. And strangely it is often found that many saints use erotic vocabulary, specially those following the Bridal Mysticism.

Writers make a distinction of it from similar changes. Counter-conversion in Christian literature refers to the change of a Catholic priest to a free thinker. Reversion is to the older faith. Return refers to the turn to the older life. Development has no overturning of values but is gradual. Recognition involves vital realization, and crises of conscience are less searching, as from one political party to another.

The time taken for religious conversion varies, though an immediate awareness of the reality of God is clearly discernible. But in the instances of saints like St. Paul, St. Augustine and John Bunyan 'there is evidence of a long preparatory stage and often the whole process appears to move gradually and evenly to its consummation.'

In the Hindu tradition nothing is taken as sudden. There is a distinct process of development. The cases of sudden spiritual awakening that are evident in the lives of saints are explained by a definite development in previous lives and are so due to the results of accumulated merit. When perfection is taken as the innate nature of man, conversion means only the unfoldment of his real nature or recognition, albeit sudden, of this fact.

In Buddhism too the same idea persists. But there are instances of sudden awareness of the transitoriness of life and the realization of enlightenment simply on hearing Buddha preach the Dharma. Even Buddha and Asoka had sudden changes in their lives, definitely turning away from ordinary life. The idea of conversion in religions believing in Karma and rebirth is naturally slightly different from the idea in Christianity. Here the stress is more on gradual developments through a slow, determined process of spiritual discipline. But in the lives of many saints the suddenness of awakening to the awareness of God is very clear. Of course, because of the philosophical background, less stress has been given on this suddenness.

In the Hindu tradition, this idea is accepted in this sense. The idea of a second birth with the initiation into Vedic studies making one a Dwija, twice-born, is there. The Upanayana ceremony, of having a subsidiary eye, as well as the Divya-cakshu, divine eye, mentioned in the Gita, open up a new vision. In them a sort of suddenness is implied. Various types of realized souls have been mentioned in the *Gospel of Sri Ramakrishna:*

'There are five kinds of Siddhas (perfect men) found in the world. They are: (1) The Svapna-siddhas, or those who attain perfection by means of dream-inspiration. (2) The Mantra-siddhas, or those who attain perfection by means of a Mantra or sacred 'name' of God. (3) The **Hathat-siddhas,** or those who attain perfection suddenly, like a poor man who at once becomes rich by finding a hidden treasure or by marrying a rich wife. Similarly, many who are sinful somehow become pure all of a sudden and enter the Kingdom of Heaven. (4) The Kripa-siddhas, or those who attain perfection through the grace of God. As a man in clearing a forest may discover some ancient tank or house and himself need not construct one with pain and trouble, so some fortunately become perfect with very little effort on their own part. (5) The Nitya-siddhas, or those who are ever perfect. As the vine of a gourd or pumpkin brings forth first its fruit and then its flower, so the ever perfect soul is born a Siddha, and all his seeming exertions after perfection are merely for the sake of setting an example to humanity.'

The broader division of saints through efforts or grace will cover the first four types. But grace of God is essential even for efforts. Discussion is there in mystical literature about the place of grace and free will in this experience. The Catholics hold that 'sacraments convey grace and confer character'. The Protestants consider that 'sacraments declare in symbolic form a change which has already taken place as the result of an act of faith on the part of the individual'. All the devotional schools generally stress the grace of God. It is needless to say, the grace of God is the predominant factor, but for a lasting effect a long effort has been found to be essential. Anyway, it is with regard to the suddennesss of the external manifestation of the change that we use the term sudden conversion.

A dramatic change is common in all such conversions of not only those who became saints but others also. But still each one is unique in its expression. There are, however, certain broad types. Often the drama of conversion centres on 'the birth of a new and higher selfhood', integrating, healing and energizing. Starbuck has pointed out that despite a considerable number of backslidings and recurrences of struggles with old attitudes and habits (about 40%), it appears, from an intimate study of many hundreds of confessions, that something of permanent value is carried over into later years. Psychologists consider conversion fundamentally as 'a blossoming, or fruition, of the basic biological and psychological urges and drives'. The sublimation the saints practise is of a higher type. As it has been said by a writer:

Is not this event, however, a sublimation also of self regard, (the seeking of personal salvation); of fear, (of final destruction); of gregariousness, (fellowship of the saints); of self-expression, (missionary zeal); of appreciation, (the beauty of holiness); and perhaps a dozen or score of other fundamental 'instincts' or propensities, which in their blending or fusion constitute the kingdom of righteousness in the heart. The sweet singer of Israel, realizing the majesty and glory of the heavens and of the universe, exclaims 'The Law of the Lord is perfect converting (or restoring) the soul.' (V. Ferm: *Encyclopaedia of Religion and Ethics*, p. 202.)

Conversion signifies the resolution of a conflict, e.g., between sin and righteousness, and involves, a change of values and acceptance of a faith 'unto salvation'. Ethical conversion consists in having a positive attitude towards morality.

With all this discussion in tracing the nature and suddenness of conversion, we must not forget that this idea is a little wide and away from the orthodox meaning of the word. The outstanding lives of definite preparation, growth and culmination, of years of religious devotion and service are before our eyes. And the vast majority of the people who accept spiritual disciplines consciously, also will fall in the category of gradually developing persons. The effect of the strong emotional experience that is felt during the awakening must be permanent. 'The test of a conversion lies not in the form which it takes but in the completeness with which it results in a life of which God has become the inspiration, centre and goal.'

For conversion a sort of psychological crisis is essential. If it is absent, then it can be called a gradual development. It is precisely because of this stress on crisis, it is found in many religious sects that a sort of an eager expectation is kept up, ending ultimately in a crisis. Generally this sudden change occurs in persons who are highly emotional. And as emotion is predominant in many people, its importance cannot be minimised. To such people things and values which were till now marginal and vague, suddenly become focal and clearly defined. But that may not mean a deep instantaneous final illumination. It is held in practically all the systems that on hearing of God, Truth, Mahavakyas or Mantras, an immediate illumination takes place. But generally a long practice of contemplation, japa and repetition is necessary for the consummation. John Bunyan considered his conversion as starting from the time when he began a higher life, but he had to pass through different stages of mystic suffering to get the unification.

Among the Christian sects the Methodists, Salvationists and others give much stress on this factor. John Wesley's idea of a 'new birth', which is a rebirth from sin and profanity, is well known. The evangelists believe in this to a great degree. This is why it is found that some of the noted evangelists create a congenial mood through their lectures or services in which such changes take place, not to a few but to a large number of people. It will be considered valuable only if it has a lasting effect, and is not a momentary thing resulting from emotional upheavals and loss of emotional balance. Some of the devotional sects in India practise this type of upheaval through singing and dancing. But unfortunately the effect is often demoralizing. It has been pointed out that a little rising of the Kundalini Power may give rise to some visions, etc. If it is not backed up by definite moral and spiritual preparation, the mind is apt to sink lower when the spell is over.

Much study has been made of conversion by writers on mysticism and theology, as well as by psychologists, both sympathetic and critical. It has been pointed out that a large number of cases occur during adolescence. This seems to be needless for our purpose, for scores of other instances are available of older people having this experience. However, the opinion of the writer on Conversion in *Encyclopaedia Britannica,* regarding psychological conversion of all people, seems to be a balanced one.

'The most that can be said is that the period between ages of 15 and 25 is the time when the greatest changes occur in human personality, and that therefore this is the most propitious epoch for the occurrence of decisive events in the history of individuals. Adolescence is only an extrinsic or indirect cause, a provocative stimulus to an intellectual and ethical transformation which requires for its completion the additional presence of a psychic factor. Indeed, the psysiological causes of conversion can be greatly exaggerated.'

From the study of the views of the writers some favourable conditions for the conversion have been given in the above article..

1. The presence of general religious tendencies deriving either from heredity, from the family or from earlier impressions. 2. A habitual tendency of the intellect towards absolute convictions. 3. A tendency of the individual spontaneously to fix the attention beyond and above the realities of the senses. 4. A richness of potential or psychic energy held in suspense by the individual. 5. The tendency of the individual to transfer his chief interests to questions of origin, purpose, destiny and so forth. 6. The recurrence of painful experiences.

This is true about general conversion in the psychological sense. Spiritual conversion is more definite and all-consuming. By the very nature of the experience, the sudden conversion does not seem to be predictable in point of time.

The fact that many such mystics have left behind them their autobiographies or experiences in songs, shows that their emotional experience created a deep impression in them because of its depth and suddenness. On the other hand, many other illumined saints and holy men who passed through a definite preparation and development were not struck by its uncommonness to feel it necessary to narrate it.

In the religious tradition more importance is given to definite discipline. And different experiences following particular Sadhanas have been meticulously described. The Yogis consider the suddenly converted saints and prophets as 'stumbling into religion'. Of course, the later flowering forth of their life takes away the sting from this remark. As for lesser people, it is felt that their capacity is limited and that is why so much of upheaval and external manifestation are seen in them. As Sri Ramakrishna said:

> 'Do you know the nature of this ecstasy? It is like boiling one ounce of milk in a big pan. The pan seems to be full of milk, but remove it from the stove and you would not find a single drop. Even the little quantity that was there would have all stuck to the pan.'

This sudden change in the life is not essential, though in every case there is evidence of some suddenness, at least during the first awakening to higher values, even if the change is not dramatic. Of course, the idea that without it no spiritual realization is possible cannot be accepted, for there are hundreds of other saints, and the vast majority of saints for that matter, in whose lives there was no dramatic change.

However, the idea of sudden conversion must be accepted as occuring in the spiritual realm. As it produces saintly characters it is surely of profound significance. The study of the lives of saints is for both individual good and social betterment. In the development of the saintly qualities lies the ultimate solution of all human problems. The lives of saints, as we have seen, point out that a large number of them were leading ordinary lives till an awareness of God suddenly dawned in their consciousness. Such examples will hearten man that, weak though he is, he has the required spiritual potential which can develop when the grace of God descends on him. Then all doubts will vanish and spiritual certainty will replace despair, uncertainties and fears. Then will the life be raised, in the words of Dr. Radhakrishnan, above 'the meaningless existence of dull despair' and have direction and purposiveness which are so essential for the contemporary world.

SOCIAL REFORM AND THE RAMAKRISHNA MOVEMENT

SOCIAL rules are created by the necessity of time. As the latter changes, a shift in the outlook also results. The change of outlook in turn is followed by social change. There are physical, biological, technological and cultural factors that influence social change. Much depends on the scheme of values already operating in the particular social situation. When the change is consciously done or attempted, it may be said to be coming strictly under social reform. When we study the history of different societies, we realize the fact that the greatest changes came through new discoveries and inventions requiring the complete overhauling of the lifepattern. Thus the nomadic men settled down and became the agricultural communities, which earlier were more or less exclusive. With the coming in of easy communication and growth of industry, the pattern of life had undergone again a major change. The Industrial Revolution of the 18th and 19th centuries is the one single factor having the greatest impact on human society.

Though the above is quite true, we must not ignore the fact that changes, though not of the same magnitude, were taking place right down from the beginning of human history. They were more or less dependent upon changes of the pattern of life. With the coming in of higher religions there was a conscious effort to make the higher ideals real in life. The later ethicists, humanists and political philosophers are all in the line of the higher religions. Mostly their inspiration was even consciously religious.

So social reform in some form or other is seen from the dawn of written history. Our life is such that it depends on exploitation of some kind or other. When it is too much, it may be called an oppression which in its turn produces discontent. In two ways oppression can be minimized or eliminated. Either the oppressed join together and demand a change, or a group of sympathetic, thinking people from the privileged group try to remedy the evils. These efforts may be designated as social reform dealing not so much with economic affairs as with other social injustices or inequalities. Religious teachers down the ages had the vision of equality of man, and out of their overflowing sympathy for the weaker sections they exhorted their followers to render service to them and to abolish the inequality. Taking the cue from them many other thinkers too worked for it and dreamt about ideal social conditions in Utopias, Ramarajyas and the like. Various communities were established for a common life of equality and social justice. The world probably is not yet ready for complete equality. Hence in spite of their efforts, social evils persist. When a particular evil is too nauseating, effort is made to remedy it.

Social reform primarily deals with correcting the defects or injustices done to the weaker sections of the community. In the Indian context, the caste system draws the immediate attention of critics. Improving women's rights and privileges is another important item. This along with economic betterment are world problems. Caste in different forms, i.e. prejudices against other sections of the community, also may be said to be a common problem for the social reformers throughout the world. In the western countries the reform movements are striving more or less towards parliamentary electoral reform.

It is often contended that persistent injustice is often

traced to the tradition or scriptures. In the Indian situation there was practically less difficulty on this score though caste has been often supported with scriptural quotations. But all the religio-philosophical systems stood for the equality of all human beings for reaching the highest goal of life. Vedanta speaks of the divinity of human souls, and if equality was not possible in the mundane sphere, it stressed its workability in the spiritual realm. This idea of the divinity of man removes all barriers of man for his progress. Swami Vivekananda loudly proclaimed this divinity of man with all its implications and claimed equal treatment for all. Because the Vedantic ideas dominate the Indian consciousness, no difficulty was felt in India after freedom to give franchise to women and the socially backward people, sometimes with special advantages. Overnight, governors, ministers and other top ranking administrators could be selected from them without any opposition.

The modern economic forces are a great leveller. It is said that the feudal order was completely changed by the Industrial Revolution, the transition being through commerical revolution. But the European mind was prepared for total changes through the development of the idea of brotherhood, rationalism and writings of the precursors of the French Revolution. Industrialism has broken down the communal and national isolation and brought about the world relationship. Religious, political and social philosophers are preparing the mind of man for complete acceptance of this new relationship.

Though it is time and the social and economic situation, that are mainly responsible for vast social changes, the spear-heads for these changes are great men and movements that bring about reforms on smaller or larger scales. In that context only can we discuss the services rendered by the

Ramakrishna Movement in the reformation of society in modern India.

Social reform has three factors: first, preparing the proper mood for it, second, to give a programme for reform, and third, creating institutions to carry out that programme. In the first, the teachings of Sri Ramakrishna and Swami Vivekananda had the greatest effect. In the giving of a programme, their Movement did not go straight to the reforms. The stress was more on education—education of women and the masses. Asked once what he thought of widow-remarriage, Swami Vivekananda retorted: 'Am I a widow to decide whether a husband is necessary? Give them education and let them decide for themselves'. He gave still more stress on the education of the masses and was anxious for their material improvement. The study of Hindu social structure down the ages shows it clearly that material prosperity, education and culture are the three factors that bring a group to a higher rung of the ladder. He thought that it was better for reformers not to waste their energy on attacking the social evils, which he thought originated through social ill-health, which in turn must be cured through education and material amenities. He encouraged the educated upper classes to go to the service of the suffering millions, the Daridra-Narayanas, with the idea of Divine worship. This idea had taken deep root in the Indian consciousness, and Mahatma Gandhi popularized it further through his efforts for Harijan uplift.

But it must not be forgotten that the nature of society is such that it cannot be fully dictated to. The most that reformers can do is to supply the leaven of culture and the atmosphere. This the Ramakrishna and other movements did. The actual changes that we see now-a-days cannot be said to be the direct result of any one man or movement. The changes

have come through forces which cannot be fully calculated
or determined. Economic changes, easy communication,
growth of industry and cities, western education and ideas and
lastly the national movements under Gandhiji, and economic
conditions after war, independence and partition are the direct
causes that actually have hammered all the opposition and
brought about the changes that were undreamt of in the
preceding years. All these changes cannot be said to be for
good, but desirable changes also have taken place. The
function of the religious teachers and idealists is to prepare
the common mind for changes for the better as also to impress
on the rulers the necessity of bringing in the desirable changes.
The idealistic writers and preachers try through preaching and
propaganda to prepare the people for impending changes.

What exactly is the contribution of the Ramakrishna
Movement in the social reform of the country? Before
trying to find out the exact services by the movement, over and
above the supplying of ideas and enthusiasm for reform, let
us see what the other socio-religious movements of the last
century tried to achieve. That will give an idea of the
concurring and distinctive services of the Ramakrishna
Movement.

The Brahmo Samaj was more of a social reform movement. Raja Ram Mohan Roy, through his personal effort
as well as through the Samaj, tried to bring about some
reforms. Of these the abolition of Suttee is well known.
Efforts for widow-remarriage, stopping of polygamy, and
abolition of caste through inter-caste-marriage and giving up of
the sacred thread also must be taken into account. Of course,
these are not things that could be introduced in full through
legal measures. But they did create a questioning and a
mood to change among the educated elite, though in reality,
very few of them actually accepted them in their own life.

Some of the Brahmo leaders were the first to go to foreign countries, which was a taboo in those days. The Brahmo Samaj along with preaching of the harmony of scriptures, reason and faith, and monism and social reforms, advocated universal brotherhood.

The Prarthana Samaj also stood for abolition of caste and child-marriage, and advocated inter-dining, inter-marriage, widow remarriage and equal status for women.

The Arya Samaj too advocated some reforms. It advocated going back to the Vedic age of simplicity and castelessness. It introduced a spirit of social service and was preoccupied with social reclamation through Suddhi, Sanghatan and education.

The Theosophical Society, being an international organisation, did away with caste within the group, spoke about universal brotherhood and encouraged the study of comparative religion and occultism.

Needless to say, all these movements remained confined to the elite and followers of the particular groups. They could not touch the vast Hindu society. But surely, all these movements removed all opposition to these forms from the mind of the educated. Whole-hearted acceptance, however, did not result.

The Ramakrishna Movement came on the scene at that time, almost by the end of the 19th century. Its stress on the spiritual essentials without disturbing too much the ritualistic forms gave it a unique status. It did not attack too directly any of the accretions which were created due to exigencies of time, and only mildly pointed out that society could change without requiring any change of religion. This suggestion was more acceptable to the people of the land who swore by their religion and were afraid that reformers would kill their religion too. It is in this field of preparating the Hindu mind that the Ramakrishna Movement had the greatest contribution to make. Ideas of reform by members from within the community become more appealing and forceful. The followers of Sri Ramakrishna remained fullfledged members of the Hindu community and thereby were heard with more sympathy and less opposition. As the Movement did not secede from the body politic and form a separate sect, changes in the lives of its followers brought about changes in the larger society. To achieve greater success in reform without much opposition, it is necessary to build on the past without attempting to demolish the superstructure. This method of work was followed by this Movement. As a result, its ideas permeated the society and unobtrusively liberalized it to a large extent. Through its religio-social institutions it preached these ideas and effected some changes, for a world outlook was at the back of all its activities. Many other people and groups followed this idea and helped in the social reforms.

Any movement to be effective must create institutions of social service. The reforms are brought about through the pattern of life in these institutions. An account of the institutions created and run by the Ramakrishna Math and Mission may be given here. There are altogether 138 centres of which 72 are mission centres and 66 math centres. Of these 86 are in India. There are also over 20 sub-centres in India and abroad. The Mission does temporary relief works in different parts of India faced with flood, fire, refugee, epidemic, earthquake and other problems. In the medical field there are 12 indoor hospitals and 60 outdoor dispensaries. In the educational field there are 53 students' homes, 3 colleges, 2 teachers' training colleges, 3 engineering schools, 1 agricultural school, 1 rural institute, 35 high schools, 127 lower grade schools, 1 institution for training auxiliary nurses and midwives. The number of students in all the institutions taken together are nearly 54 thousand, a third of them being girls. Spiritual and cultural work is done in most centres in the form of regular classes and occasional lectures, libraries and reading rooms. Ten principal publication centres with 5 magazines in English and 5 in the Indian languages are also bringing out numerous books in different languages to popularize the ideas. Over and above these there are almost an equal number of unofficial centres bearing the names of Sri Ramakrishna, Swami Vivekananda and the Holy Mother, carrying out similar work for the benefit of the society.

Thus it will be seen that in the field of social service the Ramakrishna institutions working without any extraneous consideration had something to offer. The greatest service for social reform was, however, in the field of ideas. The teachings of Sri Ramakrishna and Swami Vivekananda stressed spiritual values and tried to purify social life and create abundant sympathy for suffering sections of the society and generated enthusiasm for the amelioration of social injustices. Their teachings are general and universal and not directed particularly to some social evils and so have the potency to render the same services for generations to come. Time cannot limit the value of the eternal verities they spoke of and the implications of their realization of the divinity of man and equality of life will surely guide the society through the corridors of time.

MORAL AND RELIGIOUS EDUCATION

THE essence of moral education is to present in the form of stories and anecdotes, moral ideas that will become real and part of a child's nature through personal experience. Man lives in society. His interests sometimes come to clash with others. There is also a moral struggle between self-interest and duty, or Sreyas and Preyas, as the Upanishads say. The existence of the evil of selfishness is a reality. It must be counteracted by training and education. Hence there is the necessity of moral training. Nowadays it is specially proposed as a remedy for certain tendencies that undermine the social morale and cultural standard, and are giving a destructive turn to the youthful energies of boys and girls. Not only the domestic and social authority is threatened by this lack of integration, even the governmental authority is in difficulty. The help of moral education is sought to bring about peace more naturally through education than through force.

True morality is natural, not forced. It is the external manifestation of the inner goodness of man. Efficiency in work comes through moral ideals, through a feeling of equality and not through fear and want, as some people think. Through religious and ethical training only, willing co-operation and responsible work without supervision are possible, for the drive is internal and not external.

India for centuries was guided by a religious pursuit; politics and administration were looked upon as mere auxiliaries. The making of manhood, the development of character, was its goal. The British, with the Western development of ideas, introduced secularism in India. Secular morality was the dominant note of English educational institutions and of English life itself. Moreover, modern inventions of science and easy communication have changed the outlook, bringing about a revolution of ideas. Hence the contemporary unrest is a part of the social upheaval due to a change in the pattern of life because of industrialization and technological development.

Not only India but the whole world is passing through moral confusion. Higher ideals are being thrown to the winds, ignoring the fundamental principles of civilization, and the lower conceptions of life are being preached vigorously. The result is tragic. Thinkers with the future welfare of man at heart are trying to find a solution. Religions down the ages were training man in the higher virtues. Their hold being slackened, a substitute in moral education is being sought.

An important factor of the modern civilized societies is the importance gained by education. As long as it was limited to the classes, the spiritual value of education was predominant. But with the masses coming in, the increased value of the educated in the labour market became more important. This commercialised view of education coupled with the self-conscious labour brought forth political theories believing in force and violence. This perverted conception of education is the root cause of restlessness in society, specially among the youth. A little moral education for youth or labour is only a symptomatic treatment of the disease without going to its root cause. The essential spirituality of man must be recognised and theories of progress and order must be correlated to it. Man is not a mere living machine; he is spirit with a body and mind and not a mere tool to produce wealth in a capitalistic or communistic pattern of social and economic society.

Proper education presupposes the conception of personality. Our conception is, each soul is potentially divine and perfect. The goal is to manifest that perfection and divinity lying hidden in us. A child is a self-conscious soul with a body, sense-organs and a mind which can be trained. So true education will mean the development of his physical, intellectual, moral and spiritual potentialities. Proper control of sense-impulses and instincts, sublimation and proper direction of feelings and sentiments and development of the will and the sense of duty must be learnt by the student. For inculcating higher virtues it is necessary to stimulate the very soul of the child. The greatest incentive to moral life is to be aware of one's pure nature and connection with the ultimate reality.

This is the age-old view of man and his place in society. The materialistic view makes man an aggregate of organs and functions. It does not recognize the spirituality of man and believes that his higher nature is determined by his education and environment. Much literature has been produced on this. The Indian idea is to recognize man's nature as spiritual; education is to remove the ignorance that hides his pure, perfect nature. As the goal of life was something non-material, to the old Indian the satisfaction of material wants and sense-enjoyment had only a secondary importance. As he loved peace and was satisfied with the minimum, he did not want conflict or disorder in the outer world too. But now times are changing. The theories of enjoyment are vigorously being preached in every country. But there too competition is inevitable As a result, the revolutionary theories developed, stressing unrest, conflict and hatred. Boys and girls are naturally affected by these. To counteract this an orientation in Western education is being tried blending technical and moral education. Industrial and technical education will teach people how to learn and live above want, and moral education will teach them the qualities of thrift, temperance, and purity and how to live with other people and the government. By such education, educationists hope that there will be a reign of contentment and happiness, law and order.

In India the situation is a little more peculiar. Here we had a developed social and moral order but a new type of civilization has been thrust upon us, bringing in its trail unfamiliar types of social evils. Conflicts of ideals and civilizations, manners and habits are the order of the day. Some of the bad habits are weedy growths, depending on the fashion. If they are to be counteracted, this idea itself must be resisted. Simplicity of life is losing its ground and multiplying things is considered a matter of prestige. So respect for the good traditions also must be kept up, at least for children. Disregard of everything old generates undesirable tendencies in children. This, however, is being corrected by some leaders nowadays.

A peaceful society requires devotion to one's allotted duty. In Indian tradition a duty is an obligatory action. Acharya Sankara points out that every act has two aspects, that of purification of the mind and yielding merits or fruits. The former leads to knowledge, the latter gives enjoyment and is destructible. One is subjective and the other objective. Practical morality requires a certain measure of definiteness. To define a duty with reference to its objective character is to keep its real nature in the dark. If duty is defined with reference to its subjective character, then Acharya Sankara's definition holds good. Whatever purifies our mind, elevates our thinking, widens our sympathies, ennobles our feelings and makes us more spiritual is a duty, an obligatory act. Devotion to duty presupposes love. To bring it to children without touching religion will be impossible. For children, love will mean not mere sentimental attachment but the idea of self-sacrifice and service. The question will arise in their mind why they should love others. The ultimate answer lies in religion only, in the idea that God dwells in every man, that all are His children. Of course, the social reason that by helping others we help ourselves too, though indirectly, is also to be pointed out. The idea of Ahimsa, of not injuring others, is a negative definition. Love is its positive aspect. But love and non-injury are possible only through self-culture. This is then a duty. Duties are directed towards others, so they make us unselfish. This love or non-injury speaks of one's own conduct and will appeal easily to children. Here both the individual and social ethics commingle. This is the beginning of moral life in man.

The demand from different quarters for moral and religious education is due to its value. In spite of secular governments, most of the countries of the world have such training. Organization being the normal working of Western life, the Christian Church also is rendering this education, though too sectarian, through its various agencies. In India religious life is disorganized. The family and the general atmosphere, however, were indirectly inculcating the moral and religious virtues in the younger people. Following the British tradition, the Government also became secular. As a result, a confusion was created among the educationists. In later days, responsible leaders tried to correct the notion about secularity. Several educational commissions also discussed about the problem and gave their well-thought-out opinions. The University Commission presided over by Dr. Radhakrishnan said:

Where conscious purpose is lacking, personal integrity and consistent behaviour are not possible.

If we exclude spiritual training in our institutions we would be untrue to our whole historical development. (p. 301).

Hence they suggested silent meditation and study of inspiring books.

The Secondary Education Commission with Dr. Lakshmanaswami Mudaliar as Chairman said that children are influenced by the atmosphere of the home, of the school and of the locality and also by public opinion regarding religious and moral codes of conduct. The Commission further said:

We, however, feel that such instruction can be supplemented to a limited extent by properly organised instruction given in the schools. One of the methods adopted in some schools is to hold an assembly at the commencement of the day's session with all teachers and pupils present, when a general non-denominational prayer is offered. Moral instruction in the sense of inspiring talks given by suitable persons selected by the headmaster and dwelling on the lives of great personages of all times and of all climes will help to drive home the lessons of morality. (p. 126).

The Sanskrit Commission with Dr. Suniti Kumar Chatterjee as the Chairman, spoke about its necessity and the role of Sanskrit in the following words:

There cannot be any objection to the introduction of "Moral Instruction" in any scheme of education. Provision should, therefore, be made in all schools for such "Moral Instruction". The general principles of personal morality and social ethics which are conducive to the well-being of the individual and the society should be inculcated in the minds of all pupils in the schools.

For this purpose, Sanskrit with its unending wealth of suitable texts and passages will be exceedingly appropriate. From the very early childhood, the average Indian boy and girl may be taught essential lessons of morality and social conduct through Sanskrit verses and tags which should be accompanied by translations in the mother-tongue. If children at a tender age are encouraged to get these by heart, both the texts and the translations, they will be equipped with a certain amount of intellectual and even spiritual wealth, with its aesthetic accompaniment because it is couched in a sonorous language like Sanskrit, and this will be an asset for them throughout their whole life. (p. 192).

The American educationists had a similar thing to offer. The Educational Policies Commission advocated religious education in a pamphlet on 'Moral and spiritual values in the public schools' and said that the public schools must increase their efforts to equip each child and youth in their care with a sense of values which will lend dignity and direction to whatever else he may learn. Human personality is a basic value, and moral responsibility and self-discipline are marks of maturity. To equip the children properly, the above Commission suggested that we must clarify essential values of our life. The sources also will have to be found out as well as the method of teaching it effectively. For this, help of other educational forces must also be taken.